3000 800055 19689
St. Louis Community College

Meramec Library
St. Louis Community College
11333 Big Bend Blvd.
Kirkwood, MO 63122-5799
314-984-7797

A HISTORY OF SOUTHERN MISSOURI AND NORTHERN ARKANSAS

The Civil War in the West

Series Editor: Daniel E. Sutherland

A HISTORY OF
SOUTHERN MISSOURI AND
NORTHERN ARKANSAS

Being an Account of the Early Settlements, the Civil War, the Ku-Klux, and Times of Peace

William Monks

Edited and with an Introduction by
John F. Bradbury Jr. and Lou Wehmer

THE UNIVERSITY OF ARKANSAS PRESS
Fayetteville
2003

St. Louis Community College
at Meramec
LIBRARY

Copyright © 2003 by The University of Arkansas Press

All rights reserved
Manufactured in the United States of America

07 06 05 04 03   5 4 3 2 1

Designer: John Coghlan

⊛ The paper used in this publication meets the minimum requirements of
the American National Standard for Permanence of Paper for Printed Library
Materials Z39.48-1984.

Library of Congress Cataloging-in-Publication Data

Monks, William, 1830–1913.
    A history of southern Missouri and northern Arkansas : being an account
of the early settlements, the Civil War, the Ku-Klux, and times of peace /
William Monks ; edited and with an introduction by John F. Bradbury, Jr.
and Lou Wehmer.
        p. cm. — (The Civil War in the West)
Originally published: West Plains, Mo. : West Plains Journal Co., 1907.
Includes bibliographical references and index.
    ISBN 1-55728-753-8 (cloth : alk. paper)
    1. Missouri—History—Civil War, 1861–1865. 2. Arkansas—History—
Civil War, 1861–1865. 3. Monks, William, 1830–1913. 4. Guerrillas—
Ozark Mountains—Biography. 5. United States—History—Civil War,
1861–1865—Personal narratives. 6. United States—History—Civil War,
1861–1865—Underground movements. 7 Missouri—History—19th
century. 8. Arkansas—History—19th century.
I. Bradbury, John F. II. Wehmer, Lou, 1952– III. Title. IV. Series.
    E517 .M9 2003
    973.7'09778'8—dc21

                                                          2003008904

Contents

Series Editor's Preface

The Civil War in the West has a single goal: To promote historical writing about the war in the western states and territories. It focuses most particularly on the Trans-Mississippi theater, which consisted of Missouri, Arkansas, Texas, most of Louisiana (west of the Mississippi River), Indian Territory (modern-day Oklahoma), and Arizona Territory (two-fifths of modern-day Arizona and New Mexico), but it also encompasses adjacent states, such as Kansas, Tennessee, and Mississippi, that directly influenced the Trans-Mississippi war. It is a wide swath, to be sure, but one too often ignored by historians and, consequently, too little understood and appreciated.

Topically, the series embraces all aspects of the wartime story. Military history in its many guises, from the strategies of generals to the daily lives of common soldiers, forms an important part of that story, but so too do the numerous and complex political, economic, social, and diplomatic dimensions of the war. The series also provides a variety of perspectives on these topics. Most importantly, it offers the best in modern scholarship, with thoughtful, challenging monographs. Secondly, it presents new editions of important books that have gone out of print. And thirdly, it premieres expertly edited correspondence, diaries, reminiscences, and other writings by witnesses to the war.

It is a formidable undertaking, but the hope is that The Civil War in the West, by focusing on some of the least familiar dimensions of the conflict, will significantly broaden our understanding of that dramatic story.

A History of Southern Missouri and Northern Arkansas, William Monks's valuable memoir of life on the Missouri-Arkansas border, was published originally in 1907. It has not been reprinted since then. The book's title is misleading in that it is devoted almost entirely to the Civil War years, including a valuable section on the way wartime animosities between Rebels and Unionists continued into the early postwar period. William

Monks was a Missourian, Unionist refugee, and sometimes Federal soldier and "scout" (or guerrilla) during the war. He also served as a militia officer in both Missouri and Arkansas following the conflict. His account of the war in the Ozark Mountains is the only one published by a Union guerrilla in that region, and his perspective provides both useful factual information and a shrewd appraisal of the effects of the war on the people of the Ozarks. His narrative not only traces the course of the principal military activities on the border (both conventional and irregular) but also pays attention to the plight of Unionist and Rebel noncombatants.

The value of Monks's memoir has been enhanced considerably by the editorial work of John F. Bradbury, senior manuscript specialist of the Western Historical Manuscript Collection at the University of Missouri–Rolla, and Lou Wehmer, a communication specialist with the Missouri Highway Patrol and skilled Civil War researcher. Like most writers of memoirs and reminiscences, Monks sometimes compresses events in his narrative, fails to identify people and events adequately, and leaves gaps in his story. All such defects have been thoroughly mended by Bradbury and Wehmer in the excellent and quite extensive introduction they have written to accompany the original text. Their introduction provides a complete biographical sketch of Monks to place him and his work in the context of the times in which he lived. They have also compiled a detailed index, entirely missing from the original volume, to make this edition of Monks's work both a riveting story and a valuable research tool. Taken together, Monks, Bradbury, and Wehmer offer a significant perspective on a little-known, yet extremely revealing, corner of the war.

Daniel E. Sutherland
Series Editor

William Monks: Union Guerrilla and Memoirist

John Bradbury and Lou Wehmer

The wonder is that William Monks lived to write *A History of Southern Missouri and Northern Arkansas*. A turbulent man in a violent time and chaotic place, he was a man to be reckoned with in the central Ozarks for two decades, beginning with the Civil War. Monks was a Unionist refugee, Federal scout and guerrilla fighter, civil and political official, lawyer and litigant, and an officer of postwar Radical Party state militias in Missouri and Arkansas. His activities and notoriety encompassed not only Howell County, Missouri, where Monks spent nearly sixty years of his life, but also the middle border counties of Texas, Ozark, Douglas, Oregon, and Shannon in Missouri, and Fulton and Independence in Arkansas. Monks fought mostly on his own turf, in an area in which he was well known and with which he was well acquainted. His was a very personal combat in a region where guerrilla warfare—the most intimate type of armed conflict—ultimately caused widespread depopulation and prolonged misery. Monks provides a striking example of the cliché that the war did not end in 1865 for many guerrilla warriors. In his case, it continued fiercely on several fronts for another decade as various partisan factions settled old scores and battled for local political control. Monks may have been a victim in the destruction of a promising region, but he also contributed to its self-inflicted wounds and perpetuated the agony. He was a Unionist guerrilla, a government official, and a lawyer. He commanded, rallied, arrested, killed, quarreled with, and sued people he knew. There could have been no lack of people with an urge to put a bullet into Billy Monks.

Monks struck plenty of sparks during his heyday, and his name still figures in local history and lore. There are still "pro" and "anti" Monks opinions—lingering indications of just how poisonous and potentially

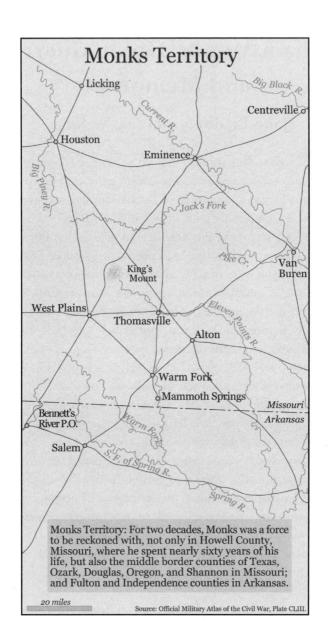

Monks Territory

Licking

Big Black R.

Current R.

Centreville

Houston

Eminence

Big Piney R.

Jack's Fork

Pike Cr.

Van Buren

King's Mount

West Plains

Eleven Points R.

Thomasville

Alton

Warm Fork

Mammoth Springs

Missouri

Arkansas

Bennett's River P.O.

Warm Fork

Salem

S. F. of Spring R.

Spring R.

Monks Territory: For two decades, Monks was a force to be reckoned with, not only in Howell County, Missouri, where he spent nearly sixty years of his life, but also the middle border counties of Texas, Ozark, Douglas, Oregon, and Shannon in Missouri; and Fulton and Independence counties in Arkansas.

20 miles

Source: Official Military Atlas of the Civil War, Plate CLIII.

deadly those differences once must have been. Common knowledge associates Monks largely with his exploits as a Yankee scout and cavalryman during the Civil War, but his greatest regional notoriety came in 1868 from the second of two "invasions" of northern Arkansas by Missouri militiamen. In fact, although he was usually called "Major" or "Colonel" Monks, his highest military rank derived from a commission as lieutenant colonel in the state militia of Arkansas, not Missouri.

He was a Union patriot and skilled guerrilla fighter for some, but others called him a bushwhacker, murderer, and thief. His enemies in the contemporary press vilified him as the "Bandit," "Brigand," or "Ruffian" Monks. He became a zealous postwar litigant in Missouri courts, punishing old enemies and protecting his reputation. The chimney of his West Plains home, painted red, white, and blue, was a thumb in the eye of former Confederates after the war. In 1874 Monks could still muster an armed band for his support. Until 1878, when he gained a newfound faith in the Christian Church, he was a subject of newspaper stories in St. Louis, Rolla, Ironton, Jefferson City, and Springfield, Missouri, as well as Batesville and Little Rock, Arkansas, and Memphis, Tennessee. Even as he gradually withdrew from public life, his reputation survived. As late as 1883, a reference to "Monks' Command" did not have to be further explained to newspaper readers. Finally, he perpetuated his memory and version of events by writing his *History*.[1]

Monks was toward the end of his life when he wrote his *History*. He had become a local Civil War relic, good for an occasional patriotic address in a schoolroom or at one of the surviving Grand Army of the Republic posts. Severe injuries in an accident at home in 1904 may have provoked thoughts of mortality, or he may have been inspired to write by the veterans' reunion he attended in 1905. By 1906, he walked only with crutches but still had some of the old combativeness about him, even if his body was infirm. He was unapologetic for his conduct and did not shy away from the lingering questions arising from the controversial years when he was a powerful man at his zenith. Clearly, he had nursed some grudges for many years.[2]

Despite its title, the book is not a standard regional history. Nor is it a full autobiography, although Monks began with a nostalgic memoir of early adulthood during what might be considered the "Golden

Age" of the Ozarks. The core of his story is an adamant account of a tumultuous fifteen-year period beginning with the Civil War. This narrative, comprising two-thirds of the book, concerns the period when he was first a Unionist refugee, then a Federal scout and captain of a cavalry company, and finally a militia officer holding commissions from the Radical Republican governors of Missouri and Arkansas. The literary effort, in which Monks refers to himself in the third person as "the author" or "the writer," is not stylish, and the tone of the narrative mixes high-mindedness with derring-do. The organization of the work displays an old man's garrulousness, repetitiveness, and disorganization. The story is chronologically confusing in places, some of the details are imperfect, and occasionally his point is nebulous. At his most interesting when he describes events in which he participated, Monks at times merely related garbled accounts of events about which he really knew nothing. And, as with many memoirists, what he did not write is as interesting as what he did.

The last part of his narrative seems to have been written as an afterthought. While it degenerates at times into a series of stream-of-consciousness reminiscent paragraphs, it also includes his account of the controversial campaign in Arkansas against the Ku Klux Klan. The *History* is illustrated with staged photographs of some of the critical events in Monks's story, recreated by aged comrades who appear to have been just barely able to hoist the muskets they held as props. The tabloid-style captions, such as "Col. Monks Arrested and Taken from Home" and "Cutting Out Rhodes' Heart," are slightly ludicrous given the aged subjects pictured in the views.

No matter its faults, *A History of Southern Missouri and Northern Arkansas* is significant as one of only a handful of memoirs by a notable participant of the guerrilla war in the Ozarks and the only one by a Union guerrilla fighter. It is also a rare account dealing with the Radical Party and Reconstruction periods in Missouri and Arkansas—for more than a decade as much a civil war as the preceding years. Monks's reminiscence is uncompromisingly Unionist but was written at the turn of the century, when his brand of radical unionism had long since become unfashionable. Monks believed the Republican Party had become the tool of big business and, far worse, that history was being stolen from the victors. Former Rebels and the Democratic Party had reclaimed their prewar dominance of state and local governments. The title "ex-Confederate" was no longer a hindrance in local affairs but rather a desirable cachet for political candidates and businessmen along the border. Monks's book is by turns a self-defense and an uncompromising affirmation of the Radical Union cause in the Ozarks. His lists of Union loyalists in Howell, Douglas, and Ozark Counties were rolls of honor of men whom he thought should not be forgotten, "While history is being written and monuments being erected to the Confederate soldiers for heroism." Monks also blackguarded his personal enemies, most of whom had long since been punished or had died of old age. The *History* was Monks's parting shot at his old foes, aimed at the historical record. By virtue of longevity if nothing else, he figured to have the last word.[3]

A History of Southern Missouri and Northern Arkansas was published at West Plains in limited numbers. The total printed is not known, but it has become a difficult volume to locate. As a primary source for regional history and an artifact of its time, the title has long been a candidate for a modern edition. A generation of modern historians has begun to examine crucial aspects of guerrilla warfare, including the treatment of noncombatant citizens, the fate of social and political minorities, the fortunes of ex-Confederates and Southern sympathizers, and the whole matter of Reconstruction. These themes are ripe for reexamination in the Ozarks, which was largely burnt out and depopulated by 1865 and where continuing political and civil violence deriving from the Civil War lasted well into the 1880s. It is appropriate that Monks's account will be readily available again.

William Monks lived his entire adult life on the middle Missouri-Arkansas border of the south-central Ozarks, first in Fulton County, Arkansas, and then across the state line in Howell County, Missouri. Geographically, the area is a subregion of the central plateau separating the watersheds of the Osage and Gasconade Rivers from those of the White River. It is an upland plateau country of rolling hills and post-oak and prairie flats, bisected by the political boundary between Missouri and Arkansas, drained to the north and east by the rugged valleys of the Gasconade, Current, and Eleven Point Rivers in Missouri. This was the heart of the great pine forest of southern Missouri that attracted first white hunters, then lumbermen, and finally the first permanent settlers during the first quarter of the nineteenth century. To the south is the White River, draining the southern slope of the Ozarks. It originates in the Boston Mountains of Arkansas, flowing generally southeastward across Missouri and back into Arkansas. The valley of the White and its major tributaries, the Spring River, Strawberry, and the North Fork of the White, had been settled by southern white immigrants following the Arkansas and White Rivers upstream. Newcomers settled the interior Ozarks from the outside in, spreading farther and farther up the major tributaries of the Gasconade and White and locating on the most favorable well-watered locations in the valleys, often at the confluences of streams or at spring sites. Areas of dry upland prairie such as those in Howell County, Missouri, were least favored and only sparsely settled well into the 1840s and 1850s.[4]

Batesville, the seat of Independence County, Arkansas, along the White River, was the oldest, largest, and most important commercial site in the region. Founded in 1810, Batesville was the business center and point at which the region's exports were likely to begin their journey to markets in New Orleans. The town was a focal area for immigration into the interior of the Ozarks and was the location of the U.S. Land Office for the White River country. Batesville's economic influence extended into the southern counties of Missouri until the early 1880s, when the "Memphis line" (the Kansas City, Fort Scott, and Memphis Railway) was built. Neighboring Salem, in Fulton County, was a small county seat. Farther north in Missouri, only Thomasville and Alton in Oregon County, West Plains in Howell County, and Houston in Texas County could claim to be towns, but they were mere straggling villages compared with Batesville.

The inhabitants of the middle border were predominantly whites of Upper South extraction. Many extended families in southern Missouri had close kin around Batesville and Bennett's Bayou; earlier ancestral connections via Kentucky, Tennessee, and the Carolinas also were common. Most had commercial, kinship, and social connections back and forth across the arbitrary state line. They were Jacksonian Democrats politically, and veterans of U.S. service in the War of 1812 living on military bounty lands were not unusual. Except for some owners of the largest farms along the White River, the people subsisted through market hunting and stockherding and raised enough corn, cotton, and tobacco for home consumption. Although slavery was legal in both Missouri and Arkansas, bondsmen never inhabited the Ozarks in great numbers except on a few large White River plantations. Minorities make virtually no appearance in Monks's reminiscence. At least in his memory, the regional population was entirely white.

Of his childhood and early years, only the details supplied by Monks himself are generally known. He was born 5 February 1830 on the north side of the Tennessee River near Huntsville, Alabama, the eldest son of James and Nancy Monks. His father hailed from South Carolina, possibly from that corner of the state near Charleston known as Moncks Corner. He was an 1812 veteran and took up a military land bounty in Alabama in the late 1820s. He must have been either restless or unsuccessful, for he moved westward three times in as many decades. He took his family to Pope (now Massac) County, Illinois, about 1835, then to Bennett's Bayou Township in Fulton County, Arkansas, in 1844. William said that his father was actually headed for Texas when Indian troubles there made him consider northern Arkansas good enough for a while. He would relocate his wife and family of four sons one more time, in 1849, to the North Fork of the White River, two miles from the Missouri border in Fulton County, Arkansas. The family's time in Fulton County was not entirely propitious. James Monks died there of "winter fever" in 1852. In addition to James's death, Nancy Monks and Henry, the youngest son, both died of the "bloody flux" in 1854.[5]

In 1844 Monks began carrying the U.S. mail between Salem, Arkansas, and Rockbridge, Ozark County, Missouri. Through this service, he became well acquainted with the North Fork country, the western edge of his territory, and known to many of the folk in Ozark and Douglas Counties in Missouri. It may have been as a mail rider that Monks first met Martha Rice, whom he married in Fulton County on 10 April 1853. Perhaps with postal wages, Monks bought land in Missouri, moving his wife and daughter to Howell County in 1858 and settling southwest of the county seat at West Plains in Benton Township. He became the local constable and began reading law. By the time of the Civil War, Monks was just a middling man, neither prominent nor wealthy. But, according to later detractors, his experience as township constable whetted his lust for power.[6]

Monks's *History* begins with a nostalgic chapter devoted to those peaceful antebellum years. He remembered the Ozarks as "almost a 'land of honey'" where civilization was but lightly dusted upon the valley and hill settlements. Peltry, deerskins, beeswax, and honey served as the regional currency; New Orleans was the primary export market. Manufactured goods came back from New Orleans either through Batesville or freighted overland from St. Louis. The natural abundance of wild game and honey made life easy despite otherwise primitive frontier conditions. Stockraising was free of expense except for salting the animals. Settlements were sparse, yet the homespun people were close knit socially. It was not uncommon for them to travel twenty-five or thirty miles for family gatherings, political and judicial affairs, and Baptist and Methodist church meetings. By this account, Monks joined other published chroniclers of the early Ozarks. But the earliest memoirists of the region, such as John Bradbury, Henry Schoolcraft, and Henry M. Brackenridge, traveled the Ozarks when it was still largely wilderness, experiencing all of the natural abundance, wildness, and vicissitudes the country had to offer. They were explorers and adventurers; they did not stay. Monks's reminiscence is more akin to the later works of John Quincy Wolf, Theodore P. Russell, and Silas C. Turnbo, all of whom belonged to the first generation of native settlers. They were eyewitnesses to the last of the Ozarks's golden age and the agony wrought by the Civil War. Later in life, all of them wrote memoirs or compiled regional histories reflecting those experiences.[7]

By comparison, Monks's account contains more nostalgia than information. He experienced frontier life only as it was ending and exaggerated the primitive nature of the Ozarks by ignoring the steady development of towns and villages. Southern Missouri and northern Arkansas underwent a round of political development and county organization in the 1850s reflecting increased settlement. The roads to Batesville and St. Louis, and between the county-seat towns, were well established, even if they were rocky, unmaintained, and difficult to traverse. By the 1850s, even West Plains, a relatively young municipality, had developed into the "neatest and prettiest" town in southern Missouri, with a population of about two hundred, a courthouse and jail, four stores, tanyard, and two saloons. There was significant economic development as well, and by the late 1850s, wagon freighters used roads leading to the railheads slowly projecting into the interior from St. Louis. Although it was not hard to find isolation in the Ozarks, Monks lived in a time when upland-hill-country inhabitants increasingly participated in and were affected by national developments.[8]

Monks lays it on a little too heavily. Things were so idyllic, he writes, that "the love of Christ appeared to dwell in each heart." Through their churches, people cared for neighbors in distress and adjudicated disputes, and there was "more real charity and religion." It was a time when the Baptists and Methodists got along, and there was no wickedness or dissipation. Locally distilled corn liquor was a common staple, but "if men became drunk on the whiskey it did not appear to make them wild and crazy as the whiskey of to-day does." Even when fights occasionally broke out, they did not feature weapons other than fists. "Men then appeared to be governed by that higher inspiration, that a man should not use anything that would permanently disable or take the life of his fellow-man." Former opponents frequently became close friends.[9]

Yet Monks contradicts his romantic musings with several accounts of whiskey-fueled brawls in which the object was indeed the permanent disability or death of an opponent. He offered several examples of belligerent drunken rowdies filling the air with obscenities and terrorizing decent people. The bravos included the likes of Dow Bryant of Fulton County, first whipped by a small man and then beaten with a board by others. There were also notable feuds between extended family clans. One of the most famous was the Tutt-Everett War, centered in Marion County, Arkansas, in the 1840s, which generated enough violence to prompt the calling out of the state militia. Marion County was also the later battleground for an alcohol-generated feud between the Coker clan and another brawler named Cage Hogan. This grew to such proportions that Hogan moved to Fulton County in fear for his life. Later, in a Howell County fracas, a blacksmith with a Barlow knife sliced him. In 1860 a drunken crowd, including toughs from Oregon County, complete with makeshift uniforms and a flag, threatened to mob a man in West Plains. Although there is no evidence that Monks was involved in it, hooliganism, feuding, and fighting clearly had a long tradition in the Ozarks, and tough customers were not hard to find. Things might not have been as sweet as Monks lets on.[10]

Monks's account of bullies and feudists gives way to his narrative of the Civil War, when life in the Ozarks and his own fortunes changed drastically. Monks had been a Douglas Democrat during the political contest of 1860. He was not remarkable in that respect, though the majority of the inhabitants supported the Southern Democrat candidate, John C. Breckenridge. Monks became prominent by his outspoken adherence to the Union when secession talk became the order of the day. His was a minority opinion, but he expressed it freely until the summer of 1861, when political and military events elsewhere brought war to the Missouri-Arkansas border. James H. McBride, a circuit-court judge residing in Houston, Missouri, was the first pro-Southern leader in south-central Missouri. He became brigadier general commanding the Seventh Division of Gov. Claiborne F. Jackson's prosecession Missouri State Guard. McBride began organizing his division of the state militia when Union forces in St. Louis, led by Brig. Gen. Nathaniel Lyon, preempted whatever slim chance remained to prevent active warfare. Lyon seized the railheads at Ironton and Rolla, occupied Jefferson City, and launched the "Southwest Expedition" toward Springfield. Although his career ended with his death at the battle of Wilson's Creek in August, Lyon's audacious campaign ultimately secured nearly all of the strategic military points in the northern Ozarks critical to keeping Missouri in the Federal fold. Most important for the middle border and also for William Monks, the Lyon campaign established permanent military control of the railhead at Rolla by Union forces.

Lyon's offensive roiled the Ozarks. Southern sympathizers predominated in the border counties, but there was a substantial Union minority as well in both states. The onset of active warfare provoked suppression of pro-Unionism throughout the region when loyalists began refusing to enroll in avowedly prosecession state units. Prominent and outspoken Unionists became the first targets. In southern Missouri, Judge McBride proclaimed martial law in June 1861. Monks had voted for McBride but "didn't consider that McBride had any right to order me to take an oath to take up arms against my country or support those who had taken up arms." The danger for Union men increased when the judge ordered them disarmed and arrested if they resisted. Monks's liberty came to an end on 7 July 1861, when he was seized at home by men of Capt. Michael Forshee's Howell County company of the Missouri State Guard. He claimed that his captors included many former neighbors who pointedly advised him "not to be so saucy" and who were generous with threats of physical harm and promises to hang him "as high as Haman." Still other acquaintances came to see the spectacle of Billy Monks under arrest, including a merchant who advised putting him in prison, predicting that "if he ever gains his liberty you are going to have him to fight." After several days during which the secessionists threatened Monks repeatedly with the ultimatum "the Confederate Army or Hell," they determined to take the prisoners for examination by Maj. Gen. Sterling Price, commander of the Missouri State Guard, who was then marshaling his forces in southwestern Missouri. McBride's men took Monks and other Unionist captives westward along the border with Arkansas. En route, Monks suffered continued abuse and threats from the soldiers, whose officers, he noted bitterly, included Baptist and Methodist preachers who did nothing to ensure the safety of the prisoners.[11]

Monks eventually escaped from his guards on the night of 2 August near Berryville, Arkansas, south of the White River. Hiding by day and traveling at night, he fortuitously encountered a Union family, who fed and sheltered him and facilitated his crossing of the White. Monks then met up with refugees making their way north and was introduced by them to Jesse Galloway and his family, Unionists formerly from Howell County. Monks reached Federal lines at Springfield several days later and was taken before General Lyon, who he says advised him not to enlist but assured him that the military would put his knowledge and talents to work. Monks left Springfield for Rolla when Federal forces abandoned southwestern Missouri after the battle of Wilson's Creek. He lingered briefly among the troops at Rolla before going to St. Louis and then went to stay with old friends in Jersey and Randolph Counties in Illinois. By virtue of a newspaper advertisement, Monks learned that his wife and family had abandoned their home in Howell County and were refugees living at Rolla in huts abandoned by the army. After a separation of many months, Monks reunited with his wife and children at Rolla at the beginning of 1862.[12]

The tale of deliverance from howling mobs of secessionists is a triumph of aggrieved innocence over treason. Monks's resentment at his treatment still smoldered many decades later, and he took pains to name his tormentors. He considered himself fortunate, however, for he knew of other Union men who had been murdered by secessionists, among them an 1812 veteran named Rhodes, killed at Bennett's Bayou in Fulton County. Monks made the grisly claim that a local physician cut out Rhodes's heart to pickle and keep it "so people could see how a black republican's heart looked." The incident cannot be verified, but even if the event did not happen quite like Monks told it, it surely could have, for the neighborhood war in the Ozarks got very harsh very early.[13]

There is only Monks's word for the tale of his arrest and escape; his escape cannot be confirmed or disproved by any available documents. But as far as is known, the facts of his arrest and escape were never proven otherwise, and other developments along the border tend to corroborate the gist of his story, if not the details. Repression of the Union minority in the Ozarks began early in the war, occurring first in Missouri, where active warfare came earlier. After Arkansas joined the Confederacy, coercion extended first to members of the loosely organized "Peace Society" existing in the northern border counties. Members of this Unionist league suffered arrest in the fall of 1861, and many were forced into Confederate service. Others escaped to Federal lines inside Missouri. Hundreds of Unionists streamed out of the border counties of Arkansas and Missouri during the last six months of 1861. Most of the able-bodied men volunteered for the Union army. In Missouri volunteer and state militia regiments, provisional enrolled militia units, and, later, Arkansas cavalry regiments, these men became the tough knot of the Federal military presence in the Ozarks. Fighting in their homeland for almost the entire war against similarly composed enemy forces, they personalized the conflict in the hills and raised the intensity of the guerrilla war.[14]

Some refugees, including Monks, found employment with army quartermasters. The government hired thousands of civilians as teamsters, wagonmasters, blacksmiths, carpenters, clerks, guides, and scouts, paying them more than enlisted soldiers received. Scouts were near the top of the pay scale. They functioned primarily as intelligence gatherers for conventional forces but also worked with provost marshals, thus combining the functions of intelligence agent and citizen-lawman under military authority. In return for higher compensation and more personal independence, scouts experienced increased danger and, if captured, very good chances of a quick and unceremonious demise. Singly and in small groups, often disguised as Confederate soldiers, Southern sympathizers, or civilian travelers making their way to Arkansas, scouts survived through boldness, guile, and knowledge of the country. When it came to locating guerrillas or bushwhackers, many developed into capable counterinsurgents in their own right. Some Federal scouts ("Wild Bill" Hickok is the most notable example) established personal reputations and continued as lawmen or government agents after the war.[15]

Brig. Gen. Samuel Curtis hired Monks as a guide in April 1862. Curtis's army had driven the Rebel army from Missouri and won the battle of Pea Ridge, Arkansas, after which it marched eastward across the border on the north side of the White River. Federal troops reached West Plains on 27 April 1862, then moved south a few days later to occupy Batesville. By the time Monks joined the army, it had been nine months since he had been taken from his home. He was assigned to the provost marshal's office at West Plains, where his job seems to have been determining the loyalty of local citizens, former Missouri State Guardsmen returning home after their six-month term of service, and miscellaneous individuals taken into custody by the Federals. Monks was in a position to pass judgment on people he knew; his determinations meant the difference between being confined in a military prison or being allowed to take an oath of allegiance and return home. As an informant, Monks would have been despised by secessionists in any event, but he evened scores with some who had mistreated him earlier. One, a man named Lusk, had been especially belligerent, threatening "to shoot his black heart out." Meeting up with him, Monks slapped his face three times but reflected that Lusk got off easy. German-immigrant cavalrymen under command of Capt. D. D. Emmons, another Howell County resident and former prisoner of the Rebels, had already beaten Lusk with boards for his earlier slurs regarding "lop-eared Dutch" soldiers.[16]

Monks returned to Rolla when Curtis abandoned Batesville in June 1862, but he would never be away from the border for long. In 1862 he became a second lieutenant of Company H, Sixty-Third Enrolled Missouri Militia, and was ordered to organize a company of scouts. By the end of 1862, Monks was in Texas County, Missouri, serving as a captain of scouts attached to the small garrison at Houston. The force was part of a screen of small outposts across southern Missouri protecting the approaches to the vital depots and regional headquarters at Ironton, Rolla, and Springfield. Fifty miles south from the post at Rolla—and another fifty miles to his old home in West Plains—Houston was well within the no man's land between the Union's strategic line from Cape Girardeau through Ironton, Rolla, and Springfield and Confederate forces along the Missouri-Arkansas border at Batesville, Mammoth Springs, and Thomasville.[17]

Both Union and Confederate armed forces infiltrated and operated in this zone, occasionally in force, but neither side permanently controlled it. The precarious military situation in the Ozarks always depended upon the demand for troops elsewhere, most notably in the Mississippi River theater. Both armies ultimately found the rugged hill country along the border too costly to hold in force for negligible strategic rewards, but it served as a convenient buffer zone. Most of the regular forces left the interior Ozarks by midwar, leaving the region to the mercies of a few conventionally organized volunteer units and a complex and changing mixture of homegrown organizations, including remnants of the Missouri State Guard, Confederate partisans, pro-Union militia, and various ad-hoc groups of irregulars for home defense. Each side fielded locally raised forces, such as the pro-Union Enrolled Missouri Militia regiments and Monks's company, and the quasi-independent units, such as those Confederate commands led by William O. Coleman, Thomas R. Freeman, Edward T. Fristoe, John A. Schnable, George W. Rutherford, and Timothy Reeves. Most of the combatants were natives of the Ozarks, intimately familiar with the terrain and inhabitants by virtue of birth and residence or, as in the case of soldiers in the Missouri State Militia units, long service in the same area. Local forces cooperated occasionally in larger army movements, such as those connected with Confederate cavalry raids into Missouri in 1863 and 1864, and executed conventional small-unit operations, such as patrolling, foraging, recruiting, conscripting, and constabulary activities. But as time passed, guerrilla-style combat—hit-and-run raids, running firefights, ambuscades, and bushwhacking—became the tactical order of the day.[18]

Another hallmark of guerrilla warfare was the increasing brutality toward the noncombatant population. All the combatants lived off the land, a practice that led to the worst abuses of civilians during the war as each side committed depredations against the other's known or suspected sympathizers. The armies rapidly depleted slim reserves of livestock, corn, and military-aged men in the resource-poor Ozarks. There were also common criminals, deserters, and draft dodgers hiding in the hills, often garbed in military mufti and indistinguishable from legitimate soldiers, who plundered local inhabitants unmercifully of everything from livestock and food to bedclothes and kitchen utensils. Conscription, forced requisitions, theft, arson, and murder, whether by regular troops, partisans, or freebooters, persuaded thousands of civilians to opt for life as refugees. Inexorably, more and more civilians abandoned the interior Ozarks for safer places as the war continued. The flight of the noncombatant populace, in turn, created a larger, unstable depopulated zone, the haunt only of armed men.[19]

Monks's narrative of the following year is chronologically confusing. He seems to have been back and forth between Houston and Rolla, and he made several visits to Howell County. Once was at the end of 1862, when he briefly returned to West Plains with Brig. Gen. John W. Davidson's Army of Southeastern Missouri. Again he settled an old account, this time with Captain Forshee, leader of the secessionists who had arrested him in 1861, who had left the Rebel army and was living nearby. Monks devoted several pages to the confrontation, frankly admitting that he went to Forshee's house to kill him. But he found that he could not shoot the man in front of his family, so he took him along for later punishment. To Forshee, who begged for his life, Monks replied "that it was too late to pray after the devil came." Ultimately, Forshee survived, but only after admitting that he had been wrong to turn Monks over to the mob. "The author had now become cool, and while he believed he ought to kill him for what he had done, he could not afford to shoot, or cause a prisoner to be shot, while he was under his charge; so on reaching West Plains, the prisoner was turned over to the guard house." Later, Monks even loaned Forshee a blanket, which he never saw again.[20]

The army declined to garrison West Plains permanently, but Monks served the remaining years of the war in and out of no man's land in his home territory. He operated out of Houston for most of 1863, leading a company of other Union expatriates as mounted rangers. Some, like Monks, seem to have been paid by the Union quartermaster at Rolla. Others got an occasional payday only when funds became available, irregularly, or served without pay in the Enrolled Missouri Militia. Monks and his men were nominally under orders from the headquarters at Rolla but served under the immediate local command of Capt. Richard Murphy of the Fifth Missouri State Militia Cavalry and Lt. John W. Boyd of the Sixth Provisional Enrolled Missouri Militia. In Boyd especially, soon to become notorious for an arsonous raid through Shannon County in November 1863, Monks would have found a kindred aggressive spirit. It is not known whether he was along with Boyd on the fiery raid, but local lore holds that Monks's activities extended into Shannon County during this period.[21]

The scouts always served at the point of anti-insurgent operations and were, in effect, regional Union guerrillas and partisans. Working alone or in conjunction with other Federal forces from Rolla, Waynesville, Hartville, Salem, and Ironton, Monks and the scouts patrolled constantly from Houston, gathering intelligence and skirmishing in Rebel strongholds around Thomasville and the Eleven Point River in Oregon County, along Spring River in Arkansas below West Plains, and in the region around the Warm Fork and Bryant Creek in Ozark and Douglas Counties, Missouri. Monks relates several close calls in his *History*, demonstrating the dangerous lives of scouts. Once he and another scout met up unexpectedly with twenty-five Rebels but talked their way out of a very dicey situation. In another confrontation Monks was nearly identified by a former resident of West Plains, a development that would have resulted in summary execution.[22]

It was during 1863 that Monks's name first appeared in the official records of the war, as army authorities sought to pay the volunteer scouts.

The post commander at Houston wrote that Monks was a good officer who had done a "great deal of service" and whose men were willing to do anything for the benefit of the United States. The district commander also endorsed the worthiness of the unpaid scouts. In July Maj. Gen. John M. Schofield authorized the temporary employment of the men as "cavalry scouts" by the Rolla quartermaster. The army seems to have gotten its money's worth. George West, another Union scout, reported to headquarters at Rolla that Monks and members of the extensive Alsup family of Howell and Douglas Counties were doing more to hurt the Rebel cause than anyone else. They were so effective, said West, that the enemy vowed to shoot them on sight. This is the first time that Monks can be documented in alliance with the turbulent Unionist family. And it was not the last time that Monks appeared in official military records, nor would it be the last time Rebels swore to kill him.[23]

In September 1863 Monks joined a Union delegation from Missouri that traveled to Washington, D.C., for a meeting with Pres. Abraham Lincoln. Many of the men in this group later become the Radical Republican standard bearers in Missouri, including Charles D. Drake, leader of the delegation. Monks was the only representative from any of the border counties to accompany Drake to Washington, where the men sought increased military assistance for Unionists in their state as well as the removal of General Schofield from command of the Department of the Missouri.[24]

Monks was back in Rolla by December 1863, when he and fifteen scouts joined a southbound expedition led by Col. Robert R. Livingston of the First Nebraska Cavalry.[25] The destination was Batesville, where Union authorities had determined to establish a permanent post in an attempt to strengthen their control of the middle border region. En route to Batesville, Livingston's command court-martialed and shot two Confederates captured in Federal uniforms at West Plains and executed two other Confederate soldiers, Calvin Hawkins and Jacob Bridges, caught robbing a house. The expedition reached Batesville on Christmas Day, 1863. The only action was the scattering of some surprised Confederates from Col. Thomas R. Freeman's command at a dance hosted by the women of the town. Monks remembered the ladies as especially vituperative at the intrusion. Livingston's troops and Monks's scouts operated out of Batesville that winter, raiding Freeman's encampments along Sylamore Creek and driving his troops eastward toward Pocahontas, Arkansas. There were some sharp skirmishes, and the Rebels snatched up forage trains and small patrols caught in no man's land, but they were not sufficient to drive the Federals away. Monks related many details of these expeditions in his *History* but neglected to recall Colonel Freeman's official complaint that two of his men had been executed after being captured by the scouts.[26]

In the spring of 1864, Union authorities reorganized veterans of the Missouri State Militia and active-duty troops of the Provisional Enrolled Missouri Militia. The object was to shift troops from state to national service so that the arms, rations, and pay of the new units could be furnished by the United States. Federal status would rationalize lines of military authority, provide a way to regularize the activities of veterans and men such as the scouts, and keep them in the field in areas where they had already established their usefulness. The War Department ultimately created two new volunteer units, the Fifteenth and Sixteenth Missouri Cavalry Regiments, and the Federal command distributed them by companies across southern Missouri in a newly reestablished screen of outposts. The small garrisons would provide early warning of enemy threats to Pilot Knob, Rolla, and Springfield and serve as the weapon of counterinsurgency against guerrillas raiding stagecoaches, merchant trains, and dispatch riders along the Wire Road between Rolla and Springfield.[27]

Monks received orders to take the scouts to Rolla and begin organizing a company of the Sixteenth Missouri Cavalry. En route near West Plains, he not only effected the release of a Union man named Krause, mistakenly arrested by other Union troops but also got on the trail of Benjamin Hawkins, a Confederate guerrilla and alleged murderer living with his wife in the appropriated cabin of a Unionist refugee. Monks shot and mortally wounded Hawkins in the doorway of the cabin when the partisan emerged with a pistol in hand. His account of Hawkins's death is quite detailed, quoting the man's dying words and observing that he laid out his corpse at the widow's request. But Hawkins had been among the men who had mistreated Monks in 1861. Rumors persisted in Howell County that Monks murdered him in cold blood, and there were legal repercussions after the war. The slur on his reputation must have rankled even the old man, for he told the story twice in his *History,* forty pages apart. Monks insisted on his version of events and wrote that truthful Rebels admitted that Hawkins was a bad man who had fired on Union troops and that he was not resting peaceably in the bosom of his family when killed.[28]

Monks spent the spring and summer of 1864 at Rolla organizing Company K. There may have been a few new recruits from the scouts or refugees at Rolla, but the men came mostly from Company K, Sixth Provisional Enrolled Missouri Militia, including the by-now notorious Lt. John W. Boyd, who became first lieutenant of the new organization. The men hailed primarily from the counties of southern Missouri, but there were a handful of Arkansans as well. Some, like Monks, had probably been driven from homes in secessionist-controlled areas on both sides of the border. From service at Houston in 1863, Monks and his men would have been familiar with each other. Company K, numbering eighty-four men, completed organization at Rolla in August 1864 and was mustered at Springfield, where Monks received his commission as captain in September. Some of the Sixteenth Cavalry engaged in the fighting during Price's Missouri Expedition, and Company K skirmished around Newtonia. This period during the fall of 1864 was the only time that the Sixteenth Missouri Cavalry engaged in conventional warfare as part of the operations of a larger army. Despite his stirring description of battle around "Utony" (Newtonia), Monks seems to have been left at Springfield with that part of the company unable to travel. Later he led a detachment escorting three hundred prisoners from Price's army to the railhead at Rolla. Returning to Springfield, Monks received orders to take his company back to Texas County and establish a permanent post south of Rolla. His mission in no man's land was to break up Confederate groups that had filtered back into the interior Ozarks in the aftermath of Price's invasion.[29]

The old scout charged back into the partisan war with a vengeance, taking Company K on a direct route eastward from Springfield through Hartville. Pressing on through heavy snow, they surprised guerrillas wintering along the headwaters of the Gasconade and Big Piney Rivers, skirmishing daily until the company reached Licking about 11 January

1865. Monks reported the killings of several guerrillas along the way, eliciting this laconic comment by the commanding general at Rolla: "Captain Monks' men must be good marksmen, as it is seldom so large a proportion of hits prove fatal." The remark hints at the remorseless nature of the guerrilla war in the hills. Monks and his men brought in few prisoners of any kind, nor was it expected.[30]

Monks established headquarters at Licking, forty miles south of Rolla in Texas County. Licking (or Lick Settlement) was ten miles closer than Houston to supplies and support from Rolla but was far enough into no man's land for mounted expeditions to reach enemy sanctuaries along the border. The small force at Licking could also cooperate with troops from similar outposts in Douglas and Wright Counties to the west, from Waynesville and Salem in the District of Rolla, and those farther east directed by the headquarters at Pilot Knob. Licking was an exposed position, and the threat of attack was very real. Monks's command probably never exceeded more than sixty effective men; reinforcement or relief from Rolla was, at best, a hard day's ride away. The first order of business was to fortify the post with a small stockade or palisaded fort—a defense proven effective for small garrisons beleaguered by raiders. Monks pressed the few remaining citizens for labor on the fortification, organized the men into a militia company, and linked his security to that of the local populace by demanding that they report guerrilla activity. Replying to the complaints of citizens that informants would be killed, Monks's brutal response characterized the rock-and-the-hard-place choices between which the locals found themselves: "I have said to you and all others that if you fail to report them I will kill you; and you say if you do report them, they will kill you; now, if you are more afraid of them than you are of me, you will have to risk the consequences; for, by the eternal God! if you fail to report them, I have said to you that I would treat you as a bushwhacker, and you well know how I treat them."[31]

Not content merely to control the immediate vicinity around Licking, Monks mounted an aggressive campaign to strike Freeman's command in winter quarters in Oregon County, Missouri, and Fulton County, Arkansas. Federal raiders skirmished near Licking, Thomasville, Spring River Mills, and along the Warm Fork in late winter and spring of 1865, leading Monks to boast that it was rare to find a regular Confederate movement north of the state line. But deserters, bands of men evading conscription and forced enrollment, and common criminals still infested no man's land. They robbed and murdered enrolled militiamen, mail riders, traveling merchants, and inoffensive citizens, plundering even the most isolated settlements. There is no doubt that these outlaws, known generically as "bushwhackers," comprised yet other armed forces roaming the interior Ozarks. Often purporting to be legitimate combatants of one side or the other, these outlaws besmirched the honorable service of regular troops while depredating against their families and neighborhoods. One of the most unusual events of the guerrilla war occurred in the spring of 1865 when Monks and Col. Thomas R. Freeman attempted to arrange a local truce between Federal and Confederates forces, which would then cooperate in hunting and killing outlaws. The plan was abandoned after one of Freeman's agents was killed by bushwhackers, but the episode was an unusual example of bitter opponents willing to cooperate against a common and even more despicable enemy.[32]

Monks and his company continued to hunt and kill armed men in the region into the summer of 1865. As late as May he proposed an expedition in force to "clean out" bushwhackers and outlaws. Remorseless as he was, Monks seemed to realize that there were limits to the behavior of Union troops. His orders, implying past abuse, consistently prohibited his men from demanding food from citizens unless it was paid for and commanded them to "Protect all citizens who show a willingness to surrender themselves up to the laws and protect the property of all law abiding citizens." He complained to headquarters at Rolla in June 1865 of a murder and other depredations by another company of the Sixteenth Missouri Cavalry. Belying his later fearsome reputation, Monks displayed a surprising tolerance when he wrote: "I think we should act in good faith if we expect good faith. . . . The people generally show a willingness to return to their allegiance and lay down their arms and do all in their power to restore law and order. I don't think such acts [the depredations] should be tolerated." The regiment mustered out of service at Springfield at the end of June. In a final report concerning the activities of his company from January through May

1865, Monks proudly wrote that his men had killed fifty guerrillas and bushwhackers and traveled nearly five thousand miles during five months of operations out of Licking.[33]

Organized fighting ceased, but the border remained a desolate and dangerous place. Not a house stood along the road between Rolla and Batesville at war's end, and West Plains was entirely destroyed by the time Monks began organizing a party of twenty-five refugee families at Rolla to return there. The Unionist had been lucky during the war: he had never been wounded, though his horse was killed under him in one engagement and a bullet passed through his hat on another occasion. But former Confederate soldiers and displaced refugees were returning to the area, and there were many local Rebels with good reason to hate Monks and to resist his return to Howell County. Asked if he did not fear going into the lair of his enemies, Monks replied, "D——n a man that is afraid to go back and enjoy the fruits of his victory." The remark revealed his attitude and determined his actions for the next decade.[34]

Arriving at West Plains, Monks sheltered his family in a converted stable on the edge of the ruined town square. He became the sheriff of Howell County, an appointment he held only briefly before being appointed to represent Howell in the Missouri legislature. Of his legislative tenure in 1866–68, Monks wrote nothing beyond expressing dismay at the corrupting influence of railroad fever in the assembly. He may have been otherwise reticent because his activities in Jefferson City seem to have been distinguished mostly by a death threat directed at him by a reporter of the *St. Louis Missouri Republican*. Monks is also said to have challenged Speaker of the House A. J. Harlan to a duel when that official ignored his requests to speak on the floor. Monks's nervous habit of sipping water between sentences in public addresses led his opponents to characterize him as a windmill diverted from its proper use and powered by water.[35]

By 1863, if not before, Monks identified himself with the Radical Republicans in Missouri. He and his men in Texas County voted solidly for the new Radical state constitution in 1865, and there was no complaint with the new regime's determination to crush rebellion once and for all. In 1866 the county clerk, prosecuting attorney, and other Radical officials at Rolla promoted Monks's appointment as enrolling officer of the Howell County militia; he almost certainly formed a personal association with Thomas Fletcher, the Radical governor of Missouri, during his term in the legislature. Although documentation of any tacit understanding has not been found, Monks's activities in southern Missouri in 1867–68 indicate that he had no fear of censure by the governor.[36]

Monks was also busy on land and legal fronts. It is not known when or where Monks was admitted to the bar, but he began a career of litigation in local courts after the war, with civil suits against William Nicks and Nathan Barnett, former lieutenants of the secessionist company that arrested him at his home in 1861. In the Union-controlled court of Howell County, Monks won judgments and personal damages from the men despite their defense that they acted pursuant to orders under martial law. Monks seized their property in lieu of payment but claims to have told them that he would deed the property to their wives and families. He finally settled on a small cash payment and land in Gunter Valley from Barnett and received several hundred acres of "tax lands" from Nicks. Monks tried to make the dual point that his old enemies could not be trusted and that he was a merciful victor, but surely Barnett and Nicks could not have been "grateful for what I had done for them." Later, with John S. Wadle and Washington F. Gieger in the real-estate firm styled Monks and Company, Monks came into possession of the land of Benjamin Hawkins, the same guerrilla he had gunned down in the doorway of a Howell County cabin in 1864.[37]

Monks soon was back in armed service in familiar country. In August 1867 the adjutant general of Missouri called into service a detachment of fifty men of the Eleventh Battalion Missouri Militia. Governor Fletcher commissioned Monks as major of the battalion, which was composed of both Union and Confederate veterans and included militia companies in Howell and Oregon Counties. Monks had orders to break up bands of horse thieves and other "desperadoes" in Oregon, Shannon, Texas, Carter, and Dent Counties. This region had provided bases for regular Confederate as well as guerrilla units throughout the war and was the winter grounds for many Rebels in 1864–65 following the dispersal of Sterling Price's army following the Missouri Expedition. Many never left after the Confederacy surrendered. The area was the prewar home for many of them, others dared not return home, and apparently a few had no allegiance to any place except away from the law.[38]

Deserters, freebooters, smugglers, and thieves, both indigenous and imported, had also congregated in the military vacuum in southeastern Missouri just out of arm's reach of Union district commanders. Many remained in the region and became powers unto themselves when the last Federal units left the Ozarks in the summer of 1865. The outlaws continued to plunder the locals and sortied from hideouts to steal horses and loot country stores south of the rail lines. They persistently defied attempts by local officials, whether former Confederates or northern carpetbaggers, to reestablish civil authority. Circuit-court officials ventured south from Rolla and Ironton only in fear for their lives. Oregon County was especially congenial to the gangs; the sheriff himself consorted with outlaws. Men led by Jim Jamison, Dick Kitchen, and other former Confederate guerrillas sheltered along the Eleven Point River near Thomasville. The former county seat of Oregon County, Thomasville had a long-established reputation along the border as a place for racing, buying, and trading fast horses. During and after the war, there were persistent rumors that it was a depot for stolen horses and a center of horse thieving and smuggling with national connections through Ironton and St. Louis. Monks had chased and tried to kill these men in 1865, and, although his men had winnowed outlaws by the score, he never got the alleged local ringleaders. Here was an opportunity to finish the job.[39]

Monks writes that he accepted the militia commission solely to ensure the security of Howell County from depredations of outlaws in neighboring counties and that Governor Fletcher asked him to take command after receiving pleas by Capt. John Alley, a former Confederate officer and the registrar of Oregon County. Outlaws had killed returning Union veterans and threatened Alley's life, preventing him from enrolling voters according to law. Monks claims too that a secret organization of ex-Confederates known as the Sons of Liberty cooperated with the outlaws. Their combined efforts were dedicated to preventing Union men from ever living in the area by any means, including intimidation, robbery, arson, and murder. The outlaw chief Jim

Jamison personally vowed to kill Monks if he ever entered Oregon County.[40]

Even former Confederates such as Alley and Capt. Samuel Greer could agree that there were outlaws and bitter former Rebels in Oregon County. Yet Monks was a Radical state representative when he accepted Fletcher's commission in 1867, and operations of the Radical militia bore political implications. Violent repressive excesses elsewhere in Missouri by Bacon Montgomery, Thomas A. Babcock, and other officers had already compromised Fletcher's Radical militia. Any use of the state's military would be politicized no matter its motives. Monks's was the first militia operation along the border, though not the last. For nearly two decades after the war, the state deployed troops to quell vigilantism and civil disturbances in counties across southern Missouri. The immediate causes for the turmoil varied, but the disturbances generally featured former Confederates against former Unionists fighting for local control of county offices, finances, and courts.[41]

Monks also operated in what were known as the "Rodmanized" counties of southern Missouri, so named for Francis A. Rodman, the Radical secretary of state of Missouri. Rodman blatantly manipulated local elections by means of voter registration, which was administered by Radical appointees and backed, if necessary, by Radical militia. He invoked technicalities to reject whole blocks of votes and assure Radical victories. In 1866 very few counties in southern Missouri held elections because the voting apparatus had not been reestablished, and, in any event, most of the electorate consisted of ex-Confederates disqualified from voting. But in 1867 incumbent senator Thomas E. Noell of the Third Congressional District in southeastern Missouri died in office, leading to a special election on 27 December. Rodman unsuccessfully attempted to void the victory of Conservative James M. McCormick by rejecting the votes of Madison, Butler, Carter, Ripley, Oregon, and Shannon Counties. In the regular election of 1868, Conservative voters reelected McCormick and threatened Radical control of county offices, whereupon the secretary of state refused to certify the votes of Oregon, Carter, Wayne, and Ripley Counties.[42]

Rodman's high-handed manipulation outraged former Rebels and Conservatives, who were effectively disfranchised while the Radicals in

Missouri promoted black suffrage. Although the Missouri Supreme Court later rejected Rodman's illegal actions in some of the most fraud-filled elections in the state's history, in the interim the Radicals maintained their dominance. Operating in this area under such political circumstances, Monks from this point on became increasingly identified as Governor Fletcher's gunman on the middle border, entirely devoted to the aggrandizement of Radical Republicans and his own self-interest at the expense of very familiar and un-Reconstructed old foes.[43]

Although Monks's mission was in Missouri, the first act of his militiamen may have been a cross-border raid to Salem, the seat of Fulton County, Arkansas, in September 1867. A band of twenty armed men, identifying themselves as Missouri militiamen in search of horse thieves, surrounded the courthouse at Salem and terrorized the citizens, attorneys, and county officials holding court. The "militiamen" ransacked a store and rode away with two prisoners. The band turned up next at the house of A. J. Smith near Salem. Not knowing the armed men in his dooryard arriving near midnight, Smith broke and ran from his house, whereupon he was shot dead; the "Ruffians" were said to have expressed regret at the killing. Monks was not identified as the leader of the Missourians in any contemporary account, though he would have surely been known to the people of Fulton County. The accusations that he led or directed the raid came a year later, when Monks was definitely with the next group of Missourians to invade northern Arkansas.[44]

Monks took the Howell County militia to Oregon County in the fall of 1867. By his own account, it was a brutal campaign. When the militiamen captured four of Jim Jamison's cohorts, the major had them lashed to a wagon, at the same time sending word to the outlaw leader that he would kill the prisoners if the militia were fired upon. Monks then proceeded into the outlaw's lair, but Jamison and his gang elected not to test his resolve. Later, some of his militiamen captured the Oregon County sheriff and tortured him by hanging him until he was ready to talk. Two companies of Oregon County militiamen, nearly all of whom were ex-Confederate soldiers, joined the Howell company, and the combined battalion dispersed the criminals. Some were captured and turned over to civil authorities for trial. Others were tracked down and killed by the Oregon County militia. Jim Jamison and Dick Kitchen left

Missouri altogether, possibly for Texas. Others may have fled to Indian Territory, expecting to evade the reach of justice, only to swing later on Judge Isaac Parker's gallows at Fort Smith, Arkansas.[45]

The Oregon County militiamen may have done the lion's share of the work. Captain Alley wrote Missouri's adjutant general that Monks's company was not doing much and intimated that he would not be displeased to see it reassigned. Monks said of the rest of the campaign only that he took his own his company north into Shannon County to prevent the gangs from escaping in that direction. His militia detachment was relieved from active service in December 1867. In his biennial report for 1867–68, the adjutant general noted expenditures for Monks's battalion of fifty men amounting to $6,328.60, but there is no record of payment for the Oregon County militia. In 1868 the Oregon County court continued its militia with funds from its own treasury, which may have been as much to keep Monks's company out as it was to combat outlaws. Monks complained that the ringleaders had been killed or driven out but left behind sympathizers who "began lying and preferring all manner of charges against the writer and his men." He insisted, "it was admitted by all honorable Confederates that I had enforced a strict discipline over my own men and protected all classes of citizens in person and property, had paid the people for all forage and commissaries that were required for the soldiers, and had driven out the worst set of bushwhackers, thieves and murderers that ever lived."[46]

The year 1868 was critical for Monks and his fortunes. During the summer, rumors circulated that he had been assassinated, and by year's end he had reached the high-water mark of his regional power as well as the beginning of the end of his influence. It was also a year of significant elections in both Missouri and Arkansas. Voters sent Radical governor Fletcher of Missouri to the U.S. Senate, and Joseph W. McClurg, with whom Monks apparently had less influence, followed Fletcher as governor. Arkansas too experienced a change in leadership when Powell Clayton, a former Kansas cavalry officer and postwar carpetbagger, became Radical governor of the state, taking over from the moderate but weak administration of Gov. Isaac Murphy in July 1868. Monks's detractors charged that in order to recoup his flagging influence in Missouri, he launched off into northern Arkansas, becoming

Clayton's hired gun and finding new fields for his roughshod methods and men.[47]

Arkansas was fertile ground for *coups de main*. It had suffered four years of guerrilla conflict during the war, exacerbated by ineffective Federal administration at Little Rock and from Washington that undercut attempts by moderate loyalists to establish a pro-Union government in the state. As one historian put it, Arkansans "were the last to abandon the Confederate cause and did so only reluctantly and with ill grace." Violence barely slackened after 1865 and crescendoed in 1867 with the advent of Congressional Reconstruction in the former Confederate states. The prewar Democratic and late Confederate powers in Arkansas had already made significant inroads toward regaining political hegemony in county courts and judicial circuits. Their power evaporated when the Radical-dominated Congress refused to recognize the governments of the former rebellious states. Readmission to the Union pended the approval of the Fourteenth Amendment and new state constitutions guaranteeing the civil rights of former slaves. Nearly all native whites were disfranchised by restrictions on former Confederates and their sympathizers while Radicals promoted suffrage for freedmen and employed them in state militias. As in other southern states during Reconstruction, Arkansas's Radical Party based its political control on the votes of African Americans, manipulation of voter registration to exclude non-Republican ballots, increased taxation, and the use of white and black loyalist militias to suppress dissent. When Powell Clayton and the Radicals gained control of state offices and engineered approval of a new state constitution in July 1868, Congress readmitted Arkansas. The Radical constitution stripped a considerable amount of political power from local officials and placed it in the hands of Governor Clayton, who quickly demonstrated his resolve to dominate the state.[48]

Disfranchised former Confederates and the prewar political elites, determined to maintain their influence at the local level and utterly opposed to black suffrage, reacted furiously to the new Radical regime. Murders of Freedmen's Bureau representatives, African Americans, Radical registrars, political officials, militia officers, and veterans of the Federal army became increasingly epidemic in 1867 and 1868, particularly in the cotton-producing Arkansas delta. One estimate tallied two hundred murders statewide in the three months prior to the November 1868 election alone. Radicals charged that the Democratic Party orchestrated the violence, directing it through the secret organization of former Confederate soldiers known as the Ku Klux Klan. Founded in Tennessee in 1865 and dedicated to maintaining white supremacy, the Klan attracted many members in eastern Arkansas, where it was led by ex-Confederate colonel Robert G. Shaver. The Radicals claimed that the murders and other civil disturbances presaged a general assault on the statehouse in Little Rock.[49]

The Radical Party seized every opportunity to blame all civil disorder in Arkansas on the Klan, including some petty crime as well as acceptable political dissent. Radicals too had secret organizations, Union Leagues, that could be employed for political skullduggery, and the assassination of Maj. Gen. Thomas C. Hindman at Helena demonstrated that former Confederates were not immune to the increasing anarchy. The rhetoric of both parties, published in partisan newspapers, verged on incendiary. Yet despite the vast predominance of Unionists, Radicals, and blacks among the victims, Democratic organs minimized the existence of the Klan and blamed the violence on garden-variety criminals, private feuds arising from the war, and even Radicals disguised as Klansmen. Newspaper editors inveighed against revolutionary Radical social initiatives involving freed blacks and came dangerously close to advocating violence, including the assassination of unpopular officials. Klansmen may have been responsible for much of the violence, especially as directed against freedmen, but their group also provided an easy scapegoat and convenient label for nonpolitical acts of personal vengeance and self-aggrandizement. Historians of Arkansas will never agree on the extent or influence of the Klan within the Democratic Party or its culpability for civil and political disturbances in the decade following the war. Modern historical opinion seems to be that most of the murders, beatings, and mobbings, while undoubtedly politically and racially motivated in the main, were more than spontaneous but less than carefully orchestrated. Yet racial issues were not paramount in the Ozarks. African Americans had a negligible presence in the mountain counties, and there were no black militia units to inflame the passions of native whites. Instead, civil war continued between long-acquainted Union and Confederate enemies. The antagonists all had a full stock of bitter grievances, and the disturbances had aspects of a protracted neighborhood feud.[50]

Whatever the truth about the Klan, Monks certainly believed the worst of the secret organization, and it became the object of one of the most controversial episodes of his career. It began on 19 September 1868, when several gunmen ambushed and killed Capt. Simpson Mason near Bennett's Bayou, Arkansas. Like Monks, Mason was a controversial character in his community. A Georgia native and resident of Fulton County by the 1850s, he had left the area with Curtis's Union army in 1862. Monks said he became acquainted with Mason during the war; they may have served together as scouts in 1863 at Houston, Missouri, and Mason was one of Monks's scouts at Batesville in 1864. He was Fulton County's representative in the first session of the Unionist state legislature, and Unionists across the northern border region acknowledged him as a leader. Mason received a militia commission from Governor Murphy in 1865 and was back in Rolla in May, where he organized a party of sixty refugees. He led them back to Fulton County in June 1865, when Mason's detractors claimed he immediately initiated a campaign of plunder that ultimately left four men dead; they also charged him with three murders in Independence County in 1864. Mason became an official of the Freedman's Bureau and a Radical county official when Governor Clayton appointed him to the Board of Registration in Fulton County. It was his political activities as registrar, so hated by disfranchised ex-Confederates, that finally aroused the fury of his assassins. Mason's activity made him vulnerable, and earlier he had written Murphy that he expected to be killed. Radicals attributed his murder to the Ku Klux Klan and pointed to a particularly inflammatory Democratic speech given at Batesville the week before. Democrats hastily disavowed knowledge of both the killing and the Klan and suggested that the murder was the result of private vengeance arising from the war.[51]

Unionists were intensely aroused by news of the killing. Perhaps as many as two hundred Arkansas militia and loyalists from the mountain border counties assembled in Fulton County to ferret out and punish the murderers. One report claimed that only appeals by Col. Logan H. Roots, a Republican candidate for Congress, and Gen. Martin Beem of Montana, who were in Salem for speaking engagements, kept the mob from lynching several ex-Confederates. Suspicion fell on a Fulton County group that included Col. Joseph H. Tracey and his brother, N. H. Tracey; Dow Bryant; Uriah B. Bush; and other former Confederates and sympathizers. The county sheriff and a group of Arkansas militiamen came to the neighborhood two days after the killing and began making arrests. Into this well-stirred pot rode Monks and a band of perhaps seventy-five Missourians who identified themselves as "militia."[52]

It is not clear how word of Mason's death reached Howell County. People in Fulton County believed it was through the Radical-appointed sheriff or the Union League that Mason had organized. Monks wrote only that "a courier" arrived with the news of the killing, reports of Union people terrorized by the Ku Klux Klan, and appeals for men and arms. Mason and the Klan aside, Unionists in southern Missouri remembered Colonel Tracey for raids into Ozark and Douglas Counties in 1863. A council of citizens convened at West Plains to respond to the appeal. Monks claims that "old men" (presumably careful and conservative) chaired the committee, which also included Monks, Benjamin Alsup, and other veteran Unionists. Led by the committee, "the loyal people of Howell county" resolved to go at once to Fulton County with all available men and arms. Monks, who controlled arms and ammunition left over from the operations of his militia battalion, helped organize a company under the command of Alsup. He saw no legal impediment to going south: "since the rebels at the commencement of the Civil war had had no regard for state lines I thought that we would have the same right to go down and help our loyal brethren to enforce the civil law." Monks also writes that he and Mason had made a solemn pact after the war that if one were murdered, the survivor would see that justice was done. The *History* features a photograph of an improbable reenactment of the event, showing an aged Monks shaking hands with a flag-bearing young stand-in for Mason, with the melodramatic caption "Making a Pledge."[53]

The Howell County posse rode into Fulton County on 23 September and met up with Sheriff Ed Spears and thirty Arkansas State

Guardsmen on Bennett's Bayou. The sheriff and Captain Richardson, the militia commander, already had in custody Uriah Bush, Joseph H. Tracey, N. L. Baker, and others implicated in the murder but had not apprehended N. H. Tracey or Dow Bryant. They reported 350 Klansmen were organizing around Batesville to attack the militia and "readily accepted" the offer of assistance from the Missourians. Monks says that while in Fulton County, he received a dispatch from Governor Clayton offering him the lieutenant colonelcy of the Seventh Arkansas State Guard, commanded by Col. George W. Dale of Independence County. Monks may have had misgivings about his earlier disregard for state boundaries, for he claims to have suggested that the Howell County posse make their actions legal by enrolling in the Arkansas militia. Disgusted with such technicalities (according to Monks), Alsup and some of the others proposed hanging the prisoners from the first tree. Although Alsup and about a third of the group ultimately returned to Missouri, Monks and the others stayed on and were mustered in to the Arkansas militia. For the next seven to ten days, the militia raided and plundered the farms, homes, and businesses of Tracey and his associates. They had already developed considerable information on Mason's murder, probably by torturing Dow Bryant after his capture. Hanging, found effective earlier with the Oregon County sheriff, evidently also worked on Bryant. He apparently named Uriah Bush as one of Mason's murderers, crediting him with boasting: "'Let [Mason] come. I can get him. I can hit an old gobbler's neck that far.'"[54]

Joseph H. Tracey and N. L. Baker, two of the prisoners, claimed that Monks called for a vote of the militia, saying, "All who are in favor of killing the prisoners, fall into line and I am with you." At about dark on 28 September, the fortuitous arrival of the deputy sheriff of Fulton County, bearing a writ of habeas corpus issued by Judge Elisha Baxter at Salem, may have saved the lives of some of the prisoners. Monks honored Baxter's writ and turned over Tracey and Uriah Bush to the deputy, who started with them toward Salem. Two miles down the road, "a party of men, with paper caps on," accosted the sheriff and his prisoners. They seized the bridle of Bush's horse, but Tracey escaped during the commotion. Tracey later said he heard Bush begging for his life, then gunfire. Bush's pleas availed him nothing, and he died on the road to Salem.

Monks's account leaves much to be desired. He writes only that "a posse of armed men" killed Bush and expresses no regret. Paper caps and gunmen masquerading as Klansmen are frequently noted in Reconstruction-era accounts. Although it is possible that Missourians thus disguised killed Bush, Monks and his men had had plenty of opportunity to execute him earlier but had not. Richardson's Arkansas militiamen are equally likely suspects. The Missourians wasted no time investigating Bush's murder and left for Howell County. Monks writes that he returned to recruit more men for Powell Clayton's Arkansas militia, but his antagonists sneered that he skedaddled when he learned that hundreds of Klansmen and outraged citizens were converging on Fulton County to drive him out. Residents flatly accused Monks of complicity in Bush's murder and charged the Alsups (presumably Benjamin Alsup and his nephew, Martin S. Alsup) with shooting him. Several days later under equally mysterious circumstances, Dow Bryant was found hanged from a tree near his home. Radicals said he had been executed by the Klan as an informant; Democrats called him another victim of the militia. Conservatives in Missouri were even more angered than those in Arkansas. The *St. Louis Times* unleashed one of the most vitriolic diatribes of the whole episode, asking: "Is it possible that there is not a single person in Missouri or Arkansas who has the courage and determination to rid the world of this fiend, Monks? What kind of blood courses through the veins of the men whose relatives he has slain, [and] whose homes he has laid waste?"[55]

Monks's return to Missouri may have had as much to do with political matters in Howell County as anything, for he was standing for reelection as state representative in the November elections. His opponent was Benjamin Alsup, scion of an extended family in Howell, Douglas, Ozark, and Greene Counties and leader of the men who refused to follow the major into the Arkansas militia. Monks surely regretted the campaign of 1868, which ended in a defeat he fails to mention in his memoir. It must have especially galled him that his opponents were Alsup and his clan, former comrades in arms and Radical allies. The Alsups had been active Unionists during the war, adamantly so after Confederate authorities arrested Ben in 1862 for assisting the first Federal expedition (a battalion of the Sixth Missouri Cavalry commanded by Lt. Col. Samuel N. Wood) to venture from Rolla to the border. The Rebels imprisoned Alsup in Little Rock, chaining him next to a mule in a bark mill or tanyard, a punishment that left him with permanent injuries. His relations served in various Union volunteer and militia units throughout the war. Those in the Douglas County Home Guard, Sixth Provisional Enrolled Missouri Militia, Forty-Sixth Missouri Infantry, and Sixteenth Missouri Cavalry were Monks's next-door allies in the brutal guerrilla war in the border region, and by war's end, the Alsup clan was the dominant Unionist group in Douglas and Ozark Counties. Their detractors accused them of persecuting former Rebels and even former Unionists with whom they disagreed and of complicity in Uriah Bush's murder. The Alsups seem to have cooperated with Monks until the election of 1868. Although the major was careful to praise the wartime patriotism of the Alsups, he portrayed Ben afterward as far more vengeful than himself. At the very least, this political contest indicated a falling out among old Radicals. It may also have been, depending on the source, either a concerted effort by moderate forces in Howell County to curb the excesses of Monks's "gang" or a greedy attempt by the Alsup clan to seize control of the county.[56]

Stung by his defeat, Monks appealed the decision in December 1868 and began assembling affidavits documenting voting irregularities among Alsup's adherents. But, adding insult to injury, Alsup countered with proof of illegal votes and improper procedures in townships controlled by Monks, even asking that the vote of his brother, Francis M. Monks, be rejected. There was also evidence that some Monks voters had been less than strictly loyal during the war, others had unsavory pasts, and another, an African American, was not entitled to vote. Ultimately, the legislature acknowledged Alsup's election, but not before the Radicals engaged in some intraparty bloodletting. The controversy delighted old Rebels throughout the Ozarks, who hooted at the trouble between "Benjamin, the Bark-Grinder" and "William the Roost Robber."[57]

The appeal of Alsup's election was part of Monks's offensive against enemies front and rear. At the same time, he recruited three companies for the Arkansas militia. His brother captained one of these; John Nicholas and John W. Rice of Howell County led the other two. No rosters of the Arkansas militia seem to have survived, but the Missourians probably included Union army veterans of guerrilla war from Howell, Texas, Ozark, and Douglas Counties. With "one hundred Springfield rifles and one thousand rounds of cartridges for each gun," Monks and his men rallied once again and rode south into Arkansas at the end of November.[58]

The Missourians returned to a state again embroiled in martial law, civil disturbances, and violence by armed bands, played out in the theater of Radical Reconstruction and the 1868 national elections. Gov. Powell Clayton had previously organized the state into military districts, named officers, and deployed a few units. Now, goaded by the murder of Mason, the assassination of Congressman James Hinds in Woodruff County, and the Klan's hijack and destruction of arms bound for the Arkansas militia, Clayton declared martial law immediately following the October elections. Two or three hundred Arkansas and Missouri militiamen assembled in Fulton County and at Batesville, where Colonel Dale levied local merchants for several hundred dollars of supplies. Authorized to live off the land in its operations, the militia commandeered buildings, livestock, clothing, shoes, and blankets as well as food and forage. The activities generated complaints of plunder wherever the militia operated, sparked an exculpatory investigation by the adjutant general, and led to equally controversial damage claims paid by the state.[59]

In January 1869 Monks received orders to report with his detachment to Brig. Gen. Daniel P. Upham, commanding the militia in the District of Northeastern Arkansas. They marched through Jacksonport, where Monks said he personally foiled a drunken assassination attempt on his life, and met Upham at Cotton Plant on the lower White River. Upham, wounded earlier in an ambush in Woodruff County, had assembled seven hundred white militiamen and was ready for an offensive against the Klan. Monks and his detachment did no fighting and suffered no casualties, but their well-armed presence tipped the balance of power in northeastern Arkansas to the Radicals. The mere arrival of the detachment at Marion lifted a siege of a militia unit there, which may speak less to the military prowess than the desultory tactics of both Klan and besieged militia. Monks and his men wound up in Osceola in

Mississippi County, where he harangued the citizens, reportedly at their own request, about the war, the Klan, Simpson Mason, and the right of Missourians to operate in Arkansas. Monks charges that the militiamen were drunken and insubordinate and that some of the officers were corrupt. He claims that he and his men restored order in Osceola, and indeed, there is some evidence that Monks's men were better disciplined than Upham's. The Jacksonport newspaper reported later that the Missourians' peaceful behavior in that town gave lie to their dreaded reputation. Ultimately, Upham's operations in Mississippi and Crittenden Counties broke up the Klan and dispersed opposition to Radical authority, but it left behind a trail of dead Democrats or Klansmen, four black militiamen executed for raping white women, and scores of plundered homes and businesses.[60]

There was some grumbling in the Arkansas legislature about Governor Clayton's embrace of Monks and the Missourians, and Democratic newspaper editors fulminated about violations of the state's sovereignty, alleged murders of its citizens, and the governor's despotism. Yet General Upham was controversial enough himself to draw most of the criticism away from his Missouri subordinate, and in any case, such charges in the northeast paled in comparison with those elsewhere, most notably in Conway County and in southwestern Arkansas, where the worst fighting occurred at Center Point between Brig. Gen. Robert F. Catterson's militia and a force of Klansmen. Ultimately, Clayton's militia secured the immediate survival of his regime and the long-term survival of the Republican Party in Arkansas. Long demonized in Arkansas histories, Clayton's mobilization of black and white militia units is now considered one of the most effective campaigns by a Radical governor during Reconstruction against Democratic insurgents and the Ku Klux Klan. In the absence of support from U.S. authorities, Monks and his Missourians were valuable allies.[61]

Clayton ordered Monks to muster out his detachment and to meet him at Little Rock in February 1869. At the time, Monks was at Marion, Arkansas, where citizens presented him a new suit of clothes when they learned of his orders. He left his command at Jacksonport and arrived in Little Rock only to learn that the governor was sick and confined to his room. Instead, he met with Clayton's adjutant, through whom the governor tendered Monks a commission as brigadier general in the militia. Monks declined. He and Clayton never met. In the interim Monks accepted a request to address the Arkansas legislature and public at the capitol. He reprised his earlier harangue against the Klan, followed by intemperate speeches by Colonel Dale and a Representative Butler from Helena, after which "the whole house rose to its feet and gave three cheers and pressed forward to give the writer a good, parting handshake." Monks's opponents no doubt bid him good riddance.[62]

If Monks returned to Missouri expecting that his reputation had been burnished in Arkansas, he was sadly mistaken. There was trouble at home: "a new political organization, composed of men who styled themselves Liberal Republicans, and democrats and rebels" and working "through some of the most vicious and unprincipled rebels," had risen against him. Monks did not shy away from the trouble, which began when he and his men joined Clayton's militia. In October 1868, Howell County citizens of the Alsup faction had produced resolutions condemning cross-border movements and Monks's militia, but the situation did not reach killing heat until men began to return home in the spring of 1869. Some of them brought back horses taken from Arkansas, whose owners then came to Howell County for civil assistance in recovering their property. When Sheriff Hugh Cordell found the livestock, the animals were in the possession of Dr. Nathan West, whose son was one of Monks's lieutenants. Two other former militiamen had given the horses to Dr. West, who was attempting to hide them from the authorities. When the sheriff caught up with him, West drew a gun and shot Cordell. The mortally wounded sheriff, "an Allsop partizan [sic]," returned fire and killed West, "a Monks adherent." Martin S. Alsup, Ben's nephew, then became sheriff. Monks does not mention Cordell or West in his memoir, only that he returned from Arkansas to find a furor over the killings. Monks then attempted to have Cordell's assistants charged in connection with West's death, but grand juries in Howell and Dent Counties refused to indict them. Old Rebels opined that the killings were examples of God taking vengeance upon the guilty; others said the murder charges were merely Monks's crass attempt to obtain a reward offered in connection with the murder. In any case, the Cordell episode added "another item to the many charges of perfidious rascality heaped against his [Monks's] name."[63]

A man named Joe Little leveled other charges regarding Monks in Arkansas. He was a questionable informant, about to be hanged at Little Rock for murder. Nevertheless, newspapers in Missouri and Arkansas published Little's confession, said to have been made to cellmates on the eve of his execution. He claimed to be a member of a criminal band of which General Upham was the captain and Monks the treasurer and said that the Missouri militiamen had been recruited with promises of "all the horses and money" they desired in Arkansas. Little also said that he had been ordered to murder his victim and voiced the timeworn complaint that he had been framed. The startling charges were never examined in any court, nor did they save Little's life. No evidence has been found that any of them were true.[64]

The remainder of Monks's memoir is brief but describes two alleged assassination attempts four years apart. Trouble first erupted on 8 June 1870, when he threatened to shoot Dr. Robert K. Belden, a New York physician who had moved to Howell County after the war lived next door to Monks in West Plains. Monks claimed that Belden (he spells it "Beldon") was a paid killer, hired by the "Ku-Klux element" that drank every morning to their health and Monks's death. Anti-Monks newspapers reported that Belden's only offense was to have shot his neighbor's dog for digging in his garden. Monks writes that he feared his life would be forfeit to a mob if he were arrested for threatening Belden, and he left to find reinforcements. He returned with twenty-five or thirty armed men, some of them former militiamen. Monks admits that his men blustered through town, threatening retribution if he were harmed, but anti-Monks reports also claimed the old guerrilla sat on his porch, casually directing the vandalization of Belden's house. The Democratic editor of the Ironton newspaper suggested that, if Monks did not have assassins on his trail, he should have: "We are of those who are satisfied that if Monks could be found dead some morning, Howell County could well afford to pay for the coroner's inquest."[65]

Belden soon left West Plains, never to return, but the trouble in Howell County fermented for several weeks. Democratic newspapers reported a "reign of terror" attributed to the pro-Monks gunmen, who threatened to kill old Rebels, Sheriff Alsup, and any officials who stood in their way. Declaring "Forbearance has ceased to be a virtue," the sheriff called a meeting of citizens at West Plains on 16 July 1870. Following speeches deploring conditions in the county, a committee (including Ben Alsup) produced a series of resolutions condemning the "lawlessness, turbulent acting and secret machinations of one William Monks and his desperate and law-defying clique." They noted the death of Sheriff Cordell at the hands of one of Monks's supporters and threats against Sheriff Alsup by the "law-subverting clique." According to the committee, the trouble arose "because at least two-thirds of the legal voters and law-abiding citizens do not countenance the unwarranted aspirations and pretended claims for office of an ignorant and unprincipled charlatan in the personage of William Monks, who has repeatedly declared that he 'would rule or ruin Howell County.'" The members acknowledged that Monks and his adherents had deadly enemies and resolved to protect them, but they warned that if the Monks gang acted out its threats, "we will visit the swiftest and severest punishment upon them." Furthermore, the committee asked that the devastating resolutions be published in the newspapers of St. Louis, Springfield, Salem, Rolla, and other locations. Democratic papers quickly obliged.[66]

Publication of the minutes of the meeting in Howell County led to a rejoinder by Monks's "gang." One hundred and fifty men, identifying themselves as the "true Radical party" of Howell County, promulgated a defense of Monks in an open letter published in Radical newspapers. They echoed Monks's charges against Belden, claimed that the colonel's life had been threatened time and again, and countered with the charge that the citizen's meeting was "purely for political and sinister purposes." Monks may have expected the notoriety to further his political ambitions, but his declaration of intent to seek the Radical nomination as state senator of the Twenty-Second District led to savage attacks on his character. One of the most extreme was by Judge Robert W. Fyan, a Union army veteran, Liberal Republican, and the circuit-court judge who had presided over some of Monks's litigation. At Gainesville on 18 July 1870, Judge Fyan called Monks "a liar, a thief, a hell-hound, and every other name known to the catalogue of crime and villainy" and rhetorically asked about "his Arkansas record—about all the old men, and defenseless captured rebel sympathizers he had murdered." Even among die-hard Republicans, Monks seems to have become too controversial to support. In August the *Rolla Express,* a Radical news-paper, chided Monks for his candidacy and published a letter, purport-edly received from him, "*verbatim, et punctuatim et spellatim.*" Addressed to "The Union Sneak," the letter was riddled with orthographic and grammatical mistakes, portraying Monks as nearly illiterate. If the let-ter was authentic, Monks characterized his enemies as "copperheads," "pimps," and "dastardly cowards," claiming that "these fault finders" possessed no principles but simply bowed to the strongest party of the moment.[67]

Monks wrote not a word about the senatorial campaign of 1870, but despite bitter opposition by Liberal Republicans, he retained enough support among Radicals to receive the nomination at the convention of the "eternal hate-ite" party at Licking in September 1870. It was not enough, however, to beat his opponent, R. Boone Palmer of Hartville, a former Union militia colonel representing the Liberal Republican Party. Palmer received nine hundred votes more than Monks, who swept only Wright County, paradoxically Palmer's home territory. In Howell County there was a near tie, indicating that the Alsup faction had not entirely triumphed over the old guerrilla fighter. If he was beaten politi-cally, Monks was not chastened. He defended his reputation fiercely, as in his published reply to an allegation of thievery in Oregon County:

> Silence ceases to be a virtue when such accusations are publicly heralded forth by the offscourings of horse thieves, cut-throats, and Ku-Klux. Now, I say that the author of the [accusations] is a calumniator, a thief, a cut-throat, a bastard, a coward and a liar of the deepest dye.
>
> And I am not afraid of the record of the past, and will, if desired, begin at Alpha and go through to Omega, and show the world who the thieves are. If you are for a showing of records, come out like men and show your colors. Wm. Monks[68]

The anti-Monks faction in Howell County was strong enough to have him indicted in 1872 for the death of Benjamin F. Hawkins in 1864. Although instigated by Hawkins's widow, the charges seem to have been largely political and may even have been promulgated by the Alsups in the wake of the contested election. Monks easily refuted the charges, aided by attorney Edward A. Seay. His defense took him into Oregon County and to Evening Shade, Arkansas, where feeling against him was very high. Monks claims that he evaded mobs and assassins and admits that he carried weapons continually, even into courtrooms. He told the circuit-court judge in Oregon County, "If these God damn bushwhackers haven't shed enough innocent blood and are still blood-thirsty, they will never have a better opportunity; so just let them come [after me]." The case never went to trial.[69]

Monks relates a last incident, from March 1874, in which "Liberal Republicans and so-called democrats" may finally have gotten his goat. This time he came out shooting. His target was James Miller, a West Plains resident and alleged assassin. Monks says that only a warning by the wife of former Confederate colonel William H. McCowan saved his life when Miller came to his house and pointed a pistol at him. Monks let loose with a shotgun blast that peppered the gunman with buckshot and knocked him down; a board fence caught most of the charge, prob-ably saving Miller's life. In a reprise of the aftermath of the Belden inci-dent, Monks fled before authorities arrived, and John Nicholas and a band of armed men rode into West Plains to protect him. Howell County citizens appealed to the governor for help, but the trouble died down before the state's assistance was required. Monks ultimately paid a fine of one dollar for disturbing the peace, though only after delaying to the point that authorities were ready seize assets in lieu of nonpayment.[70]

Monks abruptly ends *A History of Southern Missouri and Northern Arkansas* with his account of the Miller episode. Either he reckoned that he had made his case or thought the rest was better left unsaid. In the few final paragraphs, he insists that "the better element among those who had been Confederates" would admit he "was an honest man" and even "an honest lawyer," briefly acknowledging his legal defense of slan-ders against him. Although most of the defamation suits originated after the Belden and Miller incidents, the details of the cases are imperfectly known and may have harkened back to earlier events. Most were trans-ferred from Howell to other counties, especially Laclede (where the records were destroyed by a courthouse fire in 1920). Monks seems never to have lost a verdict, but juries customarily awarded him only costs of the suit. In the most significant case, a defamation suit in 1875 brought against Ben Alsup, Monks received only one cent in damages, leading to the inevitable comment that he had not had much character to defame.[71]

In 1878 Monks apparently underwent a profound midlife change, if not in attitude at least in behavior. Born to Baptist parents but never devout, he joined the Christian Church and was baptized by Adam S. Wright in a pond near West Plains. A week later a Christian Church congregation was organized at Monks's home in West Plains. His conversion cut no ice with the ex-Confederate editor of the *Rolla Herald,* who claimed that it was merely a ploy to spite the devil. It is impossible to know his conviction, but Monks afterward was far less controversial than previously. He had been popular enough in Howell County to be elected prosecuting attorney for two terms, after which he never again ran for office. In 1880 he was ordained a minister of the Christian Church. He did not pastor a church but instead devoted his time to working with congregations in the rural areas where his old comrades lived. He may have flirted briefly with populist political notions, but in 1888 he announced that he was abandoning the Republican Party for the Democrats. The editor of the *Rolla Herald* commented, "The democratic party is a strong one if it can pull through with Col. Bill attached to it." If he ever again assaulted anyone or was accused of horse theft after his baptism, it was not reported. His late-life religious awakening may well have influenced his behavior, but Monks just may have been getting old and tired of his strenuous crusades.[72]

William Monks first drew a U.S. pension, an invalid claim reflecting disability, in 1892. He had not been wounded or injured in the war, so his pension was based on his service in the Sixteenth Missouri Cavalry and approved by special congressional action; he received eight dollars monthly. Despite his age and retirement from public life, he was reminded that bygones were not bygones everywhere. At age sixty-three in 1894, in connection with an increase in his pension, Monks was ordered to appear before an examining board at Mammoth Springs in Fulton County, Arkansas. He protested and filed a notarized request to report to a different board, stating that the people there were "prejudiced against him" and that he could not get a fair hearing. Fulton County may have well remained inhospitable for former Union soldiers, scouts, and militiamen. Resident Jehoida J. Ware was a Peace Society refugee, veteran of Phelps's Missouri Infantry Regiment, and one of Monks's company of scouts at Batesville in 1864. He returned home after the war and served a term as Republican representative from Fulton County but removed to a strongly Unionist area across the border in Missouri after Democrats regained power in Arkansas following Congressional Reconstruction. It is also instructive to note that the Simpson Mason Post 328 of the Grand Army of the Republic was located in Bakersfield, a town in Ozark County, Missouri, and not in Fulton County, Arkansas.[73]

Monks lived quietly for the remaining two decades. He sustained a serious financial loss in 1894 when his country home burned. Publication of *A History of Southern Missouri and Northern Arkansas* was his most notable achievement late in life. It does not seem to have provoked any notice in the regional press, nor were there any rejoinders from old Rebels or "calumniators." If Monks still had any enemies living, they remained silent. When the old guerrilla died in 1913, the *Howell County Gazette* did not bring up old unpleasantness but printed an obituary obviously written by his family. It acknowledged Monks's controversial years with the observation, "Those were troublesome times and brave and stern men were in demand."[74]

The Civil War had been William Monks's watershed. There is no evidence that he would have otherwise risen much above obscurity. It made him important or, as his critics said, impertinent. If the war expanded his ambitions, it also left permanent imputations against his honor and accusations of murder, brutality, and thievery. To be sure, there were dead men in his wake. Monks claimed fifty guerrillas and bushwhackers killed by his Sixteenth Missouri Cavalry company. In the only known death by his hand, Monks freely admitted that he had killed Benjamin F. Hawkins, calling his victim "one of the most desperate bushwhackers and rebel desperadoes that ever was in South Missouri." He claimed self-defense and, in lieu of any other evidence, his story sounds plausible enough. As for other allegations of murder and conspiracy to commit murder, there were equally likely candidates, including the wartime Alsup scouts and Captain Richardson's Arkansas militiamen. Questionable characters are not hard to find in large groups of armed men, and Monks's crowd included killers such as "Hell Roaring Walker" and Joe Little. No murder charge against Monks ever came to trial even after Democrats gained control of county governments in Missouri and Arkansas, and as Monks defiantly points out, there was no statute of limitations on murder.[75]

There is little doubt that the colonel was personally intimidating or that his methods were brutal. His response to pleas by the citizens of Licking, the torturing of prisoners, personal assaults, and persistent belligerence all point to the preferred tactical methods of the guerrilla. Yet his complaints about depredations by Union soldiers of his own regiment, his insistence that Missourians legally join the Arkansas militia, and his punctiliousness in the face of Judge Baxter's writ of habeas corpus mitigate his overbearing reputation. Monks also points out instances of his mercy and forgiveness, such as contributing to a fund to enable the destitute widow of General McBride to return to Missouri and loaning a blanket to his old antagonist Forshee in the guardhouse at West Plains. In fact, in Forshee's case, Monks let it be known that he spared at least one Rebel who deserved killing.[76]

There were also allegations of plunder and theft, the root of which was the well-established military practice of subsisting upon local resources. Foraging by armies is as old as warfare itself and was institutionalized in the Union and Confederate forces by regulations, as was the confiscation of personal property of disloyal or reluctant civilians. Inevitably, these practices led to abuses upon private property in the guises of military necessity, vengeance, and personal greed. They tainted the reputations of officers and men throughout the chain of command. Especially as it involved foodstuffs and livestock, living off the land caused the greatest hardship and individual loss in the Ozarks. Monks handled thousands of dollars of Federal, state, and confiscated property, but there is no evidence that he ever personally profited from it or that he was a member of any criminal conspiracy. On the contrary, he won several slander suits afterward against detractors who publicly voiced allegations of theft. The only "evidence" of Monks's involvement in horse theft seems to have been the supposed pregallows confession of Joe Little, an entirely unverified account by a dubious informant. But mounted soldiers of small units in the field encounter easy opportunities for thievery, and some of Monks's men were not so circumspect about private property.[77]

Although little is known about this aspect of his life, Monks did profit from land transactions after the war, some of which were at the expense of old wartime foes. Monks acquired the land of Barnett and Nicks by civil suit, and he was also involved through the firm of Monks and Company in other transactions involving the real estate of former Rebels. One of the principals was Washington F. Geiger, veteran Missouri cavalry officer in southwestern Missouri and a Republican Party figure with political ambitions; some of the tar directed at Monks may have been meant to stick to Geiger. Yet property acquired by the firm included that formerly owned by Benjamin Hawkins, whom Monks had killed, which was at least unseemly. This may well have endeared him least to his enemies, but Monks was not alone in adding injury to insult. Ben Alsup also gained satisfaction through civil litigation against former persecutors.[78]

Monks carried on his own civil war for years against old and new enemies along the border, played out in the political arena, the courts, and the newspapers. His greatest regional notoriety effectively began with his cross-border foray in 1868. Accusations against him greatly intensified during the bitter political rivalries of 1868 and 1870, promulgated for the public in south-central Missouri and northern Arkansas largely through avowedly partisan Democratic newspapers. Of the newspapers that have survived, the *Rolla Herald,* with a former Confederate editor and serving a readership that included many veterans of Thomas R. Freeman's Confederate cavalry, was the most rabidly anti-Monks.

While old rebel enemies could be expected to heap invective, former Union comrades ultimately turned against him as well. Initially, the defense of Monks by Radical Republican newspapers was no less partisan and their reportage diametrically opposed to Democratic accounts. As an avowed Radical, Monks had linked his destiny to the likes of Thomas C. Fletcher and Powell Clayton, men who were even more domineering, widely controversial, and despised by their enemies than himself. He merely provided one more avenue by which to castigate the opposition. In the context of Conservative efforts to unseat Radical regimes in Missouri and Arkansas, Monks's fortunes diminished in proportion to those of his party on the state and national levels. Rival political candidates, Democrat and Republican alike, benefited at his expense. Locally, Monks's biggest mistake was to have become a rival of the Alsup clan, whose domineering, violent activities continued for a decade longer than his own.[79]

William Monks may have been personally brutal or extreme, but he was a product of his time and place. In his view it was his ox that secessionists gored first in 1861. Everything else, including the natural and righteous punishment of Rebels, stemmed from that fact. Ultimately, Monks may have had no choice but to write *A History of Southern Missouri and Northern Arkansas.* But it is a wonder that nobody shot him before he did.

Notes

1. The reference to "Monks' Command" occurred in a story on Andrew J. "Hell Roaring" Walker, late sergeant of Company K, Sixteenth Missouri Cavalry, accused murderer, convicted horse thief, and prison escapee. He was reported to have been "the most cold blooded murderer in southwest Missouri during the war." *Rolla Weekly Herald,* 26 Oct. 1871, 22 Feb. 1883.

2. *Howell County Gazette,* 3 Nov. 1904, 25 Aug., 25 Nov. 1905. Monks was leading a cow by a rope when the animal bolted, knocking him to the ground and dislocating his hip. By 1906, according to his pension file in the National Archives, he was a semi-invalid. William Monks Pension File, Records of the Veterans Administration, Records Group 15, National Archives and Records Administration, Washington, D.C. [hereafter cited as NARA].

3. Monks, *History,* 148. One of the best accounts of early guerrilla operations in the Ozarks is David F. Lenox, *Personal Memoirs of a Missouri Confederate Soldier* (Texarkana, Tex.: published by the author, ca. 1906). Lenox served at the beginning of the war in the command of Monks's wartime nemesis, Thomas R. Freeman. A pro-Southern memoir concerning irregular warfare around Yellville and Marion County is Thomas Jerome Estes, *Early Days and War Times in North Arkansas* (Lubbock, Tex.: published by the author, 1928). Although it is not a memoir, an excellent account of Union guerrillas operating in no man's land in Arkansas, with many parallels to Monks's story, is Kenneth C. Barnes, "The Williams Clan: Mountain Farmers and Union Fighters in North Central Arkansas," in *Civil War Arkansas: Beyond Battles and Leaders,* ed. Anne J. Bailey and Daniel E. Sutherland (Fayetteville: University of Arkansas Press, 2000): 155–75.

4. Carl O. Sauer, *The Geography of the Ozark Highland of Missouri* (Chicago: University of Chicago, 1920), 68–70; Milton D. Rafferty, *Historical Atlas of Missouri* (Norman: University of Oklahoma Press, 1982), 34; Gerald T. Hanson and Carl H. Moneyhon, *Historical Atlas of Arkansas* (Norman: University of Oklahoma, 1989), 32.

5. Monks, "Introduction," in *History,* 26; Donald S. Hubble Jr., *Bennett's Bayou, Bennett's River, 1830–1900* (Bull Shoals, Ark.: Enterprise, 1981): 46.

6. Monks, *History,* 26; Gerald Groves and Charlotte Groves, *Howell*

County Post Offices, Postmasters and Their Communities, 5 vols. (Willow Springs, Mo.: published by the authors, 1989–99), 5:17, 26; James Corrington to editor, *Rolla Weekly Herald,* 8 Sept. 1870.

7. Monks, *History,* 6–11, 63–64. For other examples of the work of the latter generation of native authors, see John Quincy Wolf, *Life in the Leatherwoods,* ed. Gene Hyde and Brooks Blevins (Fayetteville: University of Arkansas Press, 2000); S. C. Turnbo, *The White River Chronicles of S. C. Turnbo: Man and Wildlife on the Ozarks Frontier,* ed. James F. Keefe and Lynn Morrow (Fayetteville: University of Arkansas Press, 1994); Theodore P. Russell, *A Connecticut Yankee in the Frontier Ozarks: The Writings of Theodore Pease Russell,* ed. James F. Keefe and Lynn Morrow (Columbia: University of Missouri Press, 1988).

8. Monks, *History,* 23–25; Sauer, *Geography of the Ozark Highland,* 132–35; Gerard Schultz, *Early History of the Northern Ozarks* (Jefferson City, Mo.: Midland, 1937), 59–72, 89–92.

9. Monks, *History,* 10–13.

10. Ibid., 13–23, 27–29. See also Lynn Morrow, "The Coker Clan," *White River Valley Historical Quarterly* 10, no. 7 (spring 1990): 15–18; Hubble, *Bennett's Bayou, Bennett's River,* 79. Hubble writes that women in the Ozarks dreaded election days because they knew that some of their men were going to get hurt.

11. Monks, *History,* 35–36, 39, 42–44, 45–47, 57–54.

12. Ibid., 54–61, 69–71. The newspaper advertisement that led to the family's reunion has not been found. Martha Monks and her children remained at Rolla for the duration of the war.

13. In addition to Rhodes, Monks named Jesse James; men named Brown, Mawhinney, and Bacon; and Morton R. Langston as Unionists murdered in Howell, Oregon, and Ozark Counties. Ibid., 62–65, 115, 120.

14. Ibid., 60–70; Diane Neal, "Treason or Patriotism? Union Peace Societies in Arkansas during the Civil War," *Journal of Confederate History* 1, no. 2 (fall 1988): 342–46; Daniel E. Sutherland, "Guerrillas: The Real War in Arkansas," in *Civil War Arkansas,* 133, 136–37; John F. Bradbury Jr., "'Buckwheat Cake Philanthropy': Refugees and the Union Army in the Ozarks," *Arkansas Historical Quarterly* 57, no. 3 (autumn 1998): 236–42; James J. Johnston, "Peace Society in Fulton County (Anti-Secession Sentiment)," *Fulton County Chronicles* 11, no. 2 (fall 1996): 26–44.

15. Joseph G. Rosa, *They Called Him Wild Bill: The Life and Adventures of James Butler Hickok* (Norman: University of Oklahoma Press, 1974), 53–71; see also Rosa, introduction to "The Civil War Letters of Lorenzo B. Hickok," *Newsletter of the Phelps County Historical Society* 5, nos. 3–4 (Oct. 1986): 2–5. Historians of western gunfighters have paid more attention to guides and scouts than have authors of the war, but none have examined the activities of thousands of civilians employed by Union and Confederate forces. They were indispensable to armies of both sides in regular as well as guerrilla operations.

16. Monks, *History,* 71–75. "Lop-eared Dutch" referred to the German immigrants who made up a significant part of the earliest Union forces in Missouri.

17. Ibid., 77, 116–17. Official record of Monk's commission in the 63d Enrolled Missouri Militia has not been found in the Adjutant General of Missouri Collection, Missouri State Archives, Jefferson City [hereafter cited MSA].

18. Sutherland, "Guerrillas," 142–43.

19. Carl H. Moneyhon, *The Impact of the Civil War and Reconstruction on Arkansas: Persistence in the Midst of Ruin* (Baton Rouge: Louisiana State University Press, 1994), 131–33; Sutherland, "Guerrillas," 138–39; Bradbury, "'Buckwheat Cake Philanthropy,'" 248–54. Stephen V. Ash suggests that the rise of banditry, involving soldiers, deserters, and criminals, was the most striking characteristic of life in no man's land. See Ash, *When the Yankees Came: Conflict and Chaos in the Occupied South, 1861–1865* (Chapel Hill: University of North Carolina Press, 1995), 205–9.

20. Monks, *History,* 89–92. Monks reports that Forshee is said to have died soon after the war.

21. Ibid., 77. For claims about "Monks Raiders" on the upper Current and Jack's Fork Rivers, see the chapters entitled "Dark Clouds over Shannon" and "Aunt Tabitha," in *True Tales from the Ozarks,* by Ray H. Weakley (N.p., n.d. [ca. 1953]), unpaginated. Weakley reports that the raiders consisted of cutthroats from East St. Louis, Illinois, "the dregs of humanity," who took advantage of the war to rob and plunder. He also claims they were responsible for the 1863 killing of Joshua Chilton, a death usually attributed to the Third Missouri Cavalry.

22. Monks, *History,* 95–99.

23. Richard Murphy to Capt. Lovell, 13 June 1863, Letters Received, Rolla, Mo., Records of U.S. Army Continental Commands, RG 393, Pt. 2, Entry 3334, NARA. For communications pertaining to payment of the scouts, see Thomas A. Davies to Gen. James Totten, 3 July 1863, in U.S. War Department, *The War of the Rebellion: A Compilation of the Official Records of the Union and Confederate Armies,* 70 vols. in 128 pts. (Washington, D.C.: Government Printing Office, 1880–1901) ser. 1, 22(2):353 [hereafter cited as *O.R.;* all references are to series 1]; and George West to "Commanding Officer, District of Rolla," 2 Aug. 1863, ibid., 426. For additional communications concerning the scouts, see correspondence between Davies and officials in St. Louis dated 9 and 25 July 1863 in Consolidated Correspondence File, Records of the Quartermaster General, RG 92, Entry 225, Box 1222, NARA. Special Order No. 123, District of Rolla, 22 July 1863, authorized the payment of the men on the rolls of Quartermaster Thomas O'Brien. Document in Letters Received, Rolla, Mo., RG 393, Pt. 2, Entry 3334.

24. Monks, *History,* 75–77. Monks's account of the Drake delegation's visit to Washington in September 1863 is chronologically out of place. See *Report of the Committee of the House of Representatives of the Twenty-second General Assembly of the State of Missouri to Investigate the Conduct and Management of the Militia* (Columbia: State Historical Society of Missouri, 1998), 145; and William E. Parrish, *Turbulent Partnership: Missouri and the Union, 1861–1865* (Columbia: University of Missouri Press, 1963), 161–62.

25. The quartermaster at Batesville listed Monks and the scouts on his rolls for January and February 1864. See Reports of Persons and Articles Hired (Report 1691, Lt. J. C. Thompson, 1864), Records of the Quartermaster General, RG 92, Entry 238, NARA. Monks is listed as "Chief of Scouts," for which he received $100.00 per month. There were fifteen scouts listed on the report for January and seventeen on the report for February 1864. At least two scouts, Simpson Mason and J. J. Ware, were from Fulton County. The scouts received $23.50 per month for their services and forty cents per day (an additional $12.00 per month) for the use of private horses. Monks apparently rode a government mount. The quartermaster discharged and paid off the men in February 1864.

26. Monks, *History,* 77–86. For conditions south of Rolla, guerrilla activity, and the charge that Monks's men murdered two of Freeman's men in

Arkansas, see Joseph Eppstein to O. D. Greene, 9 Feb. 1864, *O.R.,*
34(2):280–81; and T. R. Freeman to R.R. Livingston, 10 Feb. 1864, ibid.,
289–90. See also "Waugh Farm Skirmish Fought Feb. 19, 1864,"
Independence County Chronicle 2, no. 5 (Jan. 1964): 8–16.

27. U.S. Record and Pension Office, *Organization and Status of Missouri
Troops (Union and Confederate) during the Civil War* (Washington, D.C.:
Government Printing Office, 1902), 84–85; *Report of the Committee
Appointed to Investigate the Militia,* 217–18; Robert R. Mackey,
"Bushwhackers, Provosts, and Tories," in *Guerrillas, Unionists, and Violence
on the Confederate Home Front,* ed. Daniel E. Sutherland (Fayetteville:
University of Arkansas Press, 1999), 180–81.

28. Monks, *History,* 86–89, 91, 120–21, 126; Groves and Groves,
Howell County Post Offices, 4:194–95.

29. Monks, *History,* 101–2; Descriptive Book, Sixteenth Missouri
Cavalry, Records of the Adjutant General's Office, RG 94, Entry 112,
NARA; E. C. Catherwood to Monks, 4 Jan. 1865, *O.R.,* 48(1):415.
Lieutenant Boyd led the effectives of Company K against Price, an honor he
said Monks resented. See affidavit, 15 Jan. 1887, John W. Boyd Pension File,
Records of the Veterans Administration, RG 15, NARA.

30. Monks, *History,* 102; E. B. Brown to J. W. Barnes, 16 Jan. 1865,
O.R., 48(1):30.

31. Special Orders No. 22, 26 Jan. 1865, *O.R.,* 48(1):653; Monks,
History, 103–4.

32. Monks, *History,* 111; reports of Capt. William Monks, 3, 25 Mar.
1865, *O.R.,* 48(1):124–25, 135–36; Monks to John Morrill, 20 Apr. 1865,
ibid., 48(2):143.

33. Monks to John Morrill, 19 May, 6 June 1865, *O.R.,* 48(2):510,
797–98; special orders for Co. K, Jan.–June 1865, Regimental Order Book,
Sixteenth Missouri Cavalry, Records of the Adjutant General's Office, RG
94, Entry 113, NARA. Monks's final report is in *Supplement to the Official
Records of the Union and Confederate Armies,* ed. Janet B. Hewett
(Wilmington, N.C.: Broadfoot, 1996), pt. 2, vol. 25, p. 822.

34. Monks, *History,* 128. For a description of the desolation in the postwar border country, see James W. Goodrich and Donald B. Oster, eds., "'Few
Men but Many Widows': The Daniel Fogel Letters, August 8–September 4,
1867," *Missouri Historical Review* 80, no. 3 (Apr. 1986): 283–95.

35. Monks, *History,* 130–31; *Jefferson City People's Tribune,* 19 Aug. 1868. James Monihan of the *St. Louis Missouri Republican* threatened to kill Monks, and afterward the House rescinded his journalist privileges. F. 12855, Capitol Fire Documents, MSA, microfilm. The incident with Speaker Harlan is in a story on Monks's fiftieth wedding anniversary in *Howell County Gazette,* 16 Apr. 1903. John Wilson of Platte County characterized Monks as a water-powered windmill. See Missouri History Alphabetical File [no author noted], ca. 24 Feb. 1903, Missouri Historical Society, St. Louis.

36. Certification of the poll book of election in Texas County, June 1865, F. 16466, Capitol Fire Documents, MSA, microfilm. For the recommendation of Monks, see Horace Wilcox, Aaron Van Wormer, Wm. Morse, V. G. Latham, A. Dempewolf, and John W. Stephens to Gov. Thomas C. Fletcher, 4 Aug. 1865, Miscellaneous Papers, Sixteenth Missouri Cavalry, Adjutant General Collection, MSA.

37. Monks, *History,* 143–44; Groves and Groves, *Howell County Post Offices,* 2:153. Monks was not alone in obtaining civil judgments against former persecutors after the war; Ben Alsup did the same in Howell County. There were many other similar cases throughout the Ozarks. For example, see "Civil War Litigation," *White River Valley Historical Quarterly* 10, no. 4 (summer 1989): 12–13. A cursory examination of the indexes to circuit-court cases at the Missouri State Archives indicates the likelihood that there were hundreds of such cases filed after the Civil War.

38. Special Orders No. 30, 27 Aug. 1867, Adjutant General Collection, MSA.

39. In May 1864 Dr. James Reid at Ironton wrote the provost marshal in St. Louis that an extensive contraband trade was being conducted out of his town. Reid claimed that goods taken from loyal men by Timothy Reeves's Confederates and others were traded for salt and provisions smuggled from Ironton. See Reid to provost marshal, 30 May 1864, Union Provost Marshal's File of Papers Relating to Individual Citizens, M345, Roll 227, NARA. For allegations of Ironton's place in postwar theft rings, see the arrest of "Duch Boy" [*sic*] in *Iron County Register,* 10 Oct. 1867; "Bushwhacking in the Southwest [*sic*]," *Rolla Express,* quoted in *(Jefferson City) Missouri State Times,* 29 Nov. 1867; and a report on Ironton, *Bloomfield (Mo.) Argus,* published in *(Batesville) North Arkansas Times,* 11 Sept. 1869.

40. Monks, *History,* 133–34.

41. Lynn Morrow, "Where Did All the Money Go? War and the Economics of Vigilantism in Southern Missouri," *White River Valley Historical Quarterly* 34, no. 2 (fall 1994): 3.

42. For the special election to fill Noell's senatorial seat, see *Iron County Register,* 26 Dec. 1867, 9 Jan. 1868; and William E. Parrish, *Missouri under Radical Rule, 1865–1870* (Columbia: University of Missouri Press, 1965), 237–38, 257.

43. *Springfield Leader,* 15 Oct. 1868; "The Supreme Court vs. 'Count' Rodman," *Iron County Register,* 28 Jan. 1869; *Rolla Weekly Herald,* 3 June 1869; *(Batesville) North Arkansas Times,* 10 Oct. 1868.

44. *(Batesville) North Arkansas Times,* 21 Sept. 1867; *Arkansas Gazette,* 24 Sept. 1867. For the apparently first linkings of Monks by name with the 1867 raid in Fulton County, see "Invasion of the State by Missourians," *(Batesville) North Arkansas Times,* 3 Oct. 1868; and "Give Us Peace," ibid.

45. Monks, *History,* 135–39; *(Jefferson City) Missouri State Times,* 25 Oct., 29 Nov. 1867; Lewis A. W. Simpson, *Oregon County's Three Flags: Six County Seats Via the Horse and Buggy,* 2d ed. (Thayer, Mo.: Thayer News, 1983), 45–47. George Crawford and A. K. Smith were among the first men to be killed by the militiamen. An Oregon County correspondent estimated that twenty-five or thirty outlaws had been killed or sent to the penitentiary since 1865. *Iron County Register,* 3 Dec. 1868.

46. Monks, *History,* 139; John Alley to Samuel P. Simpson, adjutant general of Missouri, 20, 26 Sept., 22 Nov. 1867, 5 Feb. 1868, Miscellaneous Correspondence, Adjutant General Collection, MSA; "Biennial Report of the Adjutant General of Missouri, 1867–1868," *St. Louis Missouri Republican,* 19 Jan. 1869. Several of Monks's militiamen purchased army revolvers and surplus commissary supplies from the state when the battalion stood down. See Special Orders No. 7, 28 Apr. 1868, Adjutant General Collection, MSA.

47. Rumors of Monks's assassination derived from a satirical story entitled "Stibbs and the Militia," about a sheep-killing dog named Monks, published in the *Iron County Register,* 2 July 1868. The Radical newspaper at Springfield embellished the "painful rumor" with the detail that six citizens of Oregon County dragged Monks from his home and riddled him with bullets. *Springfield Weekly Missouri Patriot,* 13 Aug. 1868. The *Jefferson City*

People's Tribune (19 Aug. 1868) and the *St. Louis Missouri Republican* (30 Sept. 1868) also reported his alleged death. The *(Batesville) North Arkansas Times* (10 Oct. 1868) quashed rumors with a report that Monks had assaulted and severely beaten George Foreman, an old citizen of Howell County.

48. Orval Truman Driggs Jr., "The Issues of the Powell Clayton Regime, 1868–1871," *Arkansas Historical Quarterly* 8, no. 1 (spring 1949): 3; Thomas S. Staples, *Reconstruction in Arkansas, 1862–1874* (New York: Columbia University Press, 1923), 278–80; Otis A. Singletary, "Militia Disturbances in Arkansas during Reconstruction," *Arkansas Historical Quarterly* 15 (summer 1956): 141–43; Moneyhon, *Impact of the Civil War and Reconstruction,* 169, 199–205, 250–51.

49. *Little Rock Republican,* 11 Dec. 1868; Staples, *Reconstruction in Arkansas,* 291–92; Allen W. Trelease, *White Terror: The Ku Klux Klan Conspiracy and Southern Reconstruction* (Westport, Conn.: Greenwood, 1971), 149–50, 154; Moneyhon, *Impact of the Civil War and Reconstruction,* 251.

50. Staples, *Reconstruction in Arkansas,* 294, 300, 307; John M. Harrell, *The Brooks and Baxter War: A History of the Reconstruction Period in Arkansas* (St. Louis: Slawson, 1893), 69; John I. Smith, *Forward from Rebellion: Reconstruction and Revolution in Arkansas, 1868–1874* (Little Rock: Rose, 1983), 30; Trelease, *White Terror,* 151, 154; Moneyhon, *Impact of the Civil War and Reconstruction,* 251–52; George C. Rable, *But There Was No Peace: The Role of Violence in the Politics of Reconstruction* (Athens: University of Georgia Press, 1984), 105; Randy L. Finley, *From Slavery to Uncertain Freedom: The Freedman's Bureau in Arkansas, 1865–1869* (Fayetteville: University of Arkansas Press, 1996), 147. The older works by Harrell and Staples minimize the existence of the Ku Klux Klan in Arkansas and absolve the Democratic Party of complicity. John I. Smith in 1983 promulgated the proposition that the violence was Radical directed against internal and external enemies for Clayton's benefit. Trelease's revisionist work credited the Klan with great influence and charged the Democratic Party as, at least, an unindicted co-conspirator, but Moneyhon does not believe enough evidence exists to fully analyze the relationship between the party and the Klan.

51. Reports of Persons and Articles Hired (Report 1691, Lt. J. C. Thompson, 1864), Records of the Quartermaster General, RG 92, Entry

238, NARA; Mason to Maj. Gen J. J. Reynolds, 24 May 1865, *O.R.,* 48(2):583; Johnston, "Peace Society in Fulton County," 41; Higginbotham, "Reconstruction in North Arkansas," 30; *(Batesville) North Arkansas Times,* 26 Sept. 1868; *Arkansas Gazette,* 2, 6 Oct., 31 Dec. 1868; *Little Rock Republican,* 6 Oct. 1868; *Springfield Patriot,* 15 Oct. 1868; Finley, *From Slavery to Uncertain Freedom,* 146. Mason was indicted in 1866 for the murders of John Hollingsworth and Samuel Payne in Fulton County. Capt. W. O. Lattimore, of the Nineteenth U.S. Infantry at Batesville, investigated the killings. He certified that the dead men were "rebels of the worst character" and concluded: "Capt. Mason has undoubtedly rendered good service to the Government of the U.S. both during and since the war, in consequence of which he is universally hated by the Rebels. And I am convinced that no efforts will be spared to drive him from the Country." Uriah Maxfield, affidavit, 24 Sept. 1866, Union Provost Marshal's Files of Papers Relating to Individual Citizens, M345, Roll 177, NARA; Walter O. Lattimore to Hugh G. Brown, 25 Sept. 1866, ibid. Simpson is listed as a civilian agent of the Freedmen's Bureau in Fulton County in 1867. See Roster of Officers and Civilians on Duty, Little Rock District, Records of the Bureau of Refugees, Freedmen, and Abandoned Lands, M979, Roll 52, NARA.

52. For the primary eyewitness accounts for the Mason/Monks episode in Arkansas, see "Invasion of the State by Missourians," *(Batesville) North Arkansas Times,* 3 Oct. 1861; and "From Fulton County," ibid., 10 Oct. 1868. The latter account was penned by J. H. Tracey and N. L. Baker, two of the alleged conspirators in Mason's murder. The news from Batesville was reprinted, embellished, and editorialized in other newspapers. For example, see stories in the *Arkansas Gazette,* 29 Sept., 7, 11 Oct. 1868; *Little Rock Republican,* 30 Sept. 1868; and *Springfield Patriot,* 8, 15 Oct. 1868.

53. Monks, *History,* 126, 157–58, 166, 168.

54. Ibid. 158–60; "From Fulton County." Tracey and Baker accused the militiamen of torture, allegations that Monks never answered. But he did acknowledge the hanging of the Oregon County sheriff by militiamen in 1867, though not the responsibility for it. Hanging is a crude but effective means of extracting information; it is commonplace in stories of guerrillas and bushwhackers in the Ozarks. There are apparently no records of Monks's commission or the muster rolls of the Seventh Arkansas State Guard extant in the archives of the Arkansas Historical Commission in Little Rock. In his

memoir Powell Clayton notes Monks and the Missourians only in connection with later operations. See Clayton, *The Aftermath of the Civil War, in Arkansas* (New York: Neal, 1915).

55. Monks, *History,* 160; *St. Louis Daily Times,* 16 Oct. 1868. Another tirade is "History of the Notorious Robber and Murderer, Wm. Monks," *(Batesville) North Arkansas Times,* 10 Oct. 1868. It is full of inaccuracies, but there is no mistaking the bitterness toward Monks. In the same issue of the *Times* is "Fulton County Troubles," an account containing Judge Baxter's "delicate correspondence" with Monks. For the Republican attitude in Missouri, see "From Arkansas," *St. Louis Missouri Democrat,* 30 Sept. 1868. Radicals claimed that the Klan murdered not only Simpson Mason but also Dow Bryant for turning state's evidence. *Missouri Democrat,* 11 Nov. 1868. No one was ever tried for the murders of Mason, Bush, or Bryant in Fulton County. For the memoir of an Independence County Klansman who rallied to drive Monks's band from Arkansas, see S. A. Hail, "A Short History of My Long Life," *Independence County Chronicle* 20 (July 1979): 28–30. Hail claims that Arkansas Klansmen captured and probably executed two Missouri militiamen who had gotten separated from the main command. Monks does not mention this incident, and no other evidence of it has been found.

56. Monks, *History,* 65–66, 118–19, 141–42. Papers concerning Ben Alsup's arrest and imprisonment and a proposal to gain his release are in his file in Union Provost Marshal's File of Papers Relating to Individual Citizens, M345, Roll 6, NARA. The Alsups were also known for fast horses and horse racing. The controversial clan ruled Douglas County well into the 1880s, though not without casualties. See "The Hatfield Horror," *Rolla Weekly Herald,* 15 June 1871; "Bill Alsup," ibid., 21 Apr. 1881; "Alsup Discharged," ibid., 4 Oct. 1884; "The Alsup Gang," ibid., 27 Nov. 1884; Bessie J. Selleck, *Early Settlers of Douglas County, Missouri* (Berkeley, Calif.: Professional Press, 1952), 31–32, 54, 66, 68–69; and Claude Hibbard, "The Alsups of Douglas County," *White River Valley Historical Quarterly* 1, no. 3 (spring 1962): 9–11. Ben Alsup died in Arkansas under indictment for a wartime murder in Missouri. *Rolla Weekly Herald,* 28 Oct. 1880.

57. Monks wrote barely a word about the election contest with Alsup, but there are many documents from his appeal, including depositions, in F. 13238, Capitol Fire Documents, MSA, microfilm. For Conservative glee at

the turn of events in the Radical camp, see "From Howell County," *Missouri Republican,* 22 Dec. 1868, 5 Jan. 1869. For the references to "Benjamin, the Bark-Grinder" and "William, the Roost Robber," see "Alsup vs. Monks," *Iron County Register,* 27 May 1869; and "From Howell County," *Iron County Register,* 15 July 1869.

58. Monks, *History,* 161.

59. *Arkansas Gazette,* 10 Jan. 1869.

60. Monks, *History,* 164–71; Clayton, *Aftermath of the Civil War,* 122, 127, 134; Singletary, "Militia Disturbances in Arkansas," 143–45; *Jacksonport Herald* in *Arkansas Gazette,* 1 Apr. 1869. For the Democratic version of events, see *Arkansas Gazette,* 5, 9 Jan., 3 Mar. 1869; and *(Batesville) North Arkansas Times,* 13 Mar. 1869. For a revisionist, sympathetic view of Upham and his operations in northeastern Arkansas, see Charles J. Rector, "D. P. Upham, Woodruff County Carpetbagger," *Arkansas Historical Quarterly* 59, no. 1 (spring 2000): 60–75. The turmoil in Conway County lasted for years and is best chronicled in Kenneth C. Barnes, *Who Killed John Clayton? Political Violence and the Emergence of the New South, 1861–1893* (Durham, N.C.: Duke University Press, 1998).

61. Driggs, "Issues of the Powell Clayton Regime," 24–28; Harrell, *Brooks and Baxter War,* 81–94; Staples, *Reconstruction in Arkansas,* 295–300; Moneyhon, *Impact of the Civil War and Reconstruction,* 252–53; William H. Burnside, *The Honorable Powell Clayton* (Conway, Ark.: UCA Press, 1991): 29–39; Burnside, "Powell Clayton," in *The Governors of Arkansas: Essays in Political Biography,* ed. Timothy P. Donovan, Willard B. Gatewood Jr., and Jeannie M. Wayne, 2d. ed. (Fayetteville: University of Arkansas Press, 1995): 49–53.

62. Monks, *History,* 172–74; "Monks, Butler, and Dale," *(Batesville) North Arkansas Times,* 13 Mar. 1869. The Arkansas State House, where Monks delivered his farewell address, still stands and is operated as an historic site. Anyone who visits the lower chamber and considers Monks's personal vulnerability at the time of his speech must admire the man's nerve, if nothing else. Clayton says nothing in his memoir about offering Monks a general's commission.

63. Monks, *History,* 174. The Cordell affair was widely reported. See *St. Louis Missouri Republican,* 17 Nov. 1868; *(Batesville) North Arkansas Times,* 13 Mar., 26 June 1869; *Springfield Patriot,* 11 Mar. 1869; *Springfield Leader,*

18 Mar. 1869; *Southeast Missouri Enterprise,* 25 Mar. 1869; and *Rolla Weekly Herald,* 27 May 1869. Nathan D. West, a physician, and sons J. D., James D., and Jesse West, were in Monks's militia company. Missouri Militia Enrollment, 1867, Howell County, Station West Plains, William Monks Lieutenant and Enrolling Officer, Adjutant General Collection, MSA.

64. *Arkansas Gazette,* 19 May 1869. Attributed to the *Little Rock Liberal,* Little's confession also appeared in the *Rolla Weekly Herald* (3 June 1869).

65. Monks, *History,* 181–85; *Springfield Leader,* 23 June, 28 July 1870; "Col. Monks in Duress," *Springfield Patriot,* 30 June 1870; *Rolla Weekly Herald,* 21 July 1870; *Iron County Register,* 7 July 1870. Belden later fled to Springfield. Of the armed group that rode into town, at least one man, John B. Nicholas, is known to have been with Monks in the Howell County militia in 1867.

66. *Springfield Leader,* 23 June, 28 July 1870; *Rolla Weekly Herald,* 21 July 1870; *St. Louis Daily Missouri Democrat,* 22 July 1870.

67. *Springfield Leader,* 28 July 1870; *Springfield Patriot,* 4 Aug. 1870; *Rolla Weekly Herald,* 28 July, 8 Sept. 1870; *Iron County Register,* 6 Oct. 1870. The issue of the *Rolla Express* containing the letter attributed to Monks is no longer extant. The letter was "extracted" for publication in the *Rolla Weekly Herald* (1 Sept. 1870).

68. *Rolla Weekly Herald,* 29 Sept., 1 Dec. 1870. Abstracts of votes cast in the election of November 1870 are in F. 16514, Capitol Fire Documents, MSA, microfilm. The allegation of thievery by the militia in Oregon County in 1867 was published in the *Thomasville New Era,* no longer extant. This was reprinted, with the reply by Monks, as "Col. Monks on the Rampage," *Rolla Weekly Herald,* 28 Sept. 1871.

69. Monks, *History,* 174–81; *State of Missouri vs. Monks,* 8 Nov. 1872, Book B, Howell County Circuit Court Records, West Plains, Mo.

70. Monks, *History,* 181–84; *Rolla Weekly Herald,* 2 Apr. 1874; *Iron County Register,* 2 Apr. 1874; *State of Missouri vs. Monks and John Nichols [sic],* 8 May 1874, Book B, Howell County Circuit Court Records. A former Confederate officer and another of Monks's local enemies, "Billy" McCowan was later gunned down at Piedmont, Missouri, in 1885. *Rolla Weekly Herald,* 8 Oct. 1885.

71. Monks, *History,* 185; *Rolla Weekly Herald,* 21 Aug. 1873, 23 Sept. 1875. Monks was plaintiff or defendant in twenty-five cases from 1869 to

1879. See Hogan Williams and Betty Harvey Williams, *Howell County, Missouri, Direct Index to Circuit Court Records, 1855–1882* (Warrensburg, Mo., 1973).

72. *Rolla Weekly Herald,* 30 May 1878, 23 Aug. 1888; "A History of the First Christian Church in West Plains," *West Plains Gazette* 26 (fall–winter 1984): 28–34. The account in the *Gazette* was written in part by Mary Monks Green, the colonel's daughter, and by Russ Cochran, great-great-grandson of Adam S. Wright, the man who baptized Monks.

73. Monks's complaint about prejudice against him in Fulton County is in a notarized statement, 1 May 1894, in William Monks Pension File, Records of the Veterans Administration, RG 15, NARA. See also Johnston, "Peace Society in Fulton County," 27, 39–43; and *Springfield Patriot,* 23 Apr. 1868.

74. "Colonel William Monks Dead," *Howell County Gazette,* 8 May 1913. His wife, Martha, drew a widow's pension until her death in 1924. William Monks Pension File, Records of the Veterans Administration, RG 15, NARA. See also the obituary of Martha Rice Monks, *Howell County Gazette,* 20 Mar. 1924. The fire at Monks's country home may have burned some of his personal papers; descendants are said to have destroyed the remainder in the 1950s. Dorotha Reavis, interview by Lynn Morrow, 1994, Kalen and Morrow Collection, Jefferson City, Mo.

75. Monks, *History,* 179, 185.

76. Ibid., 89–92, 104–5, 138, 143, 159–60.

77. The best examination of foraging in all its guises is Mark Grimsley, *The Hard Hand of War: Union Military Policy toward Southern Civilians, 1861–1865* (New York: Cambridge University Press, 1995), 15–17, 97–110, 213–15.

78. *Benjamin Alsup vs. William Chastine and Josephus M. Howell,* Mar. 1866, Book A, Howell County Circuit Court Records.

79. Destruction of the Douglas County Courthouse by arson in 1886 precludes judicial review of the many cases involving the Alsups.

COLONEL MONKS AND WIFE.

A HISTORY

of

Southern Missouri and Northern Arkansas

Being an Account of the Early Settlements,
the Civil War, the Ku-Klux, and
Times of Peace.

By William Monks
West Plains, Mo.

West Plains Journal Co.
West Plains, Mo.
1907

Copyright 1907
by
William Monks

Introduction.

Now the author was born in the state of Alabama, in Jackson county, on the north side of the Tennessee River, near Huntsville. He was the son of James Monks and Nancy Monks. The father of James Monks came over from Ireland during the Revolutionary War and served in that war until the Independence of the United States was acknowledged. Afterwards he married a lady of English descent and settled down in the state of South Carolina. His father died when he was but an infant. His mother removed to the state of Tennessee, being left with five children, James being the youngest. Growing up to manhood in that state, he removed to the north part of the state of Alabama and there married Nancy Graham, who was a daughter of Jesse Graham. They were originally from the state of Virginia.

James Monks enlisted in the United States Army and served in the Indian war that was known as the Seminole war, in the state of Florida. After his term of service had expired he returned home and sold his farm and had a flatboat built and placed in the Tennessee River near Gunters Landing, with the intention of moving to the state of Florida. Taking his brother-in-law, a Mr. Phillips, on the boat with him, they went down the river by Decatur, were piloted through the Mussell Shoals, and at the foot of the shoals at what is known as Tuscumbia, the writer remembers seeing a part of the Cherokee Indians that were being removed from the state of Alabama to their present location. The writer can remember seeing the Cherokee Indians before they were removed from the state of Alabama.

On reaching Southern Illinois, eight miles from Paducah, my father landed his boat and looked over the country and came to the conclusion that that country was good enough, and located in what was then Pope County. Afterwards they cropped a piece off Pope and a piece off of Johnson, and created a new county and named it Massack, after the old government fort, and located the county seat, named Metropolis.

My father resided nine years in that state, then sold out and started to move to the state of Texas. On arriving in Fulton county, Arkansas, he concluded to locate in that county.

Soon after his arrival, in the latter part of June or July, 1844, the writer was employed to carry the United States mail from Salem, the county seat of Fulton County, to Rockbridge, then the county seat of Ozark county, Missouri. My father and mother taught me to be loyal to my government from my earliest remembrance, and I don't think that two persons more honest than they ever lived. They taught me from my earliest recollection to be honest and upright, and I have tried, and believe I have lived up to their teaching to the very letter; and no man or woman before the war, during the war, nor since the war, can say anything else and tell the truth. Religiously, my father and mother were Baptists, and I believe that they were Christians.

Early Settlements.

In the year 1844 father sold out and in May started to move to the state of Texas; crossed the Mississippi river at Green's old ferry, came by the way of Jackson, Missouri, and traveled the old military road made by the government troops in removing the Cherokee Indians from the state of Alabama to their present location—only road leading west—and in July of the same year (learning that it was very dangerous for a man to take his family into the state of Texas on account of the Indians) he concluded to locate in Fulton county, Arkansas, purchased an improvement and located on what is known as Bennett's river, about 25 miles from where West Plains is now located. The family at that time consisted of six persons, to-wit: father, mother and four sons, the author then being in his fifteenth year; father, being a farmer by occupation, went to work on the farm. The country at that time was very sparsely settled. The settlements were confined to the creeks and rivers, where were found plenty of water and springs. No place at that time was thought worth settling unless it had a spring on it. The vegetation was luxuriant, the broom sedge and blue stem growing as high as a man's head—and he upon an ordinary horse. The table lands, which were thought at that time to be worthless, had very little timber growing on them, but were not prairie. There were what were known as post oak runners and other brush growing on the table lands, but the grass turf was very heavy and in the spring of the year the grass would soon cover the sprouts and the stranger would have taken all of the table lands, except where it was interspersed with groves, to have been prairie. The country settled up—some of the settlements being 15 miles apart—yet the early settlers thought nothing of neighboring and assisting each other as neighbors for the distance of 15 miles. At that time Fulton county contained all of the present territory that now includes Baxter, Fulton and a part of Sharp counties; and but a short time previous to the organization of Fulton, all of the territory that now embraces Fulton, Baxter and Sharp;

Izard belonged to Independence county and Batesville was the county seat. My father located about five miles from the state line.

Ozark county, in Missouri, joined Fulton county on the state line and all of the territory that now comprises Ozark, Douglas and the west half of Howell, belonged to Ozark county and Rockbridge, its county seat, being located on Bryan's Fork of the North Fork, about 50 miles from the state line. Oregon county contained all of the territory that now comprises Oregon, Shannon, and the east end of Howell; and a short time previous all of the territory that now comprises Ripley, Oregon, Carter and Shannon belonged to Ripley county; and all of the territory that now comprises Texas, Dent, Wright and Crawford counties belonged to Crawford county. The country at that time abounded in millions of deer, turkeys, bears, wolves and small animals. I remember as my father was moving west and after he had crossed White Water near what was known as Bullinger's old mill, that we could see the deer feeding on the hills in great herds like cattle, and wild turkeys were in abundance. Wild meat was so plentiful that the settlers chiefly subsisted upon the flesh of wild animals until they could grow some tame stock, such as hogs and cattle. This country then was almost a "land of honey." Bees abounded in great number and men hunted them for the profit they derived from the beeswax. There was no such thing known as a bee moth.

Honeydew fell in such quantities as to completely kill the tops of the grass where it was open. I have known young turkeys, after they were large enough for use, to have their wings so gummed with honeydew that they could not fly out of the way of a dog—have known lots of them to be caught with dogs when they wanted to use them. There was no question in regard to there being honey when you cut a bee tree, if the hollow and space in the tree were sufficient and the bees had had time to fill it. I have known bee trees being cut that had 8 and 10 feet of solid comb that was candied and grained. When my father first located, beeswax, peltry and fur skins almost constituted the currency of the country. I remember that a short time after my father located, a gentleman came to my father's house and wanted to buy a horse and offered to pay him in beeswax and peltry, and as I had been accustomed to paper currency in the state of Illinois, I asked my father what kind of money peltry was. He laughed and remarked, "Well son, it is not money at all; it is deer skins." A man thought nothing of buying a horse or a yoke of oxen or to make any other common debt on the promise of discharging the same in beeswax and peltry in one month's time.

The immigration consisted mostly of farmers and mechanics. Among the mechanics were coopers who would make large hogsheads for the purpose of holding the honey after it was separated from the beeswax, and a man then had his choice to use either candied honey or fresh honey. I knew whole hogsheads that were full of candied honey. When men would make a contract to deliver any amount or number of pounds of beeswax, and within a given time, especially in the fall of the year, they would either take a yoke of cattle or two horses and a wagon and with their guns and camp equipage go out from the settlements into what was then termed the "wilderness," and burn bee comb. In a short time the bees would be working so strong to the bait that they could scarcely course them. In the morning they would hunt deer, take off pelts until the deer would lie down, then they would hunt bees and mark the trees until the deer would get up to feed in the afternoon, when they would again resume their hunt for deer. After they had found a sufficient number of bee trees and marked them, the morning following they would go out and kill nothing but large deer; caseskin them until they had a sufficient number of hides to contain the honey that they expected to take from the trees, take the hides to the camp, tie a knot in the fore legs of the hide, take dressed buckskin and a big awl, roll the hide of the neck in about three folds, run two rows of stitches, draw it tight, then go to their wagons with ridgepole and hooks already prepared, knot the hind legs of the skins, hang them over the hooks, take their tub, a knife and spoon, proceed to the trees, stop their team a sufficient distance from the tree to prevent the bees from stinging the animals, cut the tree, take out the honey, place it in the tub, and when the tub was filled carry it to the wagon where the hides were prepared, empty their tubs into the deer skins, return again to another tree and continue cutting until the hides were all filled with honey; then they would return home, take the hides from the hooks on the ridgepole on the wagon, hang them on hooks prepared for the purpose in the smokehouse and then the men's work was done.

The labor of the women then commenced. They would proceed to separate the honey from the beeswax, pouring the honey into hogsheads, kegs or barrels prepared for it, and running the beeswax into cakes ready for the market, while the men were stretching and drying the deerskins. As soon as the deerskins were dried and the honey was separated from the beeswax, they were ready for the market and took their place as currency, while the flesh of the deer, sometimes, when bread was scarce, took place of both bread and meat, with a change, whenever the appetite called for it, to turkey and other wild game.

At night they would hunt for fur animals, such as raccoon, fox and mink, and stretch their hides; a first-class raccoon hide would sell for 40 to 50 cents; fox 25 to 30 cents; mink for 65 to 75c. I have often known the people to pay their taxes, when the collector came around, with fur skins, such as raccoon and fox. The collector would take the hides right at the house and give them a clear receipt for their taxes, both state and county. I have seen collectors leading a horse for the purpose of carrying his fur skins. I have seen the horse completely covered with fur skins, so you could see no part of him but his head and his hoofs and tail—one could not have told there was a horse beneath the load unless he had known it.

The people then had many advantages that they are deprived of now, in the way of wild meat, abundance of honey and fine range. A man could raise all the stock in the way of horses and cattle that he could possibly look after; the only expense was salting and caring for them—didn't have to feed , winter nor summer, except the horses in use and the cows used for milking purposes. While, on the other hand, they labored under a great many disadvantages, in the way of schools and churches. During the residence of my father in the state of Illinois, we had a very good common school system, and we had three months of school every fall. My father being a farmer, sent me only the three months' term in the fall. I had acquired a limited education before his removal to Arkansas, yet he was interested in giving his children an education. At that time there were no free schools, only subscription schools; teachers generally were incompetent and employed through favoritism, and not upon their qualifications to teach. In a year or two after my father located, the settlement got together and located a school-house site, took their teams, hauled round logs, built them into walls, made a dirt floor, cut out a large window in the side, split a tree and made a writing desk, split small trees, hewed them and made benches for seats, cut a hole in one end of the house, erected a wooden chimney, what was then known as a stick and clay chimney, chinked and daubed the cracks, made a clapboard roof, hung the door with wooden hinges, then the house was considered ready for the school and had the name of teaching a three-month's subscription school; and very often half of the pupils were better scholars than the teachers. All they gained in their education was by attention to study. As the country improved in population, the people improved in the erection of school-houses and church-houses and constructed, in place of the round log school-house and dirt floor, hewed log school-houses with puncheon floors, stick and clay chimneys.

Those pioneer settlers took a great interest in each other's welfare, and the different settlements met together from a distance of 15 to 40 miles and adopted rules and customs binding each other to aid and assist in helping any person who met with any misfortune in the way of sickness, death or other causes that might occur, and I must say that there was more charity and real religion practiced among those pioneer settlers, although many of them were looked upon as being crude and unlettered. There was a great deal of sickness along the streams, especially chills and fever. Immigrants came in, generally in sufficient numbers to form a settlement; and I have known them, very often, after they had located and opened out 10 to 15 acres and put it in cultivation and broke the ground and planted their corn, for the whole family to be taken down at one time with chills and fever, not able even to help each other or administer to their wants. As soon as the information reached the other settlements for a distance of 15 miles or more, the different settlements would set a day to meet at the place with their horses, plows, hoes, wagons, etc.; also provisions, such as bread-stuff and salt. On meeting, they would ascertain the condition of the family or families and learn what they needed in the way of provision, medicine, nursing, etc.; they would then and there agree that the different settlements should divide up the time, set the day for each one to furnish waiters to wait upon them in their sickness, such medicine as they needed, provisions and everything that was necessary to render comfort, and in the morning before breakfast they would go out and kill a deer and as many turkeys as they needed, dress them, prepare them for the cook, who had been brought with them, go into the field after breakfast, plow and hoe the corn, clean out the garden, leave the families in charge of nurses and return again to their respective settlements. Those families, as soon as they were well, not being acquainted with the customs and rules, would meet them and inquire as to what amount they owed them for what they had done for them during their sickness. They would be readily informed, "*Nothing.* You are not acquainted with our rules and customs. Now, we have obligated and pledged ourselves together not to let any sick or other disabled person suffer for the want of necessary attention, and the only thing we require of you is, if any other person should move into the country and locate, and should be taken down and confined through sickness or any other cause, that you help in furnishing such aid and necessaries as they may need until they are able to again take care of themselves." Now, I have just remarked that there was more real charity and religion practiced among pioneers than there is in the present day. The people then all appeared to be interested in bettering the condition of society.

As soon as it was possible, the different settlements erected church-houses built of hewed timber, floored with puncheons, hewed seats, size of house generally from 18 by 20 to 22 by 25 feet, chinked and daubed. The churches or denominations then were Baptists and Methodist. There didn't appear to be any antagonism or hatred existing between the denominations; the doors were thrown open for any minister that might travel through and they all turned out, and you heard nothing said then in regard to "my church" or "your church." They appeared to recognize the fact that it was the Lord's church and that they were the Lord's people. In going to church, sometimes from 1 to 10 miles, they would see flocks of turkeys and herds of wild deer, both going and coming. As soon as the crops were laid by, they would agree among the different settlements as to where a campmeeting should be held; they would then erect camps or huts, make boards to cover them, erect an arbor, fill the center of it with straw, and to the distance of 25 to 35 miles they would all turn out, irrespective of denomination, and all appeared to enjoy themselves, and the love of Christ appeared to dwell in each heart, and they appeared to be proud of the privilege of meeting each other and worshiping together. If any member belonging to either of the denominations defrauded, or in any way wronged his brother, he was at once waited upon and requested to make reparation to his brother and acknowledge to his brother and to the church, or he was withdrawn from or turned out of the church. The immigration was chiefly from the Middle States, some from the Southern States and very few from the Northeastern States. They were frugal, energetic, honest, intelligent and industrious. As the country increased in population, the facilities of both schools and churches improved.

The customs and habits were entirely different from those existing now; the wearing apparel was entirely homemade; they would raise their cotton, pick it out with their fingers or a hand gin, women would spin their warp, spin their filling, get their different colors from different barks for men's wear; the women used indigo and copperas for the main colors in manufacturing the cloth for dresses, wound their stripes on a stick and then wove it into cloth; you could scarcely visit a house but what you would see a loom, big spinning-wheel and little wheel; sometimes you would see three or four wheels at one house. They made both their every day and Sunday wear; the women appeared to take great pride in seeing who could weave the nicest piece of cloth, make it into a dress, make cloth and make it into what was known as Virginia bonnets, and the men tanned their own leather, made shoes for the whole family. When the women were dressed completely in their homespun they appeared to enjoy themselves in church, in company or any other gathering, and felt just as independent and proud as the king upon his throne; they appeared to meet each other and greet each other and all appeared to realize the fact that they were human and they had but on superior and that was God. The women spun the warp, spun the wool, wove it into cloth, procured the different barks from the woods and dyed it, the general color being brown, made it with their own hands into coats, pants, undershirts; made overshirts out of homespun cotton and the whole suit was home-made, and very often a cap, made either of a raccoon or a fox, was worn on the head. When men met each other at any public gathering they appeared to be proud of meeting each other; appeared to realize the fact that they were all American citizens and human, bound together by the ties of love and affection, and the highest ambition appeared to be to make each other happy and help one another in time of need.

I don't believe there was as much dissipation by partaking of intoxicants, or other wickedness, as exists to-day among the same number of persons. It is true that then any man who was able to purchase a little still and had a spring could erect his own still house and make his own whiskey without paying any tax or duty upon the same, and anyone of his neighbors who wanted a gallon of whiskey could carry a bushel of corn to the still-house and get a gallon of whiskey in exchange for it. And if men became drunk on the whiskey it did not appear to make them wild and crazy as the whiskey of to-day does.

Men then, as well as now, would have disagreements and fall out and fight, but the custom that prevailed among that class would not tolerate nor allow a man to use weapons, and if two men had a disagreement, one of them being a large, stout man physically, the other being a small man, not equal in strength—if they were together in a public place and the large one would challenge the weaker to fight him, before he could hardly open his mouth, some man present who considered himself to be his equal in physical strength, would say to him "now then, if you want to fight, that man is not your equal, but I am; get your second and walk out and I will do the fighting for this other man." I have, on different occasions, seen the large man who was challenging the weaker man for a fight reply to the challenge and say "My friend, I have nothing against you; this other man hasn't treated me right," or set out some other reason that he ought to whip him; the man in reply would say, "I don't want to hear another word from you in regard to wanting to fight this other man, and if I do you have got me to fight." Very often I have seen the man shut his mouth and turn away and say nothing more. On the other hand, I have heard a man say to another, "If you want to fight, I am your man; the other man is unable to fight you," and in an instant the other would reply, "Well, sir, I am your man; just as leave fight you as anybody else." They would select their seconds, take a drink of whiskey together, enter into an agreement that whenever the seconds said either one was whipped, that they were to abide by it, unless they found out before their second did that they were whipped, and if so, they would manifest it by holloing "enough," when the other person was to stop at once and inflict no more injury. I have often seen them fight until they were both as bloody as butchers and in the end the seconds would have to hollo for one or the other. As soon as they were separated they would go to the same pool or place where there was water and wash themselves, and walk arm-in-arm, laughing and talking and drinking together and remark, "We are now fast friends and we have settled the matter as to which was the best man." And if a man would produce a weapon on either side his own friends would turn against him and he would be forced to put it up at once. Men then appeared to be governed by that higher inspiration, that a man should not use anything that would permanently disable or take the life of his fellow-man; but if one man became pregnant with fight or desire to maim his fellow-man, in order that he should not be disappointed, some man would readily volunteer, who believed that he was his equal physically, and deliver him of all his fighting propensities.

Dow Bryant and a Gallon of Whiskey.

I will here relate an instance that I well remember. A man by the name of Bridges lived just above where Bakersfield is now located, owned a little mill at the same place where they still continue the work of the mill just above Bakersfield. The mill ground from twelve to fifteen bushels per day; most of us carried our sacks on horseback, and ground by turns. Bridges had employed a man by the name of Math Shipman to run the mill. He was a small man weighing only about 135 pounds, and there was a man by the name of Dow Bryant, lately from the state of Tennessee, quite a large man, weighing 225 pounds, who delighted in fighting under the old style, and claimed that he had whipped two of the best men in Tennessee at the same time. Shipman had made some statement that reflected upon Bryant; so Bryant procured a gallon of whiskey, and, taking two men with him, went from Bennett's river over to the mill and informed Shipman that what he had heard he had said in regard to him, and said to Shipman that if he had said it and didn't take it back, he would have to whip him, and the only thing he hated about it would be the whipping of as little a man as he was. Shipman replied that he need not take that matter into consideration, and that his father had always taught him that if he told anything and it was the truth, not to take it back under any consideration, and that what he said was true; and as to his whipping him, his father had always taught him never to admit anything until he knew it was true; and "I have my doubts about you being able to whip me; but if you will get your second ready, as soon as the corn that is in the hopper is ground out and I refill the hopper I will get my second and we will go out into the mill yard so you can test it." They accordingly got their seconds, went into the mill yard, formed a ring, and when the word was given by the seconds, they went together. Shipman bit every finger on the right hand and three fingers on the left hand to the bone; and Bryant's friends, seeing he was going to be whipped, proposed parting them. Bryant returned home, and when his neighbors would meet him with his fingers all bound up, they would say, "Hello there. What's the matter?" His reply would be, "I went over into the wilderness and got hold of a wildcat, and it like to have eaten me up before I could get loose from it." He would further say that Shipman was all mouth, and that he could not put his hands anywhere about his head unless he got them in his mouth.

I will give another instance touching the same man (Bryant). He went over to Salem during circuit court. The sheriff of the county was a man by the name of Dick Benton, quite a small man, and the constable of the township was named Moore and a very small man. Bryant was drinking some, and wanted to fight as usual, and became noisy. The judge ordered the constable to arrest him; but when Bryant saw the constable coming, he backed behind an old building, and ordered the constable not to rush upon him. When the constable came in reach, he knocked him down, came walking around, and remarked that no tickey officer could arrest him. The judge then ordered the sheriff to arrest him. When the sheriff came within reach, he knocked him down, came walking back, and remarked, "I thought they understood me when I told them that a tickey set of officers could not arrest me." During the time the father-in-law of the sheriff had come out. Bryant walked up to him, and with a d—— said: "I want to know what you are doing here." Without any more words being passed, the sheriff's father-in-law knocked Bryant down, jumped onto him, but he holloed, and they took him off. Bryant straightened himself up right into his face again and remarked, "I have told a lie, I am not whipped." Without any more words he knocked him down again and gave him a considerable pelting. Bryant holloed again, and after they had taken him off, he straightened up and walked off about ten steps distant, turned around, and remarked, "I have told lie, I am not whipped; but I am not going to say it within reach of that old man any more." On the same day some men knocked him down, taking a common clapboard, hit him three licks while he was running on all fours, then got a piece of chalk and wrote on it, "Dow's Board," and nailed it up on the corner of the square.

The drinking class for years used all manner of language and obscenity in the streets, and even in the hearing of the court. There was a man by the name of Neely who became a candidate for circuit judge, and one of the main reasons he urged for his election was that, if elected, he would punish all offenders of the public peace, and force all persons to respect the court, and he would discharge the duties with some dignity and respect for himself and the people. Shortly after he was elected and during the first court, a man by the name of Smith, who lived just north of Salem on the South Fork, and who had worked for his election, came into the court room after the court was in session, walked around to the judge, took him by the hand and remarked, "Judge, I want to congratulate you on your success, and I hope things will change." The judge turned to the clerk and remarked, "Mr. Clerk assess a fine of five dollars against Mr. Smith." Smith soon retired from the court room and declared that Neeley was a tyrant, and that if he had his vote back he would not support him. In the afternoon the judge ordered the sheriff to bring Mr. Smith into the court room and said to him, "Mr. Smith, you were a warm friend of mine in my canvass, worked for my election, and no doubt contributed much to my success. Now I don't want to disappoint you in any promises that I made during the canvass, but after court is convened and the judge on the bench, it is contempt in any gentleman to come and take him by the hand and congratulate him on his success; and now I hope that you, with all others of my friends, and those who are not, will support and protect me in enforcing the dignity of the court." Mr. Smith at once became pacified, and said that the judge was right.

We remember another instance that occurred during the same court.

There was a young lawyer, who came into court, wearing a very fine pair of boots, and, standing on his feet, he would occasionally raise onto his toes, and you could hear his boots creak all over the court room. The judge turned to him and remarked, "Mr., what did those boots cost you?" The lawyer quickly replied, "Ten dollars, sir." The judge remarked to him, "I think you got the boots too cheap. I think they ought to be worth twenty dollars. Mr. Clerk, assess a fine of ten dollars against this man."

On the next day a man by the name of Cage Hogan, a man who was widely known, in company with others, got on the public square, near the saloon, and began to curse and swear, and use all manner of obscenity. The judge ordered the sheriff to go down and see who was making the disturbance. The sheriff went out to the place and stated to the crowd that the judge had ordered him to see who was creating that disturbance, and to arrest the party. Hogan remarked, with an oath, "You go back and tell the old judge that it is Cage Hogan, and that I suppose he has heard of me before, and I don't allow sheriffs to arrest me until I get ready." The sheriff came back and reported to the court, and the judge made an order for him to proceed at once and arrest Mr. Hogan and all others that he might find acting in a boisterous manner, and if necessary to take the power of the county, and if he didn't immediately bring him into the court room he would assess a fine against him of $100. The sheriff returned and informed Mr. Hogan of what the court had said, and that he would be bound to arrest him and take him by force if he didn't go without it. Hogan remarked that if it would be any pleasure and consolation to the old tyrant he was the man who could go into the court room. When he came into the court room, the sheriff said, "Here is Mr. Hogan." Mr. Hogan remarked, with an oath, "I am here, judge, and I would like to know what you want." The judge replied that there were some parties creating a disturbance in the hearing of the court and that he had ordered them arrested and brought in. "Do you know who the parties are?" Hogan, with an oath, replied, "I am the man; and judge, I want you to understand that I am a horse, and if you hain't become acquainted with old Cage Hogan, you will." The judge remarked to him that they had a stable and that was the place for horses, and that he would assess a fine of $50 against him, and ordered the sheriff to take him to jail until it was paid. Hogan, remarking, "I always carry the money to pay my way, and you need not put yourself to any trouble to have the sheriff carry me to jail," pulled out his pocket book, took out $50, and said with an oath, "Here is the money, and I want you to understand that I am no jailbird, and you can't stick me in your old jail." The judge then said, "Mr. Hogan seems to have plenty of money; Mr. Clerk assess another $50 fine against him." At that Hogan appeared to hesitate and reflect, and, pulling out a quart bottle of whiskey from his pocket, started to approach the judge, who was on the bench, saying with an oath, "Here judge, lets drink together and be friends and stop this foolishness." The judge turned to the clerk and said; "Mr. Clerk, assess another fine of $50 against him," and ordered the sheriff to take him forthwith to jail and keep him there until further orders, for he considered him an unlawful horse, and he did not think it safe for society for him to run at large. The sheriff, with a considerable posse, carried him to the jail, and with considerable trouble put him in and shut him up. He remained the jail two days, and at the evening session of the second day the sheriff came into court and said that Mr. Hogan was very desirous of seeing the court. The court then ordered him brought in. On his being brought in, the court asked him if he still thought he was a horse. Hogan replied, "No, sir; I am not anything now but Cage Hogan." The judge said: "As you have now arrived at the conclusion that you are human and not animal, are you willing to respect the laws of your land and the dignity of this court?" Hogan replied: "I am, judge, with all my heart." The judge then said to him, "What about that money of yours; are you able to pay the $150 fine. Hogan said, "No judge, I don't feel like I could pay $150 this evening; I don't feel as rich and as brave as I did when you first brought me into court, and I want you to be as lenient with me as possible." The court said, "Mr. Hogan if you will promise me that you will neither disturb the dignity of this court nor incite others to do so, I will remit all of your fine except $50." Mr. Hogan then and there paid the $50 fine and was released. From that time up to the end of his term there never was any disturbance of any nature in the hearing of the court, and if you went into the court room everything was so quiet that you could almost hear a pin drop.

The Tutt and Evert War.

My memory is that it was in the year 1846 that an incident occurred in Marion county that I will now relate. It was known as the Tutt and Evert war. They were once fast friends. They met in Yellville, the county seat, and while there, one of the Everts purchased a set of silver spoons at the store of one of the Tutts. Afterwards a misunderstanding grew up between them as to the payments for the spoons, which led them into a fight. Afterwards, which was often, when they would meet in Yellville, they would hardly ever get away without some fighting taking place between the parties. There was a large gathering and a public demonstration to take place within a few weeks. The Tutts declared, backed by the Kings, that if the Everts came into town that day they would kill them outright. Both parties came in early in the day, heavily armed. After coming under the influence of intoxicants to some extent, Evert went into the public square and stated what he had heard from the Tutts, and said that if they, the Tutts and the Kings, were ready for the conflict, there never was a better time than then, and that they, the Everts, were fully ready. Both parties, in short range, opened fire. One of the Kings shot Simm Evert during the fight, supposed to be through the heart. One of the Kings, just previous to the shooting of Evert, had been shot through the hips and so disabled that he could not stand upon his feet. After Simm Evert had received the wound, he turned around, and, within a few steps of the wounded King, picked up a large stone, raised it in both hands, and, stepping up to King, came down on King's head with the stone with all the force possible, completely crushing King's head. Then, turning around and walking about three steps, he remarked, "I am a dead man," and fell to the ground and expired within a few minutes. When the smoke cleared away and the fighting ceased, an examination showed that there were eight or ten left dead on the ground. The stoutest men afterwards went to the stone, but there wasn't one of them that could raise it from the ground. The surviving Kings made arrangements and attempted to leave the country. At that time the sheriff of the county was a man by the name of Mooney. A writ was placed in his hands and he arrested them. Shortly after the arrest, the Everts and their friends came upon the sheriff and his posse and demanded the prisoners. The sheriff gave them up, and they were all shot. The sheriff then appealed to the governor for aid; he sent the militia, who aided the sheriff in the arrest of the Everts, a man by the name of Stratton, and some other of their friends. The governor ordered them to be taken to Lawrence county and placed in the Lawrence county jail at Smithville, the county seat of that county. I saw the militia in charge of the prisoners pass my father's house on their way to Smithville.

In about ten days after they were put in prison, late one evening, strange men commenced dropping into the town, who were unknown to the citizens, until they reached to about the number of sixty-five. Somewhere near midnight they paraded the streets, and the jail being a log jail, they prepared levers and pried it up and let the prisoners all out, and they all left together, Evert, Stratton, and their friends proceeding directly to Texas. After their families had reached them and everything had quieted down, they sent in and notified Hamp Tutt, whom they charged with being the inciter and leader in bringing on the original trouble, that if he would "hull out" and leave the state they would not kill him. Tutt was a man of considerable wealth and declared he would not leave the state. He at once hired a young doctor, who claimed to be a very brave man, to act as his body guard, and kept himself very close to the town for about the space of two years. One day, however, he declared that he was going to take a ride out on the main public road for his health. He, in company with the young doctor, then rode out about one mile. On returning, not more than a quarter of a mile from the town, after they had passed the place where they were concealed, they, (the Everts) discharged a volley. Two balls entered the back of Tutt, and his horse made but a few leaps when he fell to the ground. The young doctor ran for dear life, reached the town, and gave the alarm. Parties immediately went out to the place, but found that Tutt was dead. On examining the place where the parties had lain in ambush, they found that they had lain there for months watching for the opportunity. So ended the Tutt and Evert war.

Indians Chase a Sheriff Ten Miles.

Now the author will relate another incident that occurred in Marion county, Arkansas, in the early settling of this country. There was a large relation of the Coker family who lived in that county. One of the Cokers raised two families, one by a white woman and the other by an Indian woman. The Indian family, after they had grown up and become men, resided a part of the time in the Nation, where the mother lived, and a part of the time they remained in Marion county where their father and other relatives lived. They were very dangerous men when drinking, and the whole country feared them. They had been in different troubles, and had killed three or four men, and if the authorities attempted to arrest them, they defied them, and would go to the Nation and remain awhile. There was a deputy sheriff in the county by the name of Stinnett, who claimed to be very brave, who said he would arrest them if he found their whereabouts. The Cokers learned what Stinnett had said, and that the warrant for their arrest was in his possession, so they got some good tow strings and vowed that whenever they met him they would arrest him and take him to Yellville and put him in jail. A short time afterwards they met him in the public road. As soon as Stinnett recognized them, and having heard of the threats they had made, he wheeled his horse and put spurs to him. They drew their revolvers and put spurs to their horses in pursuit, commanding him to halt. But Stinnett spurred his horse the harder. They pursued him a distance of about ten miles; but Stinnett's horse proved to be the best, and he made his escape. They again returned to the Nation.

The good people, generally, of the county were terrorized and afraid to raise their voices against them, and it became a question as to whether they had a man in the county who had the courage to attempt their arrest. They made it a question in the next election, to elect a man that would make the arrest, if such a man could be found in the county. There was a man living in the county by the name of Brown, who was a cousin of the Cokers, and he told the people that if they would elect him, he would arrest them or they would kill him. He was elected by a large majority, and, after he had qualified, took charge of the office. The first time the Cokers came into the settlement, he summoned two men, thought to be brave, who pledged themselves that If it became necessary they would die for him. He then went to the house of one of the Coker family where the Cokers were staying, and on his arrival found the two Coker brothers sitting in chairs in the yard. He was within some thirty feet of them before they saw him. Their guns were sitting near them, and they seized them; but before they could present them Brown had his revolver cocked and leveled at one of their heads, and told him not to attempt to raise his gun or he would kill him. Coker turned his back to him with his gun on his shoulder, secretly cocked it, and leveled it upon Brown as near as possible without taking it from his shoulder and fired, missing his aim. About the same time Brown discharged his revolver at Coker and made a slight scalp wound. The other Coker threw his gun upon Brown and fired, killing him instantly. The two men who were acting as a posse for the sheriff turned and fled, leaving Brown lying dead on the ground. After the shooting the Cokers fled to the Nation and remained there.

The author will now relate another incident that occurred in the same county. For years the Cokers and the Hogans had been intimate friends, and drank, gambled, and horseraced together a great deal. There came up a trouble between Coker and on of his brothers-in-law, and one evening Coker, in company with Hogan, went to the house of this brother-in-law. Both had been drinking. Coker swore that he would ride onto the porch of his brother-in-law, and made the attempt. His brother-in-law caught the horse by the bridle and warned him not to ride onto the porch, and that if he did he would kill him. Coker drew his revolver, spurred his horse, but as he entered the porch his brother-in-law shot him dead. Coker being a cousin of the Indian Cokers, they charged Hogan with inducing him, while drinking, to go to his brother-in-law's house, so as to give him a chance to kill him, and that Hogan's life should pay the penalty. Shortly afterwards Hogan was traveling on an old trail that led along the bluff of White river. The river here made a bend in horseshoe shape, following the bluff all around. The Cokers learned that Hogan was going to pass through this gap, and they lay in wait for him, cutting off all avenues of escape possible so he would be forced into the horseshoe for his escape. When he came in sight they raised the Indian warwhoop, and drew their revolvers. Hogan looked around and saw that his pursuers were in about a hundred yards of him. He saw his predicament, as for a quarter of a mile he confronted the bluff, and that there was only one avenue of escape. He went to the edge of the precipice and looked over. There, under the bluff, lay the deep, blue waters of White river, 150 feet below. Again he turned his eyes toward his pursuers. He knew it meant death if they caught him; so he made the fearful leap over the bluff, striking the water where it was about twenty-five feet deep. Hogan was a wicked man and cursed a great deal. He swore it didn't take him long to reach the water, but that he thought considerable time intervened from the time he struck the water until he reached the top again. He swam to the bank which was but a few feet distant. His pursuers came to the precipice, looked over, and said that they had made Hogan do something they had intended to do and that was, to take his own life, as they supposed no human being could make the leap and live. After cutting his saddle and bridle to pieces, they turned his horse loose, and reported that Hogan was killed. Hogan traveled around under the bluff for about two miles, made his way home, wound up his business, sold his farm, and moved into Fulton county, Arkansas, which ended the trouble between them.

The author will relate another incident that occurred in Marion county, Arkansas. There was a widow residing in that county, who was left with a family of children, among them a boy about twelve years of age. Her horse ran away, and she sent her boy in pursuit of it. After he had found it and was returning home, leading the horse, Hogan and one of his friends met him in the road. They had both been drinking, and seeing the boy, concluded to have some fun out of him. Hogan, with an oath, said, "What are you doing with my horse?" The boy replied, "It is not your horse, it is mother's horse." Hogan sprang off his horse, and, thinking to scare the boy and have some fun with him, said: "Here, you know it's my horse; give it up." The boy pulled a barlow knife out of his pocket, and, opening it, said, "You attempt to come near me, and I will stick this knife into you." Hogan stepped up to him and said, "You little rascal, would you attempt to cut me with a knife?' The boy, without any further words, made a stroke at him with the knife, and the blade entered his body near the left breast. Hogan declared afterward that he jumped about ten feet high. He turned to his friend and remarked: "I believe our fun with the little bugger has caused my death, or at least a serious wound." He went to a physician, had the wound probed, and found the knife had penetrated a rib and reached the inside. The physician informed him that had it passed between the ribs it would have killed him instantly. Hogan remarked to the boy, after he stabbed him, "My son, you are made out of the right kind of stuff. I had no intention of hurting you or taking your mother's horse from you, I merely wanted to have some fun; but I see I have struck the wrong boy this time. Go on and take your horse to your mother."

The author will refer to another incident that occurred in Howell county, Missouri. In the year 1860 there was a man who resided in West Plains by the name of Jack McDaniel, who was a blacksmith by trade. The same Hogan came to town, soon became under the influence of whiskey, went down to McDaniel's shop with a horse, and ordered him to shoe him. McDaniel had two other horses in the shop at the time to be shod, and said to Hogan that as soon as he had shod those two horses, he would shoe his. Hogan said, "I am in a hurry, and I want you to shoe mine now." McDaniel told him that he could not shoe his horse until he had shod the other two horses. Hogan said, "If you don't shoe him at once, I will whip you." McDaniel then pulled a barlow knife out of his pocket, and, opening it, said: "Yes; and if you fool with me, I will cut your throat from ear to ear." At this remark, Hogan moved right up to him and said, "Just smell my neck." McDaniel struck at him with the knife, and the blade entered just under the ear, cutting to the bone all the way around into the mouth. Hogan went to a physician in West Plains and had the wound dressed. He then went to a glass, looked in, and said that he had lived a long time, been in many tight places, but he had never had such a mouth as he had now, and remarked, "My mouth looks as if it was spread from ear to ear."

The people then generally gave their time to growing stock, especially horses and cattle, as hogs and sheep had to be kept close around the farms and penned of a night, especially the pigs, on account of wolves and other wild animals. I have known the wolves to kill 2 and 3 year old cattle. Farmers fed their corn chiefly to cattle, horses and mules. They always commanded fair prices. Cattle, at the age of four years and upwards were driven to Jacksonport, Arkansas and from there shipped to New Orleans. Horses and mules were driven to Louisiana, Mississippi and some to the Southern part of Arkansas and there put upon the market. Prices generally ranging from $75 to $150. All of our groceries were purchased in New Orleans, shipped to Jacksonport, from there they were conveyed by wagons. Our dry goods were mostly purchased at Lynn Creek, Missouri and brought through by wagon, but in the early settling of the country they hauled dry goods all the way from St. Louis except what were brought into the country by peddlers. The peddlers would go to St. Louis on horse back with one and sometimes two led horses, buy the goods, pack them, place them on their horses and peddle all the way from St. Louis and still further west and take in exchange all kinds of fur skins.

I have seen peddlers with one horse still loaded with goods and the other covered with fur skins, and I have seen them again after they had disposed of all their goods with all three horses completely covered with fur skins and sometimes so heavily loaded that the peddler would either be walking and leading or driving.

Money was scarce but the people spent very little money, were not in debt and lived much better and easier than they do now. Their counties were out of debt and the county warrants were always at par.

When my father first located here, there were about four or five settlers in all of the territory that now belongs to Howell county: there were but three men that resided upon what is known as the middle bayou, William McCarty and his sons, Green and Willis.

In about three years after my father settled here, McCarties sold out and located on the bayou above Bakersfield. In 1844 there was a man by the name of Thomas Hall who resided about 10 miles southwest of West Plains, a man by the name of Cyrus Newberry resided about 10 miles from where West Plains now is, and a man by the name of Braudwaters resided near where Moody is now located.

There was not a settlement in all the territory that now includes Howell valley. There had been a settlement, by a man who was a hunter, made at what is now termed the town spring at West Plains who had cleared five or six acres, but had left it. All the valleys in Howell county were considered worthless on account of there being no water.

When the country commenced settling, there was no attention paid to congressional lines. As they settled on the streams, they would make conditional lines—blaze across the bottom until they would strike the table-lands; and the next men who might come in and settle would blaze his conditional line across, and for years there was but little land entered. Men only sold their improvements, and there was a fixed law, or custom, that prevailed among them—that no man should enter the land

and take another man's improvements without paying him for them. A few such instances occurred to my knowledge. The man was at once waited upon, and informed of the rules and customs of the country; and besides the rules and customs, it was not right nor honest to take a man's labor without paying him for it; and that it was the intention and purpose of the people to see that justice was done every man; and he was therefore notified to proceed to the late owner of the improvements and pay him the value of the improvements; and if they couldn't agree upon the value, submit it to two disinterested neighbors; and if they couldn't agree let the third man be brought in, which finding would be final. In every instance if the man who had made the entry failed to comply with the terms, he was at once notified that his absence from the settlement and a speedy departure from the country would be satisfactory to the settlement; and that if he failed to comply, he would have to submit to the punishments that would be inflicted upon him. If the improvements, which were always reasonable, were paid for, the party would move off, blaze out another claim, and go to work to improve it; but if he didn't receive pay for his improvements, he remained on the land and the other fellow's whereabouts would soon be unknown; and when the land was sold for taxes, the man owning the improvements would buy it in by paying the amount of taxes and costs without an opposing bid.

When my father first located in this country, a large portion of the territory had never been sectionized. What was known as the old survey, including range seven and a part of range eight (now in this county) formed a part of the old survey. Congress passed a law graduating the price of land according to the length of time it had been upon the market. The government price was $1.25 per acre. The first reduction was twenty-five cents upon the acre; then they reduced the purchase price every few years until all the land included in the old survey went down to a bit an acre. The graduation law allowed each man to take up 320 acres by making actual settlement and cultivating it. But the land speculators took advantage of the law and hired men to go upon the land and make a few brush-heaps, and in the name of some man apply for the entry, until all of the graduated lands were taken up, and there was not a bone fide settler who had complied with the law in one out of every hundred.

Most of the land in Howell, Gunters, Peace, and Hutton valleys, and the land where West Plains is now situated, were entered at a bit per acre. After the entries, the valley lands commenced settling rapidly. When the time came to procure a patent to the land, speculators went to Washington and engineered a bill through Congress to allow the parties to prove up without making proof of actual settlement, and in that way fraudulently obtained patents to two-thirds of all the land above referred to. The next thing, the speculators went East, sold their lands (or mortgaged them) by representing that all of the table lands were bottom lands and covered with walnut, hackberry, box elder, and other bottom growth. They let the mortgages all be foreclosed.

The merchants, who procured title to the lands, sent out agents to examine the land, who went back and reported that the lands were valueless and were not worth the taxes and refused to pay taxes on them. With some few exceptions the lands were offered time and again for taxes, would not sell for the amount of the taxes and thousands of acres remained in that condition until a short time before the building of the Kansas City & Memphis railroad. All of the table lands were looked upon by the people as being entirely worthless and fit for nothing but range.

My father in the year 1849 sold out and removed from Bennett's river, Fulton county, to the North Fork of White river, in Fulton county but two miles from the State line, dividing Missouri and Arkansas. In the year 1852 father took the winter fever, died and was buried in the cemetery, three miles above the State line, known as the Teverbauch cemetery.

In the year 1854 my mother and one brother died with the bloody flux, leaving three sons of the family, William, the oldest one living, F. M. and James I. Monks. The author was married on the 10th day of April 1853 to Martha A. Rice, a daughter of Thomas and Nancy Rice. He continued to reside upon the old homestead and was a farmer by occupation. The country commenced settling up rapidly. All the land on the streams was settled, with very few exceptions, with a frugal and intelligent class of people, mostly from the middle states. In the year 1856 Howell county was created by taking a part of the territory of Ozark and a part of the territory of Oregon, to wit: Ranges 7 and 8 and a small part of 9 were taken from Oregon county and the remainder of 9 and 10 was taken from Ozark county. Andrew V. Taber, ———— Johnson (and the name of the other commissioner we have forgotten at the present time) proceeded to locate the county seat and purchased 40 acres near the West Plains spring and laid it out in lots, got the county seat near the center, as a sufficient amount of water was necessary, taking into consideration the town spring and then what was known as the Bingiman spring. The lots sold rapidly and the town grew beyond any expectation and the country was improving and settling up with the town.

In 1858 the author sold out on the North Fork of White river and moved into Howell county and located 11 miles southwest of West Plains upon sections 2 and 11, range 9, was appointed constable of Benton township and in the year 1860 was elected constable of Benton township, commenced reading law in the year 1858. In the year 1860 West Plains was said to be the best, neatest, prettiest town in South Missouri and contained about 200 inhabitants; had a neat frame court house in the center of the square, a first-class hewed log jail, had four first-class stores (for the country at that time) which kept continually on hand a general assortment of merchandise, had two saloons, tan yard and the county was out of debt, with money in the treasury; a county warrant then was good for its face value in gold, and the country was prosperous in every respect. The people generally were fast friends and their chief interest was to develop the resources of the country and aid and help each other.

How a Mob Was Prevented.

In 1860, a man resided about three miles below West Plains by the name of Collins Coffey on the farm recently owned by Thomas Bolin and some men by the name of Griffiths and Boles—(some of them resided in West Plains and some of them resided in Thomasville, Oregon county) and they and Coffey had a falling out with each other and the enmity between them became very great. So the Griffiths, who lived at West Plains went down to Thomasville and they and the Boles with a few other friends declared that they would come up to Coffey's and mob him.

They went to work and made for themselves a uniform, procured a bugle, fife and snare drum, procured a hack, made them a place for a candle and aimed to come up in the night.

Coffey owned considerable stock among which was a bull about four years old. The range then was luxuriant and there was a pond near the side of the road that led from Thomasville and West Plains and the bull with other cattle had lain down on the edge of the road about one mile from Coffey's residence. They armed themselves, procured their musicians, got into their hack, drawn by two horses and started off to the scene of action with a bright light, with a flag flying and the music playing. When they reached the place near where the male was laying, he rose to his feet, squared himself and fetched a keen bellow as though (although he was an animal) he might have some information as to their mission. They paid no attention to the action of the bull and on their driving within about ten feet of him he made a desperate lunge forward; they supposed that he intended to gore the horses, but missed his aim, struck the hack near the coupling, broke the coupling pole and turned head over heels, and fell right between the horses. The horses became frightened, made a desperate lunge to extricate themselves, and the bull at the same time was scuffling to extricate himself. Both horses fell, the bull and horses were all piled into a heap, grunting and scuffling. The occupants of the hack were all piled out in a heap, almost in an instant, and before they could extricate themselves and get onto their feet the bull had gotten up and was moving in the direction of his master's house bellowing every step as if to say, "I dare you to come any further." As soon as the posse got to their feet, having prepared, before they started, with plenty of whiskey, and being pretty well filled at the time of the occurrence, Boles got to his feet, drew his pistol, cocked it and swore he could whip any bull he ever saw, especially a one horned Coffey bull.

The hack was almost demolished and the occupants considerably bruised, both horses crippled, and after consultation, they concluded that as the Coffey bull had proved so successful they had better abandon their trip and retreat "in good order" to Thomasville, leaving their horses hitched by the roadside and the shattered hack piled up at one side of the road.

The next morning they sent out a team and brought the horses and hack back to Thomasville, and they were wiser and perhaps better men, as they never again attempted to mob Coffey.

The strange feature about this matter is that the bull was never known to be cross before this occasion, when his master was to be mobbed.

The society of the country had increased with the population, and school houses and churches were erected all over the country, nice farms were opened up, the dwellings changed from round log to hewed log and frame, the people all manifested a great deal of interest in schools and churches and the general development of the country.

Religion and Politics.

The prominent religious denominations from 1849 to 1860 consisted chiefly of Methodists, Baptists and the Christian order; but all appeared to recognize each other as Christians and would very often work together, as they had in the early pioneer days.

Everything had the appearance of pointing to the day when Howell county would become the garden spot of South Missouri.

Politically, the country was largely Democratic. In political campaigns the Whig and Democratic candidates would canvass the country together, and while on the stump speaking they would assail each other's platforms in most bitter terms. After the speaking was over they would go to the same hotel or boarding place and laugh and talk together as though they belonged to the same political party, and after the election was over the successful party would be recognized by the people as the officers of the whole people. You would see no partisan line drawn by the different courts between political parties, but the appointments of all local officers were made according to the qualifications of the man and not as to what party he belonged. The author, having been born and raised by Democratic parents, was a Democrat and acted with the Democratic party, his first vote for president having been cast for James Buchanan. In 1860 a great political question of the nation began to be agitated and a very bitter feeling was manifested from the stump between the Republican and Democratic parties.

After the Democratic party divided and the bolters nominated Breckenridge for president, the author took part in the canvas and was a strong advocate of Stephen A. Douglas, the regular nominee of the Democratic party, and at the election cast his vote for Stephen A. Douglas for president.

Missouri and the Civil War

Abraham Lincoln was elected President of the United States. Soon after the election they began to discuss the question of seceding from the Government. The author again took the field in opposition to secession, and delivered a number of speeches.

In a short time the people that had been the closest of friends and trusted a neighbor with the most sacred thing they possessed became bitter enemies and arrayed themselves against one another and as the discussion of the great question of war continued to grow more bitter the people appeared to allign themselves for and against secession. The people soon grew so bitter that they often talked of fighting each other.

Before the firing on Ft. Sumpter and after several of the states had actually seceded the Union sentiment prevailed so strongly in the state of Missouri that Clabourn Jackson, the then acting Governor, was compelled to order an election in the state of Missouri to settle the matter by a vote of the people as to whether Missouri should secede or remain in the Union. The author then took the stump and advocated that the state remain in the Union and manifest her loyalty to the preservation of the Union. In this campaign the feeling of the war grew more bitter. The result, however, of the election was that the state remained in the Union. In the mean time, Ft. Sumpter had been fired upon by the rebels.

Clabe Jackson, the Governor, appeared to be determined upon the state seceding either by fair or foul means. Without regarding a majority vote of the people of the state, Clabe Jackson, the then acting Governor, issued his proclamation convening the Legislature in extra session for the purpose of passing ordinances of secession.

At that time Gen. Frost was in the command of the militia and some state troops stationed in St. Louis Barracks but he was in heart and sympathy a rebel. Everything appeared to have been greased and prepared for the occasion.

As the Governor had the whole machinery of the state completely under his control he believed that it would be an easy matter for the legislature to pass ordinances of secession and carry the state out of the Union, but the Government authorities at Washington learned of the critical condition and deep laid scheme of the Governor to carry the state out of the Union and at once ordered Capt. Lyons of the Regular Army, (who afterward became General of the volunteer forces and fought the battle at Wilson Creek, Missouri) to come to St. Louis; he, being a captain in the Regular Army, outranked Gen. Frost, took possession of the troops, arms and ammunitions, etc., reorganized and rapidly increased the army by volunteers.

On information reaching Gen. Lyons that the legislature had been convened in extra session he at once took his available troops and left St. Louis with the intention of surrounding the Capitol and taking the members of both houses, the Governor, with all his state officers, prisoners; when the Governor learned that the Government troops were enroute for Jefferson City and their purpose, he ordered the bridge to be burned across the Gasconade river near its mouth, on what was then known as the North Pacific R.R. This delayed the troops for several hours. On their approach to Jefferson City the Governor and state officers and the members of both houses of the legislature and all the troops that had been ordered to the Capital by the Governor retreated to Boonville, Missouri.

I heard our representative in a speech delivered a short time afterwards, say they came so near getting him while he was getting out of Jefferson City that he lost his umbrella. Lyons pursued them and at Boonville they made a stand and on Lyon's arrival with his troops he attacked them and they fought for a short time. They again retreated, went into the extreme west part of the state to a place known as Lone Jack. There they made a stand again, Lyons still pursuing. He again attacked them at Lone Jack and after a short fight they retreated again into the State of Arkansas, and there Governor Jackson convened the legislature and they passed ordinances of secession declaring the State of Missouri out of the Union and that she was attached to the compact forming the Confederate States.

General Lyon returned to St. Louis, increasing his force considerably, several regiments being attached to his command from other states.

The government ordered him to prepare his troops and move west to Springfield. The terminus of the South Missouri Pacific R.R., at that time was at Rolla, Missouri. While Lyon was massing his troops and preparing to march to Springfield the most intense excitement prevailed in the entire State of Missouri.

A Big Confederate Meeting at West Plains.

The Confederate authorities at once commenced recruiting for the Confederate service and the Confederate recruiting officers published a public meeting at West Plains about the first or tenth of July and while the Confederate authorities were moving, the union or loyal element of the country was not idle, but was watching every move, openly and secretly preparing for the conflict.

A few days before the meeting was to be held at West Plains the Confederates sent to the pinery and procured a long pine pole, hoisted it at the corner of Durham's store at the northwest corner of the public square and swung to the breeze the stars and bars. At the same time, or near the same time, the Union men sent to the pinery and procured a pole. They hoisted it on the northeast corner of East Main street by the corner of McGinty's store where the S. J. Langston Mercantile Co., building now stands and swung to the breeze the stars and stripes.

It was freely published throughout the county by the Rebels that if any Union man attempted to open his mouth on that day he would be shot as full of holes as a sifter bottom. There was a beautiful grove then growing just east of the branch on East Main street running from the town spring. Large preparations were made by the Rebels for the occasion. It was published that there would be leading Confederates from all over the state and different other states to speak on that day and one of the main features of the day would be recruiting for Confederate service. A big speaker's stand was erected with hundreds of seats. When the day arrived the town was crowded with people and the friends of both parties were armed and appeared to be ready for the conflict. The stars and bars attracted a great deal of attention, being the first flag that had ever been seen by the people that antagonized the stars and stripes and threatened to destroy the United States Government.

There was soon a number of determined men gathered under each flag. A number of their prominent speakers were on hand, among them Judge Price, of Springfield, known as "Wild Bill" Price. They readily took in the situation and saw that a conflict was imminent, and as they were not ready for it they met together in council and agreed that their men should not bring on the conflict on that day. Quite a number of the parties prepared themselves at the speaker's stand. When different speakers were introduced to address the people, many of the men would sit, either with their guns in their hands or with their guns near to them, and the most firey and extreme speeches were made that I ever heard.

The author well remembers the speech of Judge William Price. He told them that the lopeared Dutch had reached Rolla, Missouri, the terminus of the railroad, and that they were complete heathens; that Abraham Lincoln had given the state of Missouri to them, if they would send enough lopeared Dutch to conquer the state, and that to his knowledge they had gone out into the country and taken men's wives and daughters and brought them into the camps, and that he saw them, in the presence of the mothers, run bayonets through their infant children and hoist them up and carry them around on their bayonets; that Abraham Lincoln had offered a reward for all of the preachers that were in favor of the South. He bursted into tears and asked the question, "I want to know who the man is, and the color of his hair, that won't enlist in the interest of his home, his wife, his children and everything that is sacred and good, to drive out lopeared Dutch, a certain class of Hessians, from our land." He urged them to come forward and place their names upon the rolls. Nearly all the preachers present placed their names on the recruiting list first.

The excitement grew still more bitter. In the afternoon they began to threaten openly that the stars and stripes should be hauled down; that no flag should be allowed to float in West Plains that countenances and tolerates heathen in our land. The Union men declared that the stars and stripes should not be lowered unless it was done over their dead bodies. Quite a number of Union men had assembled under the flag. The Union men were led by a man named Captain Lyle. He had been warned and cautioned by his friends not to open his mouth, for the reason that he would be shot full of holes. Late in the evening there was a lull in the speaking. The author walked up into the speaker's stand, called the attention of the people, saw a number of rifles grasped in their hands, and announced to them that they had been sitting all day listening to Confederate speeches, but on the next Saturday, if they would meet him at Black's store, about ten miles west of West Plains, they could hear Union speeches and the constitution of the United States would be read; thanked the crowd and stepped down. Quite a number of guns were raised in the hands of parties and a shower of groans and hisses, and remarks openly from a number that "We ought to shoot his black heart out now."

It appeared for a while that it would be impossible to evade a conflict of arms. A number of orders being sent to the Union men to draw down their flag or they would fire on it and the men who supported it, an answer was returned that the rebels were requested to draw down their flag as it was a stranger in the land and unless they lowered their flag the stars and stripes wouldn't be lowered an inch, unless it was done over their dead bodies. At last a proposition came that they would agree for the sake of averting bloodshed to commence lowering both flags at the same time which proposition was accepted; so wound up that day's proceedings.

On the Saturday following, the author, with several other Union speakers, met at Black's store where there were several rebel captains and lieutenants. The author made a speech in favor of remaining in the Union and stated that the attempt to secede by some of the states would eventually result in sad disaster, besides bringing untold suffering upon the people. Several other Union speeches were made after which the author read the constitution of the United States and urged that all lovers of republican form of government would comply with the demand of the supreme law of the land and, if necessary, sacrifice property and life in defence of the same; so ended that day's proceedings.

McBride Establishes Military Law.

As the organization of the Confederates proceeded they still grew more bitter against the Union men and declared, by meeting and passing resolutions, that every Union man should show his colors in favor of the South or be hung as high as Hamen. In the meantime the Union men had secretly organized and met together, to take into consideration as to the time when they should act.

The prevailing sentiment was, that they should remain dormant and let the rebels shed the first blood, while the minority thought the time had come for action, and that they ought to act before the rebels crippled them and tied them up in such a manner that, when the time did come, they would be entirely helpless and at their mercy.

McBride, who had been elected judge of the 18th Judicial circuit, which included Howell county, whose home was in Texas county, was made Brigadier General of the Confederate forces and commenced organizing and massing his troops. On the arrival of the federal troops at Rolla, Missouri, he became fearful that they would attack him, rout him and destroy his forces, so he concluded to march south to West Plains and make his headquarters at that place until he could organize his forces and prepare for marching west, where he intended to join the forces of Gen. Sterling Price and Gen. McCullough who then were massing their forces to march on Springfield, Missouri, to attack the federal forces who were then stationed at Springfield under the command of Gen. Lyon and Gen. Seigle. On his arrival at West Plains he opened up headquarters, issued his proclamation that all Union men or any men that were unfriendly to the Confederate cause should come in and take the oath and the civil law was declared to be suspended and the military law completely in force.

Then was when the dark day and trouble began to hang over the Union people. As soon as it was known that the civil law was suspended little bunches of rebels organized all over the country and also in the state of Arkansas. In a short time after Gen. McBride's arrival in West Plains a man who was a door neighbor to the author came into his field where he was cutting wheat, asked him if he had seen the order of McBride. My answer was "No." He remarked, "Well, he has made a general order, requiring all Union men, especially those who have been open and active in behalf of the Union, to come in and take the oath, and unless they do they are going to hang them as high as Hamen." The author replied to him that he was a Union man and he knew it; he had been open and outspoken for the Union and had voted for McBride when he was elected Judge, but now he thought he was acting outside of the law of humanity.

I had neither violated the law of my land nor harmed any man and

I didn't consider that McBride had any right to order me to take an oath to take up arms against my country or support those who had taken up arms. If this did become a general war, I thought they were making a blunder, for the Government, or the lopeared Dutch, as they termed them, would have the advantage in the way of transporting forage and commissaries and amunitions of war, while the Confederates would have to rely mostly for their resources upon the county; that I was a peace officer and while I was a strong Union man wasn't taking up arms and I thought that those who wanted to fight, if there had to be a fight, should go out into the open fields, and not force the war onto non-combatants, and that the country would suffer enough at best. Now you know I am a Union man, and I know that you are in favor of the Confederate cause, and I think this is the course that ought to be pursued at the present time. The Confederates are in control of the country, and they will come around and say they must have forage for the support of the army, and ask you if you know of any Union men; you could tell them, "My neighbor right here is a Union man, but he is not disposed to take up arms and go into the fight; take as little from him as you can possibly do with, and as little from myself; in return, if this war goes on, and the Federal authorities extend their jurisdiction, they would be out hunting rebels for the purpose of getting forage and commissaries, and I could say to them that my neighbor here is a rebel but take just as little as possible from him, and as little as possible from me, as we are going to have a hard time to get through the war any way. But if you pursue the policy you say has been adopted by the Confederates, you will force all non-combatants into arms or drive them from the country and completely depopulate it." He burst into a big laugh and remarked, "Your promises are like a broken stick, you will never see the lopeared Dutch in this country." I said to him, "My friend, if this war goes on, before the end of it you will see what you call lopeared Dutch as thick as blackbirds"; and we separated.

General Lyons Drives Rebels from Rolla.

About June 10, 1861, the rebels were having a big meeting at Rolla, Phelps county, Missouri, for the purpose of recruiting. General Lyons at St. Louis, learned of the meeting, and at once placed quite a force in the cars, well armed and closed them up so they would not be detected and started for Rolla with the intention of capturing the whole outfit.

On the day set for the rebel meeting, quite a number of them had assembled and a certain young lawyer was delivering an address, telling them that one southern man could whip five lopeared Dutch and all they wanted was just an opportunity; in the meantime Lyon's forces had reached Dillon, the next station east of Rolla about five miles distant. There the forces were taken from the cars and divided, some marching southwest and the others northwest, making a flank movement for the purpose of surrounding the whole place. While they were marching some person, who was a rebel, went with all speed possible and informed the meeting that the Dutch were right upon them; that the woods were full of them and to get out of there as quick as possible, if they wanted to save their lives.

The lawyer who was addressing them sprang from the speakers stand and holloing at the top of his voice as he went, "Get away from here, the Dutch are upon us." It was said that the lawyer ran so fast that if a glass of water had been sat upon his coat tail it would not have spilled. They scattered to the woods in all directions. The Federal force came in; but their birds had all flown and left the citizens who had remained to tell the sad tale.

The rebel forces at once retreated to Salem, Missouri, where they again concentrated their force. The Federal scout, in a few days followed them to Salem, and there again routed them and they retreated directly to West Plains, joining the command of McBride at that place. The rebels, hurriedly, concentrated their forces from all the south and southeastern counties of Missouri and from the northern counties of Arkansas.

General McBride made an order to gather all the arms, amunitions, and horses that were fit for the service, as speedily as possible and the report was put in circulation that he had given the county over to the leading rebels, who resided in it, whose action, whatever they did touching the Union men, would be indorsed and carried out by General McBride. The leading rebels of the county at once sent out word that they were going to take all the arms, amunition and available horses from the Union men and that McBride required each and every one of them to report and take the oath at once, and if they failed to comply with said order, speedy action would be taken against them.

They would either be arrested, imprisoned or forced into the Confederate army to fight and their leaders would be hung.

On the issuing of the said order the wildest excitement prevailed among the Union men. They immediately met for the purpose of consultation as to what their final action would be. There were divers opinions among them; some of them were for acting at once; others (and a majority of them) were in favor of waiting until the rebels shed the first blood. Those who refused to report and take the oath had to place themselves in hiding at once. The rebels made a general move to raid, harass and capture the Union men. Then real danger confronted a man who claimed to be a Union man. The rebels had made a general amnesty, upon condition that they would join the Confederate army and become loyal to the Confederate States. About two-thirds of the men who had been open and avowed Union men saw the danger that confronted them, and joined the Confederate army and claimed that they would be loyal to its cause. The remainder of the Union men were disarmed at once, except those who kept themselves concealed in the mountains and hills.

After they had completely disarmed them and forced many of them to join the Confederate service, had taken most of their horses, cattle and hogs for the use of the army, the leading rebels in the county claimed that they had organized for the purpose of ridding the country of all Union men who had refused to join the Confederate forces; that when McBride moved west he was going to leave the whole matter in their hands, and they intended to string up the Union men to limbs and shoot them, so they would soon be rid of the class of men who were friends of the lopeared Dutch and were nigger lovers.

The Testing of Loyal Hearts.

Small bunches of rebel troops came in from Arkansas and joined the bands that were raiding the country, and the Union men were hunted like wild beasts. Then set in the darkest day that ever any class of patriots, true to their government, had to confront.

The author remembers well when the Union men would meet together, that they took the proposition made by McBride into consideration, and it was discussed pro and con. Some men would say, "While I am a Union man and for the government, all that I have in the world is here in Howell county; my little home, my property and, above all, my wife and children. They have promised us protection provided we will join the rebel army. Had we not better accept the proposition and wait for results?" Others would arise, with tears dripping from their eyes, and remark that this state of affairs is hard indeed. "Can I afford to abandon my wife and children that I love so well and leave them unprotected in the midst of an open state of war, at the mercy of a mad and distracted people, who are thirsting for the loyal blood of the nation, and be alienated from them, perhaps, never more to see them?" Others would arise and remark that "We have seen this danger coming for months and we are satisfied that the worst has not come, and I know that I love my wife, my family, my little children, as I love my own heart; I love to meet them around my fireside and enjoy their sweet company, and I have delighted in laboring to furnish them food and raiment and shelter while they were growing into manhood and womanhood, but I have read and heard read that my highest duty was to God and my second duty was to my country; and the organic law of the nation requires at my hands that whenever it becomes necessary to preserve my government, that I owe to it my life, my honor and the welfare of my family; and the trying ordeal is now at hand and I don't know what the final result will be—if I am forced away from my family, I know they will be left at the mercy of an intolerant and unrelenting enemy, but I now and here lay my life, my family, my property and my future happiness upon the altar of my country, and let come what will, weal or woe, I intend, with all my feeble effort, to defend the stars and stripes, and stand up openly and courageously in defense of and for the preservation of the Union." That proposition prevailed and was unanimously adopted by the Union men.

At this time there was no government aid in reach of these loyal hearts, that were controlled by nothing but love of country. Uncle Sam could do nothing for them. They were completely surrounded in an enemy's country, and while they (the men), with what arms they had preserved, could by strategy evade the arrest and slaughter of themselves, their families were completely at the mercy of a mad and howling mob, thirsting for the blood of Union men.

While the loyal men in the North were enlisting in the interest of their country, Uncle Sam paid them $13.00 per month, clothed them, and their families were left in the care of friends; they knew nothing about the war, except what they read; but not so with the Union men who were surrounded in an enemy's country. They, without a single word of protection or comfort from the government for themselves or their families, but their love and devotion to their country led them to furnish themselves, to leave their families as best they could, at the mercy of a howling mob, for the defense of their country.

Rebels Defeated in Douglas County.

The loyal men in Douglas county and the north part of the county of Ozark were in the ascendency. A rebel force organized from the county of Howell, Missouri, and Fulton county, Arkansas, wanting to have some fun hunting Union men, learned that on Bryant's Fork on the north fork of White river in Ozark county there was a bunch of Union men. So they armed and equipped themselves, furnished themselves ropes, and marched to hunt the place these men were said to be. The Union men hearing of their intention hurriedly prepared a temporary barricade around the house, and about sixty of them gathered together with their squirrel rifles in readiness to repel the attack in case it was made. The rebel scout consisted of two hundred and fifty men.

Early in the morning reliable information reached the Union men that the rebel forces were well under way and would reach them some time in the afternoon. One of the Union men, who had always borne the reputation of being a brave man and would fight anything, became impatient as the time drew near that they were to be attacked. He had been a great hunter and was considered a first-class shot, and he remarked to the Union men, "I can't wait for the rebels to attack us, I want to get a shot at one so bad with Old Betsy (his gun). I know of a bald knob, about a quarter of a mile from here, where the rebel force is bound to pass. I am going there; place yourselves in waiting, and when you hear 'Old Betsy' belch, you may know there is one dead rebel, and be certain that they are coming." In about an hour after the man referred to had left, the rebel advance came in sight, but they never heard "Old Betsy" belch. They vigorously attacked the Union men inside their fortifications, and after fighting for about an hour, they retreated, leaving one man dead upon the field and one wounded. The Union men received no injury whatever. They became very uneasy in regard to their friend and "Old Betsy," supposing he had fallen into the hands of the enemy and they had used the rope on him. Search was made all along the line of march of the rebels for the missing man, but no information could be learned of his whereabouts. However, in about one week, news came from Douglas county that their friend and "Old Betsy" arrived safely at another rendezvous of Union men in Douglas county, about forty miles distant, and reported that the Union men had had a fight with the rebels, and they were all captured or killed, with the exception of himself, and he had made his escape after the fight.

Just before McBride broke camps to march west to join Gen. Price and Gen. McCullough, he made a general order that they arrest and seize every Union man possible, and after he left the country, that the committee who had been organized to take charge of the county, would at once exterminate every Union man who had failed to take the oath or to join the Confederate army, giving them full power as to what disposition they would make of them.

Rebels Capture Col. Monks.

On the 7th of July, 1861, one of my neighbors came to me and informed me that the time had come that every Union man had to show his colors and unless they reported and took the oath or joined the Confederate army, they would hang as high as Haman. While the Union men were on their guard and watching their movements, once in a while they would slip in home to see how the family was getting along. My family at that time consisted of a wife and four children, three girls and one boy. My wife had never been accustomed to staying alone and I came in home late on the evening of the 7th, thinking that I would leave the next morning before daylight. Sometime after the family had retired, not far from 11 o'clock in the night, I was awakened by a rapping on the door. My wife, suspecting who the parties were, answered them, and demanded to know what was wanted; one of them, who claimed to be an orderly sergeant, remarked that he wanted to know if Monks was at home. She replied that he was not. A man by the name of William Biffle, whom the author had been acquainted with for years, replied, "He is here, I know, for I coursed him into this house late yesterday evening." The author at once arose to his feet and remarked, "I am here, what is wanted?" A man by the name of Garrett Weaver, who claimed to be an orderly sergeant and in charge of the squad, also a neighbor to the author said, "I have been ordered by Gen. McBride to arrest you, bring you in and make you take the oath." I owned at that time a first-class rifle and there was also another rifle gun in the house. I took my gun into my hands and my wife took hold of the other gun. I told them that a general order had gone forth, so I was informed, that they wanted to hang all the leading Union men and "if that is your intention I will die before I surrender." Weaver replied they were not going to hang me, but they were just going to take me to McBride to take the oath and I should be protected. Upon those terms I agreed to surrender, made a light in the house and found that the house was surrounded by a posse of twenty-five rebels. As soon as the light was made, a part of them rushed into the house, took my gun and jerked the one my wife had in her hand out of her possession, almost throwing her to the floor, began a general search of the house for other arms and such things as they said the army needed.

As soon as I dressed, they ordered me to move. They didn't even give me time to say good-bye to my wife, nor to imprint a kiss upon the cheeks of my loving children. Closely surrounding me, they marched me about 250 yards, came to their horses, where two more of their posse guarded the horses, they having dismounted, to approach the house on foot so they might not be heard.

"Billy, You Ought Not to Be So Saucy."

When within a few feet of the horses the author was halted. It was just starlight. I noticed a man by the name of Wilburn Baker, a man with whom the author had been acquainted from a boy, go to the horn of one of the saddles, lift therefrom a coiled rope and move toward the author. The author quickly arrived at the conclusion that the time had come to enforce the order of hanging. Baker ordered the author seized by the arms, drew them behind him and securely tied him. The author asked, just as they had completed the tying, "What do you mean? Are you going to cage me?" Baker replied, "Billy, you ought not to be so saucy, for you don't know the danger you are in." I was at once ordered placed on a horse. One of the posse rode up to my side and placed the other end of the rope around his body and the posse moved west. A short time before daylight they arrived at the house of William Nicks, who was a rebel lieutenant. They dismounted and took the author into the house. There appeared to be a general rejoicing among them. Nicks

COL. MONKS ARRESTED AND TAKEN FROM HOME.

said, "You have got him, have you? We had become uneasy about you, and thought it might have been possible that he had his Union forces around him and that you had met with disaster; but I feel satisfied that we have now captured the leader and the counselor of the Union forces and the remainder will be easily extinguished." Gen. McBride in the meantime, being uneasy for fear Federal troops would attack him, had removed his forces from West Plains to the south part of Howell county, camping at what was known as the Flag pond.

I was closely guarded until daylight. McBride's forces had broken camp at the Flag pond on the morning of July 8th and were marching west with the intention of joining the forces of Gen. Price and Gen. McCullough, who were then moving in the direction of Springfield, Missouri, with the intention of attacking the Federal forces at that place, commanded by Gen. Lyon and Gen. Siegel. Very early on the morning of the 8th the party started in a southwest direction, with the author closely guarded. On coming near the head of Bennett's river, Fulton county, Arkansas, the posse commenced cheering and remarked: "Listen! Do you hear the drums and the fife? That is Gen. McBride's command moving west to kill them lopeared Dutch that you Union men have brought into the state of Missouri. Do you know what we are going to do with such men as you are? Those of you that we don't hang, the first fight that we get into with the lop-eared Dutch, we will make breast-works out of to keep the bullets off of good men."

About a mile further we came in sight of the moving column. We rode along the line, when there was general cheering until we reached a company that was organized in Oregon county and commanded by Capt. Simpson. Simpson said, "Why have you brought a Union man in here alive! If my company had possession of him, he could not live ten minutes."

We soon reached a company commanded by Capt. Forshee which was organized in this county to whom the whole posse made the arrest, belonged. The author was well acquainted with all of them and over half of them resided in the same settlement and were his neighbors. On reaching the company Captain Forshee walked out of the line and remarked to them, "Why have you brought him in here alive?" Some of the posse remarked, that he had been a neighbor and they had all been friends up to the war and they hated to kill him. Forshee said, "When I saw him at West Plains at the speaking when he got up and contended that there was a union and the government ought to be preserved, I wanted to shoot his black heart out of him and I feel the same way yet."

The author was kept in close confinement and on the night of the 8th the command went into camp near what is known as the old Steve Thompson farm. The author, with several other prisoners, was placed in the guard house and orders were given that he be closely guarded.

After they had taken their suppers, men that the author had been acquainted with from his boyhood, and men who had been acquainted with his relatives, came to the guard house in considerable numbers and remarked, "Hello, Monks?" "I never expected to see you under arrest." "What have you been doing that they have arrested you? I thought you was a good Democrat." "Have you left your party." "The Democratic party is in favor of the South." The author replied to them that when they thought he was a good Democrat they were right. But that he was not a slave to party and that he held country higher than party and if Democracy meant secession and nullification, that was one part of the principals of Democracy that he had never learned; that true Democracy, as understood by the author, taught every man that in case his country was invaded either externally or internally that he owed his honor and property in the support of it and for those reasons he was for the preservation of the Union at all hazards. Some remarked that "We ought to hang him right now without waiting any longer." Others remarked that "We have been acquainted with his people both on his mother's and father's side and they were all southern people and Democrats and they are all of them, almost, in favor of the South. It is strange indeed to see the course that he has taken." The author remarked that "There were always some shabby sheep in a flock and I suppose from your reasoning that I am one of them." They all retired, the officers giving orders that the most vigilant watch be kept over the prisoner. After he had retired a gentleman by the name of Joseph Teverbaugh who resided in Ozark county, a merchant and the owner of about twenty negroes, who had been well acquainted with the author from boyhood, brought up the conversation as to what disposition they thought ought to be made of the author. The author could easily hear all the conversation inside of the guard line. Many opinions were expressed. Quite a number said, "Hang him outright." That was the only way to get shut of the Union men, to make short work of it, and forever rid the country of that element.

Others said that appeared to be too harsh, that they were in favor of taking him to Little Rock and confining him in the penitentiary until the war was over, for it wouldn't take but a short time to rid the country of the lopeared Dutch and those who were friends to them. Others remarked that "that would be too easy for a man who was in favor of the lopeared Dutch; that we are in favor of taking all like him right into the army and making them fight and if they won't fight, the first engagement we get into, pile them up and make breastworks out of them, so that they will catch bullets off of good men." At this juncture Teverbaugh remarked, "I have been acquainted with Billy from a boy and you never can force him to fight against what he believes to be right," that he was a good boy and since he has grown up to be a man he has been an honorable and straightforward man and quite an active man politically and my advice would be to confine him in the State Penitentiary until the war is over, for I tell you now if he ever gains his liberty you are going to have him to fight."

Sold as a Beef Cow.

On the morning of the 9th they broke camp and marched near the mouth of Bennett's river and went into camp at what was then known as Talbert's mill. A short time after we had been in camp Capt. Forshee, who had charge of the prisoners, came to the guard house and the author requested him that he be allowed to take the oath and return home, as his wife and children were almost scared to death owing to the reports that were currently circulated all through the country, his wife would believe they had hung him. The captain replied that they were not going to allow him to take the oath. They had plenty of proof against him, that he had been communicating to the lopeared Dutch and as soon as they had formed a junction with Price and McCullough he would be tried as a spy. He gave orders to the guard to see that he was kept in close confinement, and about 11 o'clock in the night as near as the author can guess, it being starlight, the Captain came down to the guard house in company with one of his men, Frank Morrison.

The author was lying on the ground pretending to be asleep. The Captain came inside of the guard, called out, "Monks, are you asleep?" The author raised up in a sitting position and said, "Captain what is wanted?" The Captain remarked, "I want you to go up to my campfire," which was about 75 yards distance from the guard house. The author said, "Captain, this is a strange time of night to come down and order me to your camp fire." He said, "Not another word out of you, rise to your feet." He ordered Morrison to step behind him with the same gun that he had recently taken from the author and cock it and "if he makes a crooked step from here up to the campfire shoot him through." The author heard Morrison cock the gun and about half way between the guard house and the camp fire the Captain remarked to the author, "Do you know Kasinger?" The author, suspecting that he was going to be delivered to a mob, said "I know him very well; we have grown up together from boys." The Captain said, "I thought he was a mighty nice man. I have sold you to him for a beef cow." The author remarked there was but one thing he was sorry for; that if he had known he was going to be delivered to a mob he never would have surrendered and had some satisfaction for his life. The Captain said, "I thought I was doing mighty well to sell a black Republican or a Union man for a beef cow where we have as many good men to feed, as we have here."

His camp fire was under a gum tree with a large top. The fires had all died down, it being in July and nothing but the stars were giving the light. On coming within two or three feet of the tree the Captain ordered the author to halt. He and Morrison walked about ten paces and said, "I have brought you up here to liberate you. We have got plenty of good men here to feed without feeding men who are friends of the lopeared Dutch." The author replied to the Captain, "You may think you are dealing with a fool. I have neither violated the civil nor military law; have demanded a trial and you refuse to give it to me. You can't bring me up here at this time of night and pretend to turn me loose for the purpose of escaping the responsibility of an officer and deliver me into the hands of a mob."

The Confederate Army or Hell.

The author was satisfied that he could then see a bunch of men standing in readiness. The Captain replied, "Sit down or you will be shot in half a minute." The author sat down and leaned against the tree. He had on strong summer clothing, wearing an alpaca vest and coat. In an instant, about twenty-five men, led by Kasinger, and a man by the name of William Sap, approached the author; Kasinger, holding a rope in his hand with a noose in it, walked up to the author, held the noose of the rope above his head and said, "Monks, you have half a minute to say you will join the army and fight, or go to hell, just which you please."

The author replied that it was said that "hell was a hot place," but he had never been there, and that he had always been counted a truthful man until he had been arrested, and since his arrest he had been asked divers questions of the whereabouts of the lopeared Dutch, and that he had told them in every instance he knew nothing of them and had been cursed for a liar. "If I was to say that I would join the army and fight, I might have a cowardly set of legs and they might carry me away; and in the next place, I am a Union man, first, last and all the time. I suppose your intention is to hang me, and there is only one thing I am sorry for,

A NARROW ESCAPE FOR COL. MONKS.

and that is that I ever surrendered; but there is one consolation left, when you kill me you won't kill them all, and you will meet plenty of them that won't be disarmed as I am now."

Kasinger replied, "No damn foolishness, we mean business," and made an attempt to drop the noose over my head, which was warded off with my arms.

At this juncture the author appealed to the Captain for protection from the mob, saying that he was a prisoner, unarmed and helpless, and if he suffered him to be murdered by a mob his blood would be upon the Captain's head. No reply being made by the Captain, all of the parties being considerably under the influence of whiskey, Sap raised his left hand, pushed Kasinger back and remarked, "I have been shooting and wounding some of these black Republicans who are friends of the lopeared Dutch, but I intend to shoot the balance of them dead." At the same time he drew a pistol from his right-hand pocket, cocked it, stooped over, ran his fingers under the author's clothing, gave them a twist and commenced punching him around the chest with the muzzle of the revolver, and after, as the author thought, he had punched him some fifty or sixty times with the revolver, the author said to him, "William Sap, there is no question but that your intentions are to kill me, and you want to torture me to death. You know that if I was armed and on equal footing with you, you would not do this." He made a quick jerk with his left hand, intending to jerk the author upon his face, remarking to the Captain at the same time, "Captain, you promised him to us and we are going to take him." The author, with all force possible, leant against the tree, Sap's hold broke loose, tearing off all the buttons that were on the vest and coat.

The author again appealed to the Captain for protection from the mob. The Captain then remarked to Sap, "Hold on for a moment, I will take a vote of my company as to whether we will hang him or not." The company at that time was lying on the ground, most of them apparently asleep. The Captain called out aloud to his company, "Gentlemen, I am going now to take a vote of my company as to whether we will hang Monks or not. All in favor of it vote, aye; all opposed, no." He then took the affirmative vote and the negative vote. They appeared, to the author, to be almost evenly divided. Sap again remarked to the Captain "You promised him to us, we have bought him and paid for him and he is ours."

The author again appealed to the Captain for protection. The Captain replied to Sap, "He claims protection and as I am an officer and he a prisoner I reckon we had better keep him until we reach McCullough and Price and then we will try him for a spy and there is plenty of evidence against him to prove that he has been writing to the lop-eared Dutch and after he is convicted will turn him over and you men can take charge of him." At this juncture a brother-in-law of the Captain said, "Captain, I have one request to make of you. I want you to take Monks in the morning and tie him hard and fast, with his face to a tree, and let me shoot with a rest sixty yards and show you how I can spoil a black Republican's pate." The Captain replied, "As soon as he is convicted you can have the gratification of shooting him just as often as you please."

The Captain and Morrison again took charge of the author, carried him back and delivered him to the guard with instructions to the guard to be diligent in keeping him closely confined so that he would have no possible chance of escape. On the morning of the 10th we broke camp and went into camp that night just beyond where Mountain Home now stands. Dr. Emmons, of West Plains, who was a strong Union man and who afterwards became captain in the 6th Missouri Cavalry, attempted to go through to the Federal forces but was pursued by the rebels, captured somewhere in Texas county and brought back to the camp. He was also a prisoner at the same time; but being a master mason, was paroled to the limits of the camp and on the night of the 10th made his escape and got through to the Federal lines, enlisted and was made captain. Of him we will speak later.

In Camp at Yellville.

On July 11th they broke camp and reached Yellville, Marion county, and on the 13th reached Carrolton, a small town in Arkansas, and went into camp. The author well remembers the spring. It ran out of the steep, rocky gulch and the branch ran a little south of west and a beautiful grove of timber surrounded the spring. The prisoners were marched down within a few feet of the spring and there placed under guard. As usual, the abuse that had been continually heaped upon the prisoners during the march was renewed and in a short time a man who was said to be from one of the counties north of Rolla, Mo., commenced making a speech and inciting and encouraging the soldiers to mob the prisoners at once; that he had disguised himself and entered the camps of the lop-eared Dutch at Rolla, and that to his own personal knowledge they had men's wives and daughters inside of their camps, committing all manner of offenses possible, and that they were heathens; didn't resemble American people at all and that he would not guard nor feed any man who was a friend to them; that they ought to be killed outright.

The men who enlisted in the Confederate army from Howell and adjoining counties, before starting, went to the blacksmith shops and had them large butcher knives made; made a belt and scabbard and buckled them around them, and said that they were going to scalp lop-eared Dutch. In a short time the tenor of the above mentioned speech had incited over 400 men and it had become necessary to double the guard. The grove of timber was filled with men and boys looking over, expecting to see the prisoners mobbed every minute. There was a man who drew his pistol, others drew knives and made different attempts to break lines and mob the prisoners. The man in possession of the pistol declared that he intended to shoot them. He was on an elevated place and they called him "Red," and there were three or four men holding him to prevent his firing. The author remarked to him that: "The time will soon come when you will meet men who are not disarmed. You had better save your bravery until you meet them, and my opinion is that you won't need any man to hold you then." Just about this time on the north side of the spring—the land dropped toward the spring, on a descent of about 45 degrees—the author heard the voice of a man order-ing the guard to "open the lines and let these ladies come in." The author at once arose to his feet and spoke out in an audible voice to the guard to give away and let the ladies come in and see a Northern monkey exhibited, that the monkeys grew a great deal larger in the north than they did in the south. At this juncture it appeared to take one more man to hold Red who said that "he would kill the saucy scoundrel if it took him a week to do it."

When the posse came in we saw that the ladies were accompanied by eight or ten Confederate officers with about fifteen ladies. All the ladies carried small Confederate flags, the first ones that the author had ever seen. On coming very close to the prisoners they halted and one of the officers remarked, "These are the Union men that are friends to the lop-eared Dutch. Couldn't you tie the knot upon them to hang them?" I think almost everyone spoke out and said "we could." After heaping other epithets and abuse upon the prisoners they and the officers retired outside of the line. The speaker was still talking, urging and insisting that the prisoners should be mobbed at once, that they should not be permitted to live.

At about this stage of the proceedings a man's voice was heard on top of the bank saying, "Men, I believe your intentions are to kill these prisoners. You have all started out to fight and you don't know how soon you might be taken prisoner and you would not like to be treated in any such manner; I know Billy, (referring to the author) and all you have against him is the political side that he has taken and I order the orderly sergeant to double the guard around the prisoners so there will be no possible chance for the mob to get through, and move with the prisoners south to a large hewed log house and place the prisoners therein, and place a guard around the walls and suffer no man to approach the house without an order from the officers."

As the prisoners began to move, the excited soldiers, who were wanting to mob them, brought out an Indian yell, and it appeared to the author he could almost feel the ground shake. After they were put into the houses, among the prisoners were some who were deserters, the author whispered to the Union men and told them to lie down close to them so that they could not distinguish from the outside one from another. The author was informed by Maj. William Kelley, of the Confederate army, who resides at Rolla, Phelps county, Missouri, at the present time, that he was the officer who made the order to remove the prisoners into the house and place a heavy guard around them to prevent their being mobbed. This ended the excitement for the evening.

The author had always been a believer in the realities of religion. About one-tenth of the officers appeared to be Baptist and Methodist preachers, and frequently when they would go into camp would call a large number of the men together and very often take the prisoners and place them near by under a heavy guard, and then convene religious services. They always took for a text some subject in the Bible and the author remembers well of the taking of the subjects in the book of Joshua, where Joshua was comanded to pass around the fortifications of the enemy and blow the ram's horn and the fortifications fell, and, the God of Joshua was the same God that existed to-day and there was no question but that God was on the side of the South and all they had to do was to have faith and move on, attack the lopeared Dutch and God was sure to deliver them into their hands.

The author could not help but add, in his own mind, that when the attack is made that God set the earth to shaking and all around where the lopeared Dutch are standing that the earth will open and swallow them up just leave their heads above the surface; so that those Confederates who were so furious could take their big knives and scalp the Dutch as they had said on divers occasions they intended to do.

Makes His Escape.

The author was determined to make his escape whenever the opportunity offered; and he could learn all about the whereabouts of the Federal soldiers from the excited Confederate scouts who would ride along the lines and say that the lopeared Dutch were as thick as rats at Springfield, Missouri, moving around in every direction and they might be attacked at any time and General McBride was looking every day to be attacked by the Federal forces to cut off his forming a junction with Generals Price and McCullough.

In about four or five days they reached Berryville, near where the Eureka Springs are, and went into camp just west of Berryville right at the spurs of the Boston mountain. The prisoners were placed in the guard house near a little creek that was then dry. Captain Forshee's company went into camp next to the company commanded by Captain Galloway of Howell county. As the weather was very hot and dry and the author had been marched barefooted (one of his shoes having worn out) until his feet were badly blistered, he was lying down, feigning sickness. The guard has become a little careless. Just about sundown heavy thunder set in in the west. The clouds continued to increase, the elements grew very dark. In the mean time they had put out a chain guard all around the encampment and said guard was about thirty steps from guard house. The low lands were all bottom, covered with heavy timber and a large oak had fallen across the creek and reached from bank to bank and the bark had all slipped off. About thirty feet from the top of the tree the foot of a steep mountain set in. The guard fire was about sixty yards south of the guardhouse. The clouds soon came up and a heavy rain set in, with terrific thunder and lightning, and as the army had temporary tents the guards all crawled in under the tents and left the author by the fire. The rain soon quenched the fire.

The chain guard were walking up and down the dry creek and they met at the log referred to. The author thought now was his time to make his escape, if ever; knowing that he would have to have a shoe, slipped to one of the tents, got hold of a shoe, and then the thought struck him that he would like to have a revolver, but on further examination found their revolvers to be placed in such a position that it was impossible to get one without waking the men. He then slipped to the butt of the log and heard the guard meet at the log and turn again on their beat. He at once crossed on the log on the other side, walked into the brush, reached the foot of the mountain about twenty steps distant and halted. Everything appeared to be quiet, the release around the guard fire were singing, whooping and halloing.

The author then took the mountain which was about one quarter of a mile high, and it always has appeared to the author that he crossed the log and went up the mountain as light as a cat. On reaching the top, still raining heavily, the thought came into his mind that "I am once more a free man, but I am in an enemy's country, without friends," and at once determined in my mind to reach Springfield, Missouri, if possible. I sat down, pulled on the shoe that I had taken and it just fitted without a sock; I then procured a dead stick for the purpose of holding before me as I traveled for fear I would walk off of some steep cliff or bluff, as it was very mountaineous.

Having the guard fire for a criterion I moved northwest, soon struck the leading road west that the army was marching on, traveled the road for about one mile, came onto the pickets, surrounded the pickets, struck the road again, traveled all night until just gray day, directly west or nearly so. A slow rain continued all night. As soon as it became light enough to see I found myself in a country completely covered with pine timber. I turned square from the road, went about 350 yards up to the top of a high knob, found about one quarter of an acre level bench. A large pine had turned out by the roots and the hole was partially filled with old leaves. The author always had been afraid of a snake but the time had come when he had more fear of a man than a snake, so he rolled himself down into the hole in the leaves and at the time had become chilled with the steady rain. About 9 or 10 o'clock, as well as the author could guess, he heard the beat of the drum which told that the army was marching on the same road that he had traveled in the night. In a short time the army passed where the author was lying in the sink. The author could have raised himself up and have seen the procession pass but he had seen them just as often as he wanted to and he remained still. Late in the evening a company of about 65 men passed. The author was informed afterwards that they had been detailed to make search for the prisoner, with orders if they found him, to shoot him at once. The author was further informed by Confederates who belonged to the command that as soon next morning as it was reported that the author had made his escape that the chain guard declared that no man could have passed between them and they were satisfied that the author was still inside of the lines.

They at once made a large detail and commenced searching. There were quite a large number of box elders with very heavy, bushy tops. They said every single tree, every drift and possible place of hiding, was examined. Orders were at once issued by the commander, who sent word back to the home of the author, that he had made his escape and to watch for him and as soon as he came in home to arrest him and either shoot him or hang him at once.

In the afternoon of the same day it cleared off and just as soon as dark came, the author was determined to try to reach Springfield, being in a strange country and knowing that if he was re-captured it would be certain death. He knew somewhere about the distance he had traveled west. He located the north star which he used as his pilot or guide and set out for Springfield, having no arms of any kind, not even a pocket knife and had become very hungry. He came to a slippery-elm tree, took a rock, knocked off some of the bark, ate it and proceeded on his journey, traveling all night. When gray day appeared again, he went to a hickory grub, broke the grub off with a rock, cut the top off with a sharp edged rock, to be used for a weapon, placed himself in hiding, remained all day. As soon as night came, again he proceeded on his journey, traveled no roads except when they run in direction of the north star. On the second morning he went into a small cave surrounded by a thicket, about 10 o'clock in the day he found that he was near enough to some rebel command to hear the drilling. As soon as dark came on he proceeded on his journey. The nights were dark and only star light until the after part of the night. He went near a spring house, but when he got to it, there wasn't a drop of milk in it. He passed through an Irish potato patch, grabbled two or three small Irish potatoes and ate them; passed through a wheat field, rubbed out some dry wheat in his hand, ate that; ate a few leaves off of a cabbage. On the third morning, went into hiding, remained until the darkness came again and resumed the journey.

On the morning of the 4th at daylight I had reached an old trace, pulled off my clothes and wrung them and put them on again as the dew was very heavy and every morning my clothes would be wet. I went about 30 or 40 yards from the old trace and thought to myself, if I saw any person passing that was not armed, that I would approach and learn where I was. Hadn't been there more than a half hour when I heard a wagon coming. As soon as the wagon came in sight I saw there was a lady driving, accompanied by a small girl and boy, I got up and moved into the road, walked on, and met the wagon, spoke to the lady. She stopped the wagon and I asked her if she would be kind enough to tell me where I was, that I had got lost, traveled all night and didn't know where I was. She told the author that he was in Stone county, Missouri, and asked where he was from. I told her that I was from the state of Arkansas. She wanted to know if there was much excitement there. I told her that there was; that men were enlisting and going into the Confederate service and the people were generally excited over the prospect of war. I asked her if there was any excitement in this country. She replied that there was—that the rebels a day or two ago had run in, on White River, and killed four Union men and drove out about 40 head of cattle and "that's why I am going out here in this wagon. My husband belongs to the home guards and has come in home on a furlough and is afraid to knock around the place for fear he will be waylaid and shot by the rebels."

I then asked her if she would allow me to ask her a civil question. She replied that she would. I asked her what her politics were, and she told me that she was a Union woman. I told her, then, that I would tell her the truth; that the rebels had had me prisoner and that I had made my escape from them and had been traveling only in the night time; that this was the fourth morning since I had made my escape, and I asked her how far it was to the house; that she was the first person I had spoken to since I had made my escape. She said it was about 350 yards around the point, to go on down to the house, and as soon as she got some light wood she would be back. I went to the house, halloed at the fence, a man came to the door and invited me in. I walked in, and at once I began to look for arms, and to my great delight I saw a Springfield musket lying in the gun rack, with a cartridge box with the letters U.S. on it. O! the thrill of joy that passed through my mind. I had often heard the old adage quoted, that "a friend in need is a friend indeed," but had never before realized its full meaning. In a short time the lady returned. She went to work cooking, soon had me something to eat, but I had almost lost my appetite, having fasted so long.

After I ate something and while she was preparing provisions to carry with me the man told me there was but one place that we could cross White river without being placed in great danger of being captured by the rebels, for they were patroling up and down the river every day. I told him I never had attempted to travel a foot in daylight since I had made my escape. He told me he thought if we could get safely across the river, he knew of an old trace that led across the mountains and intersected Taney county and as soon as we reached that settlement they all belonged to home guards and a man would be in no danger in making himself known.

The woman baked enough biscuit and tied up bacon and red onions with them, the author thought, to have lasted a hungry man three days, for him to carry with him and we at once, after taking leave of the good woman followed by her best wishes that I would get through to the Federal lines safely, started for White river, about two miles distant. Just before reaching the river he left the author standing in the road, went into the house near by and soon came out with two other men in company with him. On reaching the river where there was a canoe tied to the bank they stepped aside by themselves, held a short consultation; then all got into the canoe, carried me across the river, piloted me across the river bottom to where the old trace left the bottom; there we separated, they hoping that I would get through to the Federal lines safely.

They didn't think there was any danger in traveling in daylight, because there wasn't a single settlement for the entire distance of 25 miles.

The author traveled on until dark had overtaken him. The moon gave no light until the after part of the night. The author laid down by the side of the road, took a nap, after the moon came up proceeded on his journey and in about two miles came to a house. Hallooing at the gate, a lady came to the door and said: "Come in." They appeared to have a very savage dog. I remarked to the lady that I believed the dog would bite me and noticed at the same time that she stood off to one side of the door. She remarked: "Go in; that dog will not bite you." As I stepped into the door I was confronted by a man standing in the middle of the floor in his night clothes with his old Springfield musket cocked and presented and he called out, "Halt!" The author halted, of course, and the next remark was, "Who are you and where is the balance of your crowd?" The author replied: "There is no balance of them and there is not much of myself left. The Confederates have had me prisoner and I have made my escape from them and I am now trying to reach Springfield, Missouri."

The man ordered his wife to strike a light, and after viewing the author critically, placed his Springfield musket near the bed and invited the author to take a seat, while he dressed himself. Being not more than two hours until daylight, his wife asked me to go to bed and rest. I told her that I wasn't fit to lie in bed; that I had lain on the ground like a hog ever since I had been arrested. She said that it didn't matter how dirty a Union man was, he was welcome to sleep in her bed, and to lie down and she would proceed at once to get breakfast; that there were some refuge wagons, about two miles distant, making their way to Springfield, and that she would have me up in time to reach them. Accordingly, after eating breakfast before daylight, and starting with the purpose to reach the wagons before they broke camp, the man remarked to the author, "My captain lives just this side of where the wagons are camped and I know he would love to see you and learn about the movements of the rebels."

When we got to the house, he hallooed and the captain came out, asked the author his name, where he lived and when he was taken prisoner. The author gave him his name and place of residence, and on learning that he was from Howell county, asked him if he was acquainted with a man by the name of Washington Galloway. The author informed him that he was well acquainted with him. He inquired as to which side he was on, the Confederate or Union. The author informed him that he was on the rebel side and was a captain commanding one of the rebel companies; that I saw him and had had a conversation with him on the evening before I made my escape. He said, "He is an own brother of mine. My name is Jesse Galloway"; and the tears ran from his eyes like a whipped child. He said, "Get down; you are not in a condition to travel any further at the present time." He gave me a change of clothing and had my clothes washed and sent me through to Springfield by one of his men on horseback.

About three weeks after I left him the rebels slipped up near his house, lay in ambush, and when he came out into the yard they shot him to death while he was holding an innocent child in his arms.

Arrives at Springfield.

On reaching Springfield, I was conducted directly to the head quarters of Gen. Lyon, gave him all the information in my possession and told him I had been entirely stripped, had no means with me for support and I would like to join the army. He remarked to me, "I don't want you to join the army; we intend to move south next spring and you are one of the men that will be in great demand. We have a position for you and the Government will pay you good wages."

A short time after I arrived I met a man by the name of Percy, a lawyer, who resided at West Plains, a bitter rebel, who was in there as a spy. I was alone and there were very few persons that I was acquainted with living in Springfield. Percy had been posing as a Union man and offered that if I would go with him, he would carry me safely through home; tried to get me to agree to go outside the lines with him after dark, but knowing that he was a bitter rebel and had been taking an active part in the rebel movement I discarded him as quick as possible. In a day or two Benjamin Alsup, who resided on Hutton Valley, Howell county, happened to meet him in town, and he being acquainted in and about Springfield, had him arrested at once. A man by the name of Moore, who was a strong Union man, lived about two miles from

Springfield on the Wilson creek road took me home with him for the purpose of resting up. He was the owner of a fine dapple gray gelding four years old. He made Gen. Lyon a present of him. About five days before the Wilson Creek battle it was reported that the Rebels were on Cane creek, west of Springfield, in considerable force. Gen. Lyon moved out with a considerable force, riding the same horse, but on seeing the federal forces approaching they retreated. On the 8th day of August the rebels appeared in large force, being commanded by Gen. Price and Gen. McCullough.

General Lyon Killed at Wilson Creek.

Gen. Lyon sent out scouts with glasses for the purpose, if possible, of ascertaining their number. The rebels had gone into camp about ten miles from Springfield, with the avowed purpose of attacking Gen. Lyon the next day at Springfield, and as the scouts were not able with their glasses to see the largest force of rebels, which was encamped around a point out of sight, reported as to what they thought the number was. Lyon and Siegel came to the conclusion that by strategy they could easily whip them, so on the morning of the 10th, about midnight, they broke camp at Springfield, taking all of their available men. The morning being very foggy and misty, they easily surrounded the pickets and took them prisoners without the firing of a gun, then drew up and fired the artillery into them before they knew they were there.

So the memorable fight known as the battle of Wilson Creek was begun. Gen. Lyon rode the horse above referred to at the time he fell on the battlefield. Both the Confederate and Union side were founding all their future hopes upon the result of that battle, as to settling the question in Missouri. The author heard the artillery all day. Late in the evening word came to the Union men that Gen. Lyon had been killed and that the Federal army was retreating in the direction of Rolla, Missouri, and that all the Union men and the home guard would fall in and meet them at once. O! the scene that followed. Men would hurriedly ride around, meet their wives and children, tell them that the battle was lost and they were then retreating and they had only time to come around and bid them good-bye, and to do the best they could; that they didn't know that they would ever be permitted to see them again. We could hear the wife and children crying and sending up the most pitiful petitions to God to have mercy.

Everything on the Union side appeared to be dark, although it was a drawn battle and the rebels commenced retreating at the same time, and retreated about twenty-five miles west, but on learning that the Federal troops were retreating, they faced about, taking possession of the battle-ground and all of the southern and western portion of the state; and then the rebels, being encouraged by the late victory, determined to rid the country of all Union men at once.

About that time about 350 men mostly from Oregon county commanded by two very prominent men, made a scout into Ozark county, Missouri. On reaching the North fork of White river they went into camp at what was known as Jesse James' mill. The owner, a man of about 55 or 60 years of age, as good a man as resided in Ozark county, was charged with grinding grain for Union men and their families; at the time he, and a man by the name of Brown, were cutting sawlogs about two miles from home in the pinery. They went out and arrested them, arrested an old man by the name of Russell and several others, carried them to a man's house, who was a Union man, and had fled to prevent arrest. They took Brown and James about 300 yards from the house, procured a rope, hunted a long limb of a tree, rolled a big rock up to the first rope where it was tied to the limb, placed the noose around James' neck, stood him on the rock, rolled the rock from under him and left him swinging, rolled the rock to the next rope, stood Brown on it, placed the noose around his neck, rolled the rock out and left Brown swinging in the air, went to the third rope, placed Russell on the rock, and just as they aimed to adjust the noose, word came that the home guards and Federals were right upon them in considerable force. They fled, leaving Russell standing upon the rock and both Brown and James dangling in the air.

Their Wives and Other Women Bury Them.

Every Union man now having fled in fear of his life, the next day the wives of Brown and James, with the help of a few other women, buried them as best they could. They dug graves underneath the swinging bodies, laid bed clothing in the graves and cut them loose. The bodies fell into the coffinless graves and the earth was replaced. So the author is satisfied that the bones of these men still remain in the lonely earth underneath where they met their untimely death with no charge against them except that they had been feeding Union men, with no one to bury them but their wives and a few other women who aided.

Some of the men who were in the scout and present when the hanging was done are still living in the counties of Howell and Oregon.

A General Jackson Soldier Shot Down.

A short time after this hanging there was a man by the name of Rhodes, who resided on the head of Bennett's Bayou in Howell county. He was about eighty years of age and had been a soldier under General Jackson.

HANGING JESSE JAMES AND MR. BROWN.

His head was perfectly white and he was very feeble. When he heard of the hanging of Brown and James he said openly that there was no civil war in that, and that the men who did it were guilty of murder.

Some two weeks from the date of the hanging of Brown and James, about twenty-five men, hearing of what he had said, organized themselves and commanded by Dr. Nunly and William Sapp, proceeded to the house of Rhodes, where he and his aged wife resided alone, called him out and told him they wanted him to go with them. His aged wife came out, and being acquainted with a part of the men, and knowing that they had participated in the hanging and shooting of a number of Union men, talked with them and asked: "You are not going to hurt my old man?" They said: "We just want him to go a piece with us over here." Ordering the old man to come along, they went over to a point about one quarter from the house and informed him of what he had said. There they shot him, cut his ears off and his heart out. Dr. Nunly remarked that he was going to take the heart home with him, pickle it and keep it so people could see how a black republican's heart looked.

They left him lying on the ground, proceeded directly to Joseph Spears', who resided about six miles west of town on the Yellville road, declaring that they were going to treat him the same way. They reached his house about two hours in the night, all full of whiskey. When they arrived there Spears was sick in bed. They dismounted, came in, ordered their suppers and their horses fed. Spears at that time owned a negro

CUTTING OUT RHODES' HEART.

man, and he ordered him to put up the horses and feed them, and his wife to get them supper. After supper, they concluded to remain until morning. During the night they became sober, and concluded, since Spears owned a "nigger," that it could not be possible that he was a Union man, and the reports that they had heard that he was a Union man might be untrue, and they would let him alone until they could investigate further.

In the meantime, Rhodes not having returned home, and not a single Union man left in the country that Mrs. Rhodes could get to look after him, and having heard when they reached Joseph Spears' that the old man was not with them, although very feeble, she still continued the search; on the second day, about fifty yards from the road and about a quarter of a mile from home, while she was looking for him, she heard hogs squealing and grunting as though they were eating something. She proceeded to the place and found the hogs were just about to commence eating the remains of her husband. The Union men having fled, she notified some of the neighbors, and the women came in and helped dress the body and buried him the best they could; and neither at the taking down or burial of Brown and James and the burial of the old man Rhodes did a single rebel put in an appearance.

There never was a man arrested by the Confederate authorities, or a single word of condemnation uttered, but as far as could be heard there was general approval. It was said that the means used were desperate, but that was the only way to get rid of the men and strike terror to them so they could neither give aid nor countenance to the lopeared Dutch.

Benjamin Alsup Taken to Little Rock.

In a few days following they proceeded to arrest Benjamin Alsup, residing in Hutton Valley, who was a strong Union man, took him to Little Rock, placed him in the state penitentiary, and kept him there until after Little Rock fell into the hands of the Federals, when they exchanged him with other prisoners. While they had him in prison they worked him in a bark mill by the side of an old mule, with a strap around his breast and two leather hand holds. He pulled so much in the mill that his little finger was calloused and he almost entirely lost the use of it.

After they had hung, shot, captured and driven from the country all of the Union men, they called a public meeting for the purpose of taking into consideration what should be done with the families of the Union men, which meeting had a number of preachers in it. After discussing the premises, they arrived at the conclusion that if they let the families of the Union men, who had escaped and gone into the Federal lines, remain, they would return and bring in the lop-eared Dutch. They didn't believe that both parties could ever live together, and as they now had the country completely rid of the Union men, they would force their families to leave. They at once appointed men, among whom were several preachers, to go to each one of the Union families and notify them that they would not be allowed to remain; because if they let them stay, their men would be trying to come back, and they didn't believe both parties could live together. They stated at the same time that they were really sorry for the women and children, but nobody was to blame but their husbands and sons, who had cast their lot with the lop-eared Dutch. Also, as they had taken up arms against the Confederate states, all the property they had, both real and personal, was subject to confiscation and belonged to the Confederate authorities; but they would allow them to take enough of the property to carry them inside of the lines of the lop-eared Dutch, where they supposed their men were and where they then could care for them.

Loyal Women Driven from Their Homes.

They said they might have a reasonable time to make preparations to leave the country, and if they didn't leave, they would be forced to do so, if they had to arrest them and carry them out.

The wildest excitement then prevailed among the women and children. They had no men to transact their business and make preparations to leave. Little had they thought, while they were chasing, arresting, hanging and shooting their men, that they, too, would become victims of the rebel hatred and be forced to leave house and home, not knowing where their men were or whether they were dead or alive. All they knew of their whereabouts was, that those who escaped arrest had left their homes, aiming to reach the nearest Federal lines.

Women were at once dispatched to reach the nearest Federal lines, if possible, and inform them of the Confederate order, and procure help

MRS. MONKS AND CHILDREN BEING DRIVEN FROM HOME.

to take them out. Their homes and houses were being continually raided by small bands of Confederates roaming over the country, claiming that they were hunting Union men, taking all classes of property that they might see proper to take, without any restraint whatever.

When the Union men heard that an order had been made requiring their families to leave, not thinking that a thing of that kind would ever occur, having left them with comfortable homes and plenty to eat, the wildest consternation reigned amongst them.

The Federal authorities were willing to give them aid, but were placed in such a condition that they needed every man in the field, and for that reason couldn't give them any help in getting out. The women had to speedily fit up as best they could, close their doors and start for the Federal lines, leaving the most of their property in the hands of the rebels. The rebels proceeded at once to take possession of and occupy most of the homes.

The suffering that followed the women and children is indescribable. They had to drive their own teams, take care of the little ones, travel through the storms, exposed to it all without a man to help them, nor could they hear a single word of comfort spoken by husband, son or friend. On reaching the Federal lines, all vacant houses and places of shelter were soon filled, and they were known and styled as refugees. Many of them went into soldier huts, where the soldiers had wintered and covered the tops of their huts with earth. They had to leave home with a small amount of rations, and on the road the rebels would stop them and make them divide up the little they had started with, and reaching the Federal lines they would be almost destitute of food and many of them very scantily clothed.

They would at once commence inquiring for their husbands and sons. Numbers of them never found them, as they had been captured, killed and imprisoned while attempting to reach the Federal lines. O! the untold misery that then confronted them! After they had traveled and half starved and suffered from cold and exposure, promising themselves that when they reached the Federal lines they would again meet their loved ones who could again care for them, they were doomed to disappointment, in a large number of instances.

Those who did meet their husbands and sons were also disappointed; they had either joined the service or been employed by the government as guides and scouts, and the small amount of pay they received from the government, wouldn't provide food and raiment for their families. They were compelled to still be absent from their families, although they were suffering greatly for all of the necessaries of life and for clothing and shelter. The women's task of caring for and looking after the family and the little ones was just as great after they had reached the Federal lines as before. The government ordered that wherever aid could be given, rations should be issued to the families, and while the government did all it could in this way, it was not able to furnish shelter and houses for their comfort. Winter came on and they underwent untold suffering; disease set in from exposure, besides the contagious diseases of smallpox and measles, and hundreds of them died for want of proper attention, while their men were in the lines of the service of the government.

Here let the author speak a word in behalf of the devotion and patriotism manifested by those loyal women who had given their husbands and their sons to be placed upon the alter of the country, and sacrificed their homes and their firesides, had become exiles and wanderers, without home or shelter, had undergone untold suffering, had faced disease and death, had seen the little ones die, calling for papa, shivering with cold, suffering with hunger—all for the love of their country. Yet when they would see the Federal troops move by, with the stars and stripes unfurled, they would cheer the boys in blue as they would pass, and urge them to save the country they loved so well and had made so many sacrifices for and were still willing to suffer and wrestle with all the ills that a desperate war had brought upon the country, and wanted to live to once more be returned to their own hearthstones and be permitted to live under their own vine and fig tree, where no man dare molest them or make them afraid, to again enjoy all the sweet comforts of life.

We revere and honor every Federal soldier who enlisted in the interest of his country from the Northern States, where they knew nothing about war except what they read, their families being left in comfortable circumstances, with plenty to eat and wear and friends to speak words of comfort to them, while their husbands and sons had gone to the front and were willing to sacrifice themselves on the alter of their country, if it became necessary. But O! the comparison between the sacrifices made by the loyal element in those portions of the country where they were completely surrounded by the enemy.

Those who were willing to lay upon the alter of their country, their fathers and sons, their wives and children, their property and their sacred honor in support of the government they loved so well, with no protection from the government; no arms, amunitions, rations, clothing or pay from the government, was thought of for a moment. The only question that prompted, ruled and controlled them was their patriotism to their God and their country. When we come to compare the sacrifices, privations, suffering and services between the two classes of loyalists the first referred to, sink into insignificance.

O! never let us forget to honor and revere patriotism and sacrifices that were made by the loyal men and women that were surrounded in the enemy's country and continual fighting without and within. Their husbands and sons were shot and hung and imprisoned all over this country, whose bodies never were even honored with a burial. Orders being made by the rebels that they should not be buried; but yet they live and speak in thunder tones to the living. Let us plead with the living to revere and honor the stars and stripes that were maintained and supported by the blood and lives and sacrifices of the loyal men and women of the South.

After the rebels had completely driven all the loyal element out of the country and had but one political party left they exclaimed, "Now the means that we have been forced to use are very harsh but the line has been drawn and all of the parties who are giving aid and comfort to the lopeared Dutch are all outside of the Confederate line and we will never be troubled with them and the lopeared Dutch any more."

The author went back in retreat with General Siegel, after the Wilson Creek battle. On reaching Rolla, Missouri, Siegel went into quarters for the winter. The author was almost worn out with exposure and traveling, and as General Siegel informed him that there would be no advance made south until the spring of 1862, and as his family had been left in comfortable circumstances, with plenty to eat and wear, and he, being acquainted with some men by the name of Cope, who lived near Jerseyville in Jersey county, Illinois, went to that place, remained a month, and being taken sick with lung fever, came very near dying. He told his friends where he was staying that if he died, he would die dissatisfied; that he wanted to live and be able to move with the Federal command in the spring of 1862 when it moved south. After he had partially recovered he learned that a Mr. Cope, who was living neighbor to him at the time of his arrest and capture, had moved into Randolph county, Illinois. He visited the family at once, hoping to hear from his family at home, and remained there about a month. His wife, among many others, being notified to leave, had been informed that the author had made his escape, reached Springfield, and had gone back with Siegel in his retreat to Rolla. She was permitted to dispose of just enough of the property, at the rebels' own prices, to enable her to move, the family consisting of herself and five small children. She was followed on the road and her wagons searched for arms, and the rebels threatened to take her to Little Rock, Arkansas, but to enable her to reach Rolla, Missouri, she posed as the wife of a rebel who had gone into the Confederate service, and said she was trying to reach her father, who resided near Rolla. By making that impression, her wagons were not disturbed any more.

On reaching Rolla, she went to Colonel Phelps, who was afterwards governor of the state, and inquired if he knew anything of the whereabouts of the author. He informed her that he had no knowledge of his whereabouts at that time, but he would take her name, place an advertisement of her arrival at Rolla, in the paper, and if he was alive it might reach him.

Every house and cabin was full, it being in the dead of winter, and a deep snow upon the ground, but through the aid and assistance of one Cyrus Newberry, who had escaped through the lines in Howell county, she procured a shelter about three miles north of Rolla, which was very uncomfortable; her clothes were partially frozen on her at that time. In a short time the advertisement reached the author in Randolph county, Illinois. He at once set out for Rolla, Missouri, to meet his family. The house that she had first got into was used by her but a short time, and she had been forced to go into one of the huts that had lately been occupied by the soldiers and had been made vacant by their moving west to Springfield.

On the arrival of the author, O! the horror and the joy that were intermingled! I was proud to once more meet my wife and children, but in a moment the thought would pass through my mind, "I left you in a comfortable home, with plenty to eat, and now to see you here in this 'dug-out,' suffering for food and shelter! O! the war, the horrible war! What is it that men won't do?" I set out at once to procure a comfortable shelter for my family and to get in readiness to move south with the army. Gen. Curtis, then in command of the western department, was preparing to make a general move south. I was employed by the government as a guide, receiving $1.50 per day, with rations and clothing.

Establishing a Federal Post at West Plains.

The army soon broke camp and moved southward. On arriving at West Plains, the Federal army located a post there. Capt. McNulty, of the First Illinois cavalry, who had been wounded in a battle with Gen. Mulligan, was made Provost Marshal. The author was at once detailed and placed in the Provost Marshal's office as assistant, as he was well acquainted with all of the people in the surrounding country. The Provost Marshal would order the author to be seated in a conspicuous place in the office, and as a general order had gone forth from Curtis requiring all rebels and rebel sympathizers to come in and take the oath, and as hundreds of them were daily coming into the office for that purpose, the Provost Marshal ordered the author to watch every person who entered the office and whenever any person entered who had been taking an active part in committing depredations, just to put his hand upon his forehead and move it down over his face, and he would order them to the guard house for further examination, without any further words being said at the time.

Many of the rebels who were taking the oath couldn't see how he could draw a line between the different persons; let some take the oath and be released at once, and others ordered to the guard house without a word being spoken. Among the persons who came in and took the oath and were released, was the man who was present at the time Capt. Forshee attempted to deliver the author to the mob, who asked the Captain at the time to tie the author with his face to a tree, and let him shoot him in the back of the head, to show him how he could spoil a black Republican's pate.

The author remembers one incident that occurred during the stay at West Plains. A man named Lusk, who was constable of Howell township, and resided in West Plains, was a strong Union man at the beginning of the war; when the general order was made that every man who had been a Union man had to join the Confederate service and show his colors or be hung, Lusk enlisted in the Confederate army and went out with McBride's command.

Three or four days after the capture of the author by the rebels, Lusk came up to him in a braggadocio manner and says, "You ought to have your black heart shot out of you." Lusk had taken the oath and been released before the author reached West Plains. The author met him in West Plains and remarked to him: "Hallo, Lusk! How are you getting along? And what are you doing here?" He replied that he had taken the oath; that he was tired of fighting. The author asked him if he felt like he did when he wanted to shoot his black heart out. Lusk replied: "Captain, I am sorry for what I did, and Captain Emmons so maltreated me the other day that I could scarcely sit in my saddle." The author remarked to him: "I will just give your face three good slaps with my hand." After giving him three raps, the author let him pass.

Lusk Sees Some Lopeared Dutch.

Soon meeting Captain Emmons, who belonged to the 6th Missouri Cavalry, had asked him what the trouble was between him and Lusk. He said that while he was prisoner Lusk came to him with his big knife belted around him, and said that he was just equal to ten lopeared Dutch and he had that knife for the purpose of taking ten Dutch scalps before he returned home, and otherwise abused him for being a Union man and a friend to the Dutch.

On the arrival of the troops in West Plains he inquired of the citizens if Lusk had returned home. They informed him that he had and was residing on Spring Creek, about six miles from town. About half of Emmons' company were Germans. He went immediately to his company, ordered the Orderly Sargeant to make detail of ten men and he wanted them all to be Germans. He ordered them to be mounted and ready for a scout at once. Taking charge of them in person he proceeded to the house of Lusk, about six miles west of West Plains at the head of Spring Creek, rode up to the house and holloed. Lusk immediately came out into the yard and recognized Dr. Emmons and said "O! Doctor! Is that you? I am proud to see you." The Doctor said to him, "I am proud to see you, too." The Doctor at once informed him of what he had said to him when he was a prisoner in regard to being equal to ten lopeared Dutchmen and how he had his knife prepared to take that number of scalps before he came back home, and wanted to know if he got the scalps before he came home. Lusk replied that if he killed a single Dutchman he didn't know it and that he got all of the fighting that he wanted, didn't want to fight any more.

The Doctor wanted to know if he ever saw any lopeared Dutch and Lusk replied that he "didn't know that he had." The Doctor replied, "I have selected ten of the smallest sized of the full stock and I want you to step over the fence and view them." He then ordered the scouts to dismount and form in line. Lusk told the Doctor he didn't want anything to do with them whatever. After they had formed a line the Doctor made him step in front and view them; asked him what he thought of them. He said, "They are good looking men." The Doctor said to him, "If you didn't get the chance when you were out in the service to fight ten of them, and you say you didn't get any scalps, I have brought these ten down and intend that you shall fight them." Lusk pleaded with the Doctor that he didn't want to fight them and for God's sake not to let them hurt him. Emmons said to him, "Why Lusk! you said you were equal to ten of them and intended to bring back ten of their scalps and there will be nothing now unfair about this fight. I intend to give you a fair show." He ordered Lusk to get his horse and get onto it and get ready to march.

There were some four-foot clapboards stacked up near Lusk's house, and Emmons ordered six of the Germans to get a board apiece. They were all soon mounted and moving toward West Plains, soon coming to a "horsen" log. Emmons ordered them to dismount and form a line, placing the men about ten paces from Lusk, then said to Lusk, "Now, prepare yourself, and if you can whip these ten lopeared Dutch I will let you go back home and give you a chromo." Lusk pleaded pitifully to not let the Dutch abuse him. Emmons ordered the six who had the clapboards to move one pace in the rear, leaving four of the number to attack Lusk; he then ordered the four men to seize Lusk, take him to the "horsen" log and take down his clothes. Two of them were to take him by the hands and two by the legs and buck him tight against the log; if they succeeded, the six would proceed, one at a time, and strike him three licks across that part of the body that he generally used for sitting on.

He then turned to Lusk, saying, "Prepare to meet them; if you are a better man than they are, down them and pile them up." At the command of Capt. Emmons, the four men advanced on Lusk, who did not attempt to move, seized him by the arms, led him to the log, bucked him over it, two holding him by the arms and two by the legs, ordered the six men to advance, one at a time, strike three licks with the flat side of the board, march on a few paces and give room for the next.

After the performance had been completely carried out as commanded, the Captain declared that he could have heard Lusk holloing a mile distant every time the clapboard hit him.

After he had received the boarding, Emmons said that Lusk's setter was blistered where the boards had hit him, and that he never saw ten Germans enjoy themselves as much in his life. He then asked Lusk, in their presence, how he felt now in regard to fighting lopeared Dutch. Lusk declared that he had nothing against the Dutch and that he never would want to fight another one as long as he lived, and he hoped that Dr. Emmons would not let them do him any more harm. He dressed himself, they were all mounted, formed a line, and Lusk was brought into West Plains and took the oath, under the promise that he never would fight another lop-eared Dutchman.

Goes to Washington City.

After the post was discontinued at West Plains, the author was again ordered back to Rolla. The state had made a proposition to the Federal authorities that if the government would arm, feed and clothe the troops, it could place a number of regiments of state troops in the service, and they would be able to send some of their regular troops to the front. A delegation was appointed by the state to visit Washington City, wait upon the President and see what the government could do for the state. The author was appointed as one of the delegates, and on the night following the departure of the delegation for Washington City, a rebel scout appeared at the house where the author's family was living and demanded the author. His wife replied that he was not at home, that he was one of the delegation that had left that morning for Washington City. She distinctly heard one man remark: "I expect that is so, for there was a delegation left this morning for Washington City." The house wasn't more than a quarter of a mile from the picket posts.

After parleying for some little time, they left the house, marched west about a mile, where some refugees were located in a house, and demanded their surrender. The house was full of women and children, there being also one boy and two men, to-wit: Peter Shriver and a man named Johnson. They ordered the doors opened; the inmates refused; then the rebels knocked down the door, and fired a volley right into the house. Shriver and Johnson being armed, returned the fire, killed one of the rebels on the spot, and fleeing through the rear part of the house, made their escape. The rebels killed one boy and severely wounded a girl and young Johnson, and retreated south, leaving their comrade dead.

It was learned afterwards that most of the scout were men from Howell county who had learned that the author had placed his family just outside of the Federal lines and had marched all the way there, with the avowed purpose of capturing the author and either shooting or hanging him.

On arrival of the delegation at Washington City they organized the delegation and made Chas. D. Drake their spokesman. He was afterwards elected to the United States Senate. Soon after the arrival President Lincoln informed us that he would be prepared to meet the delegation in a large hall, near the mansion, at which time and place he desired to be introduced to the whole delegation. When the delegation entered the hall the President and his secretary were seated together.

The Delegation Meets the President.

The delegation entered the hall in a single file. Chas. D. Drake approached the President and when within a few feet of the President and secretary, they arose to their feet and as the delegation marched by each one was introduced to them. Afterwards they were seated, and the petition and address of the people of the State of Missouri was delivered in an audible voice by Chas. D. Drake. In the opening of the address we addressed the President and called ourselves his friends.

As soon as the address was read the President rose to his feet and proceeded to deliver an address to the delegation and the author never will forget the impression that was made upon his mind in a part of that address. He said: "You should not address me as your friend; I am the President of the whole people and nation and while I am President, I expect to try to enforce the law against all violators of the law and in the interest of the whole people of the nation; but if I have any friends in Missouri I suspect you men compose a part of them. I listened to your petition and offers, which make me proud for the patriotism that you manifest, in offering your services to your country in the darkest hour of her peril and I would be glad if the government was able to grant every request that you have made. The government at the present time is not in condition to furnish clothing and commissaries for the number of men that you propose to put in the field, but the government will furnish all the arms that they can possibly spare, ammunitions and commissaries and authorize the state to organize and put in the field any number of state troops, not to exceed sixty regiments." He said he would do all in his power to feed them but in the present condition of the government the state would have to pay them.

The delegation returned and informed the state of what promises the government had made and at once went to organizing and putting state troops into the field. The author was commissioned as lieutenant of Company H, and the regiment was ordered into active service for the period of sixty days. At the expiration of the term of service, the government ordered that a company of scouts be organized and that the author be made Captain of the company, to receive first lieutenant's pay and be clothed and fed by the government, be ordered on duty at once and placed under the direct command of Captain Murphy, who was then commanding the post at Houston.

The company scarcely saw an idle day, it was kept continuously scouting and fighting. The counties of Texas, Dent, Wright, Crawford, LaClede and Phelps, outside of the post, being completely under the control of the rebels. Not a single Union man nor his family could remain at home outside of the post.

Incidents of 1863.

In the fall of 1863, Colonel Livingston, who was acting in the capacity of Brigadier General, was ordered to proceed to Batesville, Arkansas, and there erect a post. The author was transferred, by order of the government, and made chief of scouts receiving Captain's pay and ordered to move with the command of Colonel Livingston and be under his command and control until further orders. On or about December 15, 1863, Colonel Livingston, who was Colonel of the 1st Nebraska regiment and the 11th Missouri Cavalry regiment, broke camp at Rolla, and marched in the direction of Batesville, Arkansas. Colonel Livingston, on leaving Rolla, issued a general order and sent the same in all directions, that all rebels, or "bushwhackers," who were captured wearing Federal uniform, would be court-martialed and shot; or all persons who were captured in robbing or plundering houses would be court-martialed and shot.

On our arrival in West Plains the advance of the command captured three Confederates dressed in Federal uniforms, near what was known as the Johnson farm. One of them broke from custody and escaped; the other two were court-martialed and shot, while the command was camped at West Plains. After those men were shot, some of the Confederates, dressed in Federal uniforms, came inside the Federal lines, while in camp at West Plains, just after dark, and took nine black cavalry horses from the line and made their escape. The soldiers saw them take the horses, but thought it was their own men taking them to water.

The command, breaking camp at West Plains, marched in the direction of Batesville, passed through Salem, Ark., and on Big Strawberry encountered the rebels and had quite an engagement. The weather was quite cold. I remember that after the fighting ceased, some of the soldiers had been fighting with their revolvers, and their hands had become so benumbed that they had lost the use of their fingers, and couldn't return their revolvers to their scabbards, and the revolvers had to be taken from their hands; the hands of some of them were badly frost-bitten.

The command again renewed its march for Batesville. Small bands of bushwhackers and rebels kept up a continuous fire every day on the advance, and committed depredations by pillaging; claiming they were Federal forces, most of them being dressed in Federal uniforms. The pillaging grew so annoying that Col. Livingston, just before breaking camp, divided the advance into two columns, marching from a mile to two and a half miles apart. Late in the afternoon, one wing came onto a number of those irregular Confederates, or bushwhackers, robbing the house of a Union woman whose husband was in the Federal army. Nearly all of them were dressed in Federal uniforms, claiming to the woman to be Federal soldiers. They had all dismounted and gone into the house to plunder it, except their captain, Elliott, whom they had left on guard. The road came around in a short bend and concealed the approach of the Federals until they were within a hundred yards of the house. There was a large gate in front of the house. The woman was standing in the yard about ten steps from the gate. She saw the troops coming before they were discovered by the captain, and supposed them to be of the same command. They were all cavalry. As soon as they saw the captain, they put spurs to their horses, and with revolvers in hand, charged upon them. The captain gave the alarm, and fled as rapidly as possible on horseback, a part of the Federals in hot pursuit after him.

Every avenue of escape was cut off from those who were in the house, and they were forced to retreat through a ten-acre open field, before they could reach the timber. The woman of the house, seeing them flee, knew at once that they didn't belong to the same command. While the Federals were approaching the gate at full speed, she ran to it and threw it open, so that they would not be checked in their pursuit. They overtook them about two-thirds of the way across the field, as the rebels were cut off from their horses and were on foot. Three of the rebels were killed, and three were taken prisoners. They had everything in their possession—bed clothing, domestic, knives and forks, and even axes, that they had been taking from Confederates as well as from Unionists; also a number of women's dresses. All of the dresses were given to the woman whose house they were robbing at the time of their capture. The soldiers had a fine time after they reached camp, by turning the domestic into new towels.

Just after supper, the author was notified to appear at the provost marshal's office, to see whether or not he could identify the prisoners. On his appearing and entering into conversation with the prisoners and inquiring their names, one claimed to be named Smith, another Taylor and the other Johnson. One of them lisped a little when talking. The author soon recognized one of them and said to him: "Your name is not Smith. You had just as well give your proper name, for I know you." The Provost Marshal asked him if he knew the author. He hesitated to answer. On the Provost Marshal urging him to answer, he said: "I ought to know him, as he was one of my near neighbors when the war commenced. My name is Calvin Hawkins." The author replied, "That is correct," and turning to the other prisoner for a second look, recognized him. He remarked, "Taylor is not your proper name." The Provost Marshal asked him if he knew the author. He hesitatingly replied he did. His proper name was then demanded, which he gave as Jacob Bridges. The other was a boy named Hankins, 13 years of age.

Court Martialed and Shot.

The Provost Marshal asked them if they had ever read or heard of the general order that had been issued by Col. Livingston. They replied that they had. He said to them: "You have violated the order in every particular; you are wearing Federal uniforms, and have been caught robbing and pillaging citizens' houses. Tonight your cases will be submitted to a court martial, except the boy's." He then ordered the author to take them to a room and inform them that they would certainly be convicted by the court martial, and the only way they could escape death would be to give the rendezvous and names of all irregular troops in their knowledge, and agree to pilot a scout to the different places of resort.

The author informed them of what the Provost Marshal had said, and further informed them that Col. Livingston, then acting in the capacity of Brigadier General, would have the only power to commute their sentences, after they were convicted. They refused to give any information that would aid the authorities in capturing the different irregular roving bands. The author bade them good-bye, told them he was sorry for them, that they were in a bad condition, but had brought it upon themselves and each of them had better prepare for death, for they were certain to be court-martialed that night. He then left the prisoners, the guard taking charge of them. The court-martial convened that night; charges and specifications were preferred before the Judge Advocate of violating both orders. They were accordingly convicted, and the next morning, before we broke camp, the author saw the detail that had been selected to execute them; saw the prisoners under guard moving out to the place selected for the execution, heard the discharge of the guns, and soon learned that they both had been shot. Somewhere on the head of Big Strawberry, in Izard county, the boy's mother came to us, and he was turned over to her.

The command broke camp and proceeded on the way towards Batesville, with more or less skirmishing with the rebels every day; and on the 25th of December, 1863, we had come to within about three miles of Batesville, Independence county, the rebels in considerable force then being in possession of the city. They had a strong picket about a quarter of a mile from the main city, leading right down Poke bayou. Another road turned to the right and entered the lower part of the city. The commander halted and threw out a considerable force in advance. The author was placed right in the front of the advance, with orders to charge the pickets, and on their retreat, to charge the enemy, and if they found them in too strong a force to fall back on the main command.

The rebel ladies had procured a large hall in the city, situated upon High street, leading west through the city. They were all dressed in gray, and had any amount of egg nog and other delicious drinks in the hall and all through the public parts of the city. A large number of the Confederate soldiers were in the hall dancing, a number of them belonging to Col. Freeman's command. On reaching the rebel pickets, they fired, and the commander ordered a charge with revolver and saber, and we followed close upon their heels. On reaching the city, the firing became promiscuous. The rebels retreated south, a number of them retreating in the direction of White river, and swam the river with their horses, while many of them abandoned their horses and swam the river. One part of the rebel command filed to the right, thinking that it was a Federal scout, and attempted to retreat upon the lower road. The Federals saw them coming, and knew from their actions that they were retreating. They at once deployed two lines in front of the command, one on each side of the road. Before the rebels found out their real condition they were completely into the trap, and they surrendered without the firing of a gun.

How Received by the Batesville Ladies.

After the fighting had subsided, the author, with a part of the command, rode up High street to the hall where they had just been dancing. There must have been as many as two hundred and fifty or three hundred ladies in the hall and on the roof. Some of the boys dismounted, went up into the hall and drank some of their eggnog, although there were strict orders against it.

The main command reached the east end of High street, marching in a solid column of two, with a brass band and drums and fifes playing, and striking up the tune of "Yankee Doodle," they came marching down High street, in the direction of the hall. The women began to use the strongest epithets possible in their vocabulary against the Union soldiers, calling them "nigger lovers," "lopeared Dutch," "thieves" and murderers." The author spoke to them saying, "You are mistaken. These men are gentlemen, sent here by the government to establish a military post, and if you treat them nicely you will receive the same kind of treatment."

About this time the front of the command had moved up to the hall. At once a number of the ladies began to make mouths at them and spit over the banisters toward them, calling them vile names. The soldiers then began to hallo at the top of their voices: "O, yonder is my Dixie girl, the one that I marched away from the north to greet." "God bless their little souls, ain't they sweet; sugar wouldn't melt in their mouths." "I am going to get my bandbox and cage up one of the sweet little morsels and take her home for a pet."

The voices of the soldiers completely drowned the hearing of anything the women were saying. In a little while the women hushed. As the column was passing by, one of the women remarked, "I believe that gentleman gave us good advice; I think we had better stop our abuse and we will be treated better." We marched down to the west end of High street, marched across to the next main street, then the head of the column turned east again up Main street, and striking up the tune of "Hail, Columbia, My Happy Land," marched up to the east end of Main street, and ordered a guard placed around the whole town, to prevent the escape of the rebel soldiers that were concealed in the town. The author never saw as much confusion as there was there, for a short time, among the citizens, especially the women. Some were laughing, some were abusing the soldiers, some crying, and some cursing.

After things had quieted down the soldiers went into camp. Colonel Livingston began to hunt suitable buildings for his head quarters and for an office for the Provost Marshall and Judge Advocate. It became a fixed fact with the citizens of the city that the Federals were going to locate a permanent post at that place.

While they were in pursuit of the rebels the author remembered an incident that attracted his attention. There were four or five negro men standing upon the street corner and one of the officers holloed out to the negroes, "Which way did the rebels go?" On one corner of the street there was a bunch of rebel citizens standing and as soon as the corner was turned and they were out of sight of the rebel citizens they answered the officer, "Massa, we don't know which way the rebels went; one of them dodged around the corner in an instant," and in a low tone of voice, and with a motion of his hand, said, "Massa dey went right dat way," almost in an instant came back around the corner and said in hearing of the rebel citizens "Massa, I declare I don't know the way dem rebels went."

The next morning Livingston issued a general order for all persons who claimed protection from the Federal army to come in and report and take the oath. The author remembers an incident that occurred on the evening of the fight. There had been two or three men killed just across the bridge and they placed a guard there with orders to let no person cross it without a pass. Shortly after dark a young lady who had secreted around her waist under her clothes, two pistols, a belt and scabbard which belonged to a Confederate soldier, just after dark came to the bridge and wanted to cross. The sargeant of the guard asked her if she had a pass, to which she replied she had not. He informed her that he could not let her go over. Among the guards was an Irishman and the young lady remarked to the sargeant that "it was very hard" that she "had a relative that was killed just across the bridge and she wanted to go over and see him and that a woman couldn't do any harm and they might let her go over without a pass."

The Irishman sprang to his feet and remarked "Be Jasus, women can do a divil of a sight of harm, can convey more information, can carry more intelligence through the lines to the rebels than twenty men and there are so many of our officers, if she happens to be good looking, would let her pass through." The sargeant believing that she was a near relative of one of the men that was killed a short distance from the bridge, let her pass over, and that night she delivered the pistols to the Confederate soldiers. She afterwards admitted this when she was arrested for refusing to take the oath.

If You Will Grease and Butter Him.

She declared that she "wouldn't swallow old Lincoln," and the commander ordered all persons who refused to take the oath, either men or women, arrested and sent to Little Rock. When she found that she had to take the oath or go to Little Rock, she said to them that "if they would grease and butter the oath she would try to swallow it." Afterwards she became very intimate with one of the young Federals, married him and when the command broke up left the post, left the country and went with him.

The author remained there all that winter, being in active service almost every day, capturing some of the worst men that there were in the country. In a short time after the post was located the west side of the river was all in the control of the rebels. The rebels began to boast and brag that those Northern Yankees could stay around the open field and around cities but whenever they crossed the river they would show them just how rebel bullets would fly. Colonel Freeman's head quarters were near the head of Silamore creek, they would get on the mountains, on each side (as the Yankees knew nothing about mountains) and roll rocks down on them and what they didn't kill with rocks and bullets would be glad to get back across the river to Batesville.

There were no ferry boats on the river, they had all been sunk or run out by the rebels.

The weather was very cold. White river froze over solid. The old residents there said it was the first time they ever knew of the river freezing over solid. The ice was so thick that it would hold the weight of horses and wagons. Col. Livingston ordered lumber hauled and laid the planks flat on the ice. He then sent some men who resided in Nebraska when at home, to make a test. They reported that the ice was safe for a command to pass over. The commander at once organized a force, crossed the river on the ice, and took up the line of march for the purpose of attacking Freeman's forces, which were distant about ten or twelve miles. As soon as the rebel forces found that they were moving up Silamore creek in the direction of Freeman's headquarters, they placed men on the hills on each side of the creek, and as soon as the Federals forces came within reach, they opened fire, and commenced rolling stones. The commander halted, deployed skirmishers, ordered them to fall back, march on foot and flank the rebels, while they would continue the march up the creek and attract their attention until they would have them completely flanked, and then close in on them. While the main force moved up the creek slowly, under almost continuous fire, all at once a general fire opened up on both sides of the hills. I never before saw rebels running and dodging in all directions, trying to make their escape, as they did then. A number of them were killed and wounded, and the others taken prisoners. The remainder got down from the hills, wiser men, and made a hasty retreat up the creek. Upon the Federal column reaching the headquarters of Freeman, it was so unexpected that he had to retreat, leaving all his camp equipage, his trunk and clothing, and about $5,000 in Confederate money.

They retreated in an almost northerly direction. Our force returned to Batesville. The scouts, with a small force of troops, were sent up White river to find where the line of march of the rebels was. They found that they had crossed White river near the mouth of the north fork and were moving in the direction of Pocahontas. There had been two Federal companies detailed and sent out northeast in the direction of Spring river. Freeman's command surrounded them and made prisoners of one of the companies. The other company, commanded by Capt. Majors, made a charge on the lines and cut their way through.

Reinforcements were at once dispatched in the direction of the moving columns of rebels. In the meantime, the rebels had reached Pocahontas, on Black river, and had effected a crossing onto the east side of Black river, except the rear guard, which were in their boat about midway of the river, when the Federal forces reached the west side of the river. They fired on the parties in the boat, wounding some of them, but they succeeded in reaching the bank, and turned their boat loose. A strong line of rebels was drawn up on the east bank of Black river, and opened fire on the Federal forces on the west side. After considerable firing, both sides ceased. The rebels appeared to move east; the Federal forces again countermarched and returned to Batesville.

The country on the west side of White river was still under the control of a strong force of rebels commanded by Col. Weatherford and three or four other Confederate commanders. About three weeks after their return, an order was issued for two wagon trains with six mule teams and a detail of two companies, to escort it. The train moved out, for the purpose of getting corn and other forage, about fifteen miles distant on White river. After they had arrived at their destination and were loading their wagons, a large force of rebels surrounded them, charged on them, and made prisoners of about half of the escort. The Federal captain, who belonged to one of the 11th Missouri companies, surrendered, handed his pistol, about half shot out, to a rebel soldier, who turned his own pistol on him and shot him dead. The scouts who escaped capture, retreated with all possible haste to Batesville.

In the meantime, the rebel forces cut the wagons down, piled them in heaps and set them on fire; while the mules, with all their gear and breeching on were put into White river and swam across to the other side. As soon as the news reached headquarters, a force was speedily organized, and started on a forced march. Upon reaching the scene of action the rebels were all safely across on the other side of the river, harness and wagons were just about completely burned up. No chance of any boats to cross the river and the river being full, they countermarched and returned to Batesville again.

The whole winter was taken up in scouting and fighting small bands of rebels. Sometime in the latter part of the winter the commissaries and forage were becoming scarce and the nearest Federal post down White river was at Duvall's bluff. The commander called on the author, who was Captain of scouts, for a detail of two men who could procure a canoe and try, if possible, to reach Duvall's Bluff and inform the Federal authorities there of the conditions of the post. The author detailed a man by the name of Johardy Ware and a man by the name of Simon Mason. They were to procure a canoe and travel in the night, drawing it, when daylight came, into thick brush, and in that way, if possible, reach the Federal post. They succeeded in reaching the post and in a short time commissaries and provisions, with forage, were forwarded up the river on two small transports, with a number of troops to force its passage up the river. Sometime in the latter part of the winter the boats reached Batesville and supplied all of the wants and short rations of the soldiers and again made everything merry and happy.

Give an Oyster Supper.

In April, 1864, the author had promised to return to Rolla for the purpose of aiding and recruiting a regiment, known as the 16th Missouri Cavalry Volunteer. He informed the commander and asked for his recommendation which was granted. He wanted to know when I wanted to start so that he could make preparations to send me around by water. The author informed him that he intended to march through by land. The commander thought it was a thing impossible, that scouting bands of rebels had possession of the country, from a short distance outside of Batesville almost to Rolla, Missouri. The commander and Provost Marshall gave the author an innovation, made an oyster supper for him and his company of scouts, said they were loath to give them up, that they had performed so much valuable service, and he didn't know where he could get any other men to take their places.

After taking leave of the officers and soldiers, the author took a small flag, fastened upon a staff, fastened it to the browband of the bridle and remarked to the officers as he bid them good bye, that the stars and stripes should float from Batesville to Rolla or the author would die in the attempt. The company then set out for Rolla, Missouri. Colonel Woods of the 11th Missouri cavalry had been on detached service and Lieutenant Colonel Stevens had been commanding the regiment. He had received orders to join his regiment at Batesville, Arkansas, and, with a considerable force of men, reached the state line about 12 o'clock, and came in sight of the command.

They saw our company approaching, at once drew up in line of battle, and as many of the rebels had procured Federal uniforms, both parties sent out couriers to ascertain who the forces were. On learning that both sides were Federals, we marched up and went into camp with them. The author was immediately taken to Col. Wood's headquarters. He informed him that he had camped near West Plains the night before, and that the bushwhackers had kept up a continuous fire until after they got a considerable distance down South Fork; and he believed it impossible for as small a force as I had to reach Rolla without great disaster and perhaps annihilation. He said that the author and his company of scouts were the very men he wanted, and offered to increase his salary to $7.00 per day if he would go back with him and remain with his command. The author told him that he was honor bound to return to Missouri and assist in organizing a regiment of cavalry for the United States service, and if the bushwhackers didn't keep clear, he would give some of them a furlough before he reached Rolla.

After dinner Woods broke camp and moved in the direction of Batesville, and we in the direction of Rolla. Near where the last firing was done they had arrested a man named Craws, who really was a Union man, and the author had been well acquainted with him before the war commenced, but Woods' soldiers could with difficulty be restrained from shooting him. On my informing the Colonel that I was well acquainted with the man and that there was no harm in him, he agreed to turn him over to the author and let him bring him back home with him. After we had started, Craws informed the author that he knew the parties who had been firing on the Federal troops; that their headquarters were about two miles from where he resided; and that he was satisfied from the last firing he had heard, that they had turned off from the main road and gone up what was called the Newberry hollow. After passing the old Newberry farm, they had a plain trail that turned to the right and led directly to the camp. They were commanded by two men named Hawkins and Yates.

On reaching his house he agreed to continue with us to the road he thought they had gone, and then return home. I think he was the happiest man I ever saw when he found he had been turned over to my care, believing that Woods' command intended to shoot him.

On reaching the road, we found a fresh rebel trail leading right up the creek; we moved on until near the Newberry residence, which we had been informed by Craws was occupied by Hawkins' wife. We turned from the road and halted, and the author, with two or three of his men, being familiar with the country, reached a high point from which we could distinctly see one horse standing at the door. Supposing the rebel scouts were all there, we went back to the company, moved cautiously toward the house, and gave orders to charge upon them as soon as our approach was discovered. On coming within fifty yards of the house, which was unenclosed, a woman stepped outside the door, looked toward us, and then wheeled for the house and we charged. Hawkins' horse was hitched to a half of a horse shoe driven in at the side of the door, the bridle rein looped over it, his halter rein being already tied over the saddle horn. The author had ordered all to charge with pistols in hand. As Hawkins reached the door and made an attempt to take his bridle rein, he saw that it was impossible. The author demanding his surrender, he attempted to draw his pistol and had it half way out of his holster and cocked, when the author fired upon him. He fell back, still holding his pistol. The author, supposing more of the enemy were inside the house, dismounted, and rushing to the door, demanded the surrender of every person that might be in the house. As the author entered the door, he heard Hawkins, still holding his pistol, remark: "Monks, you have killed me." The author replied that that was what he intended to do, and he must let go of that pistol or he would be shot again. He took his hand loose from the pistol and in a short time was dead. His wife asked the author to lay him out, which request was complied with.

We mounted and again took the rebel trail and by this time it had grown so dark that we lost it and went on to the residence of Captain Howard, dismounted, fed our horses and got our supper.

Captain Howard afterwards informed the author that he had just been home and started back to the rebel camp and heard the horses feet, stepped behind a tree and that we passed within fifteen feet of him; said if it hadn't been dark we would have been certain to have found the rebel camp; that that day some of the rebel soldiers had killed a deer, stretched the skin and had it hanging up and the camp wasn't more than two hundred yards from the main road. After we ate our suppers and fed our horses we again resumed our march and reached Rolla, Missouri, on the second day afterwards.

Another Meeting with Captain Forshee.

In the spring of 1863 General Davidson was ordered to move from Rolla, Missouri, directly south to Little Rock. On breaking camp and marching in the direction of West Plains the author, with his company of scouts, was ordered to report to him for service. On reaching West Plains he went into camp. West Plains and vicinity were completely covered with tents and troops. All of the hills adjoining West Plains were literally covered with tents, Davidson's headquarters being inside of the town. The author being sent out on a scout, came to the home of a man named Barnett residing in Gunter's Valley and not being able to reach town, went into camp near Barnett's. In a short time Barnett came in home. He had been a lieutenant in the company where the author was prisoner. He informed the author that he had been to Thomasville Mill and that Captain Forshee, who lived about one mile below, had also returned with him.

The author at once placed a guard around Barnett's house (Barnett being the father-in-law of the Captain) detailed two men to accompany him, prepared, mounted, and started to the residence of Forshee fully determined to kill him. The author instructed his men that if Forshee remained in the house and didn't attempt to run, to play off and tell him that they belonged to Colonel Woods, a Confederate officer on White river. The author then being clothed in Federal uniform and having but a limited acquaintance with Forshee before the war did not think he would recognize him. On reaching the house we repaired to the door, halloed, and his wife invited us in. The author had his pistol under the cape of his coat still determined upon killing him. On entering the house, found him in bed with one of his children, his wife did not have the supper on the table. The author asked him if he had ever been in the Confederate service; he answered that he had, went out in the six months provisional Confederate service; didn't stay his time out, resigned and came home. The author asked him if they had taken any prisoners while they were in service; he hesitated a moment and replied that they did. The author asked him if he remembered the names of any of them; he said he remembered the names of two of them well. The author asked him if he knew what became of them; he said that Black enlisted in the Confederate service, served his time out and then substituted himself and was now in the eastern Confederate army; he again hesitated. The author asked him if he knew what became of the other man; he said that he didn't; that he made his escape from the Confederate army and he had heard that he was a captain in the Northern army. The author said with an oath "How would you like to see him"; he replied "I would not like to see him very well." The author then said, with an oath, "I am here, look at me and see whether you think I am worth a beef cow or not." At this his wife sprang between him and the author and he said to the author, "Captain, there ain't one man out of ninety-nine but what would kill me for the treatment you received while a prisoner but I have always thought that if I ever met you and you would give me the time to explain the cause of it, you wouldn't kill me, and I want to live to raise my children."

The thought passed through the mind of the author that he could not kill him in the lap of his family; but he would take him to Barnett's house where he had some more prisoners and on the next day he would kill him on the way; ordered him to get out of that bed; Forshee again appealed and said that he would like to know whether the author was going to kill him or not; that he wanted to live to raise his children. The author replied to him with an oath that "you ought to have thought of these things when you was pulling me away from the bosom of my family, never gave me time to bid them good-bye; get out of that bed." There was about a six months old child in the cradle. He slid out of the bed, kneeled down by the cradle, and was in the act of praying, his wife still standing close by. The author ordered him to get up; that it was too late to pray after the devil came; that I had been appointed by the devil to send him up at once and he had the coals hot and ready to receive him and that I didn't want to disappoint the devil. He arose to his feet and again asked the author if he was going to kill him; said he wanted time to give me the whole truth of the matter; went on to say Hawkins, Sapp, Kaiser and others were the cause of all the mistreatment, but would admit that he done wrong in agreeing to deliver the author to them for the purpose of having him mobbed and for abusing him, himself.

His wife had hot coffee on the table and she asked that he be allowed to sit down, saying that she wanted to see him sup coffee once more. The author told her that they never gave him time to bid his wife good-bye, let alone to sup coffee with her. After taking a few sups of coffee, the author said that he couldn't fool any longer with him; that he must strike a line and move out. His wife said that she was going with him, but her husband told her she had no business going, as it was then snowing and the ground was considerably frozen. The author told her that if she was determined to go, the boys could take her and the children behind them, but the Captain would have to walk right in front of the author, and if he made a crooked step from there until he reached Barnett's, he would shoot him through. The boys took his wife and children on the horses, and the author started the Captain in front of him. He had thought that he would be compelled to shoot him on the way, but he could not shoot him in the presence of his family; so he thought he would take him to the guard house and keep him until morning, and then on the way to West Plains he would make a pretext to kill him, for he thought he must kill him.

In the morning, after breakfast, we broke camp and moved in the direction of West Plains. The author had now become cool, and while he believed he ought to kill him for what he had done, he could not afford to shoot, or cause a prisoner to be shot, while he was in his charge; so on reaching West Plains, the prisoner was turned over to the guard house.

The morning following was very cool, and the ground was covered with snow. Gen. Davidson had ordered out a large scout for the purpose of marching towards Batesville and White river, to feel the strength of the enemy, and the author's company composed a part of the detail. After the command was mounted and waiting for orders to move, the sergeant of the guard came out and inquired if there was a Captain Monks in that command. The Colonel informed him that there was. He said there was a prisoner in the guard house who wanted to see him. The author got permission to ride to the guard house, and on reaching the door, who should meet him but Capt. Forshee, who told the author that he had almost frozen the night before, and wanted to know if the author couldn't loan him a blanket. He was told that he was the last man who should ask the author for the use of a blanket. Forshee replied: "That's so, Captain; but I believe that you are a good man, and don't want to see a man, while he is a prisoner, suffer from cold." The author asked him if they had any gray backs in the guard house. He said he had none on himself, but didn't know in what condition the others were.

The author had two new government blankets that he had paid $5 apiece for a short time previous, on the back of his saddle. He told Forshee that he didn't know as he would need them both until he had gotten back from the scout, and would loan him a blanket until he returned. Forshee replied: "I will never forget the favor." The author handed him one of the blankets, and immediately started on the scout. While the scout was south reconnoitering with the enemy, Gen. Davidson received orders from headquarters countermanding the order to march to Little Rock by land, and that he would march his forces to Ironton, Missouri, and there await further orders. He at once broke camp and resumed his march in the direction of Ironton, carrying the prisoners with him, with orders for the scout on its return to move up and overtake him, as they were all cavalry. So the author never saw Capt. Forshee nor his blanket any more, but was informed that he was parolled at Ironton, took the oath, returned to Oregon county, and died shortly after the close of the war.

Upon the return of the scout to West Plains, a part of the command that belonged to Gen. Davidson's forces moved on after the army, while the author, with two companies, remained in West Plains about half a day for the purpose of resting up. While in West Plains a rebel that the author was well acquainted with, came to him and told him he had better be getting out of West Plains, for a force of five hundred rebels was liable to come into West Plains at any moment. The author pretended to become considerably alarmed, and reported that he was going to march directly to Rolla with the two companies then under his command. After marching about fifteen miles in the direction of Rolla, he made a flank movement, marched into the corner of Douglass county, was there reinforced, and the next day marched directly to the west end of Howell county. The rebels, believing that the Federal troops had all left the county, came in in small bunches from all over the county. The author made a forced march and reached the west end of the county about dark, turned directly toward West Plains, took the rebels completely by surprise, had a number of skirmishes with them, reaching West Plains with more rebel prisoners than he had men of his own. On the next day we turned in the direction of Rolla, and by forced march reached Texas county. On the next morning we reached the Federal post at Houston, in Texas county, and turned over the prisoners, among whom were several prominent officers. Capt. Nicks was one of them. On the night of his capture the author said to him: "It appears to me that it is about the same time of night that they brought me prisoner to your house." He answered: "I declare I believe it is." After the rebels found the small number of the force that had made the scout, they declared that it was a shame to let Monks run right into the very heart of the rebels and carry out more prisoners than he had men.

Murdering Federal Soldiers.

Some time in June, 1863, a rebel scout and a Federal scout had a fight about twenty miles northwest of Rolla. The rebels were forced to abandon a number of wagons and mules, and the Federals, owing to the emergency that confronted them at the time, did not wish to be encumbered with them, so they employed a farmer to keep the mules in his pasture until the government should send for them. The Federal scouts from Rolla and Jefferson City would meet occasionally while scouting. On the scout's arrival at Rolla, another scout composed of about one company of Federals was sent out to bring in the wagons and teams. Just before reaching the place where the wagons and teams had been left, they saw a command of about two hundred and fifty men, all dressed in Federal uniforms, and they at once took them to be a Federal scout from Jefferson City. On approaching each other, they passed the army salute and marched right down the Federal line; they, being unsuspecting, believed them to be Federal troops. As soon as they were in position each man had his man covered with a pistol. The rebel scout outnumbering the Federal scout more than two to one, they demanded their surrender. The Federals, seeing their condition, at once surrendered. They were marched about a quarter of a mile, near where the wagons and teams were left, dismounted and went into camp, as the rebels claimed, for dinner. Several citizens were present. They marched the Federal company together, surrounded them in a hollow square, brought some old ragged clothing, and ordered them to strip. After they were all stripped completely naked, and while some were attempting to put on the old clothing, all their uniforms having been removed a short distance from them, at a certain signal the rebels fired a deadly volley into them. Then followed one of the most desperate scenes ever witnessed by the eye of man. The men saw their doom, and those who were not killed by the first volley rushed at the rebels, caught them, tried to wrest their arms from them, and a desperate struggle took place; men wrestling, as it were, for their very lives.

A number of the Federals had their throats cut with knives. After the rebels had completed the slaughter and hadn't left a man alive to tell the tale, they ate their dinner, and taking the mules and wagons, moved southwest with them. The citizens at once reported the affair to the commander of the post at Rolla.

The men who were killed belonged to an Iowa regiment, and the author believes it was the 3rd Iowa, but will not be positive. A strong detail was made and sent at once to the scene of the late tragedy, with wagons and teams to bring the dead back to Rolla. On their arrival with them, it was the most horrible scene that the author ever looked upon. After they were buried, the regiment to which they belonged declared and avowed that they intended to take the same number of rebel lives. The commander, knowing their determination, and being satisfied that they would carry it into effect if the opportunity offered, transferred them to another part of the country.

A Rebel Raid.

Some time in the fall of 1863 the Federal authorities at Rolla learned that the rebels were organizing a strong force in Arkansas, for the purpose of making a raid into Missouri. The rebels were under the command of Gen. Burbrage. The author, being still the commander of the scouts, was ordered to take one man and go south, for the purpose of learning, if possible, the movements of the rebels. The author left Rolla, came by way of Houston, where there was a post, thence to Hutton Valley, where there was living a man named Andy Smith, who was a Union man, but had made the rebels believe he was in favor of the south. The author approached Smith's house after dark, got something to eat and to feed his horses, and learned from Smith that the rebels were about prepared to make the raid into Missouri. On the next day the author was informed by Smith that Burbrage was then moving with his full force in the direction of Missouri. The author at once started, intending to reach the nearest Federal force, which was in Douglas county. In the meantime, Gen. Burbrage, with his whole force, reached the Missouri line, leaving West Plains a little to the right, taking an old trace that ran on the divide between the waters of the North fork of White river and of Eleven Points river, this being afterwards known as "the old Burbrage trail." The author, expecting they would march by way of West Plains and on through Hutton Valley, thought he would be able to keep ahead of them and make his report; but owing to their marching an entirely different route, the author crossed their trail. He found that a large force of men had just passed and he, in company with a man named Long, examined the horse tracks, found that the shoes contained three nails in each side, and knew at once that it must be Burbrage's command. They had passed not more than three hours before this time. Making a forced march, the author and Long followed on the same trail, and soon came to a house, holloed, and a lady coming out, we inquired how far the command was ahead. The lady informed us that they hadn't been gone more than three hours, and she exclaimed: "Hurrah for Gen. Burbrage and his brave men! The Yankees and lop-eared Dutch are goin' to ketch it now, and they intend to clean them out of the country!" We then became satisfied as to whose command it was, and their destination. We rode on about two hundred yards from the house, turned to the left, and started with all possible speed, intending, if possible, to go around them and get the word in ahead of them. On striking the road at the head of the North Fork of White river, we looked ahead of us about a hundred yards and saw twenty-five men, about fifty yards from the road, all in citizen's dress, wearing white hat bands. The state had ordered all the state militia to wear white hat bands, so that they might be designated from the rebels. The author remarked to Long: "I guess the men are militia, but we will ride slowly along the road and pass them, for fear they are rebels." They remained still on their horses until after we had passed them, then they moved forward and came riding up and halted us, and wanted to know who we were. The author told them his name was Williams and Long told them his name was Tucker. They asked us if we had ever heard of the Alsups, and we told them we had. Then they wanted to know where we were going. We told them we were going into Arkansas, near Yellville; that a general order had been made in the state of Missouri that all able-bodied men must come and enroll their names and those who were not in the state service would have to be taxed; that we didn't want to fight nor pay a tax to support those who were fighting. They ordered us to dismount, surrounded us, with cocked pistols, and ordered us to crawl out of our clothes and give up our arms. We commenced to strip. Long had on a very fine pair of boots, for which he had just paid $5.00, and while the author didn't know at what moment they would be shot, he could not help but be tickled at the conduct of Long when they ordered him to take off his boots. He crossed his legs and commenced pulling, with the remark: "My boots are tight." The pistols were cocked and presented right on him, not more than six feet away, and they told him to hurry up or they would shoot his brains out. While he was pulling at his boots he appeared to be looking right down the muzzles of the revolvers. As soon as he had pulled off his boots and pitched them over, they remarked: "Hell, a right brand new pair of socks on. Pull them off quick and throw them over." A part of these men were dressed in the dirtiest, most ragged clothes the author had ever seen—old wool hats, with strings tied under their chins, old shoes with the toes worn out, and old socks that were mostly legs; but claiming all the time to be militia. They ordered us to get into their old clothes and shoes, and placed their old hats upon us. Our clothing and hats all being new, the author thought that was one of the hardest things they had ordered him to do;

that he was just as apt to get out of the garments as to get into them. After we were dressed in their old clothing, one of them asked: "What did you say your name was?" Long replied, "Tucker." One that was standing a little back came running up with his pistol cocked, and remarked that if he was a certain Tucker (naming the Tucker): "I am going to kill him right here." Another of the number said: "Hold on, this man is not the Tucker that you are thinking of." Then their leader said, with an oath: "We belong to Gen. Burbrage's command. He is just ahead. Do you want us to take you up to headquarters?" We told him we had heard of Gen. Burbrage, and expected that he was a good man, so if they wanted to take us to his headquarters all right: but we did not want to fall into the hands of the militia, as we wanted to get through to Yellville while Gen. Burbrage was in the country. One of the men looked at the horses we were riding and remarked: "Let's take the horses. We have orders to take all horses that are fit for the service." Another said the horses were rather small for the service, and as we would have a great deal of water to cross between there and Yellville, it would be a pity to make us wade it. Then their leader remarked: "We are Confederate soldiers, out fighting for our country, and you men are too damned cowardly to fight. We have got to have clothing, and as we suppose you are good southern men, when you get to Yellville you can work for more clothes." They then ordered us to take the road and move on, and tell the Alsups that the country was full of rebels.

We mounted our horses and rode away, feeling happy on account of our escape. They remained in the road and watched us until we were out of their sight. The author looked over at Long's feet and saw his toes sticking out of his old shoes; could see his naked skin in several places through his raiment. He hardly looked natural—didn't look like the same man. We hadn't gone more than a mile until we struck a farm and a road leading between the farm on one side and the bluff and river on the other, and looking in front, saw about fifteen men coming. The author said to Long: "What shall we do? Shall we attempt to run, or had we better pass them?" We concluded that it was impossible to get away by running; the only chance left being to try to pass through them without being recognized.

We rode up to meet them, and they halted us and wanted to know where we were going. We told them we were going to Marion county,

Arkansas, near Yellville. They asked us our names and we again gave the names of Williams and Tucker. A man named Charley Durham who had resided at West Plains and had met me several times, rode up near us and asked me: "What did you say your name was?" I replied, "Williams." He asked: "Did you ever live down here about the state line?" I told him I never did, but I might have had relatives who lived on the state line. He said: "I am satisfied that I have seen you somewhere." One of the crowd asked us if we had met about twenty-five soldiers just ahead, and when we informed them that we had, they remarked: "Bully for the boys; we had better be moving on or we will be late." They moved on, and we continued down the road. As soon as we were out of sight I said to Long: "We will not risk our chances in passing any more of them; there are too many men down here that are acquainted with us. If it hadn't been for my old clothes, Charley Durham would have recognized me beyond a doubt." We then left the road and took to the woods, reaching the Federal forces about midnight. They had not heard a thing regarding the approach of the rebels. They hurriedly began to gather in all the forces, and at once set out to find, if possible, the destination of Gen. Burbrage. It was learned that he had completely cut us off from reaching either Houston or Rolla. On the next day the Federal forces met Gen. Burbrage at Hearstville, Wright county, Missouri, and there fought a battle with him. The commander of the post at Houston, who was in command of the Federals, was killed on the first fire from the artillery of Gen. Burbrage. Col. McDonald, during the engagement, was shot dead at the head of the town spring. Burbrage retreated on the same route that he had come up on. His command was separated into several divisions, to get food.

Long and I had been furnished clothes and arms. Capt. Alsup being in command, moved near the road that leads down Fox Creek, saw a rebel scout moving down Fox Creek, composed of a part of the same men we had met the day before. Capt. Alsup said he thought that by striking the road and taking the rebels by surprise we could rout them. On marching about a mile we came in sight of them, dismounted for dinner at the house of a man named Ferris. I proposed to Capt. Alsup that we charge them. He thought it might be too dangerous; that they would have the benefit of the house, and might outnumber us, and we would be compelled to retreat and might be cut off from our horses. He ordered us to dismount, formed a line, left men to hold the horses, and on moving about ten steps, the rebel picket, who was placed just outside of the line, discovered us. They opened fire from each side of the house, and along a picket fence which enclosed the house. We returned the fire. The first volley that was fired, a ball passed near my ear, and wounded the horse that I was riding. The firing continued for some time. We had them cut off from their horses, unless they came outside and faced the continual firing. One man attempted to leave the house and reach his horse, but about ten feet from the door he received a wound in the face and fell to the ground. In a moment he arose to his feet, and he and several others again retreated into the house. The firing continued for fifteen or twenty minutes, when the rebels retreated on foot, by taking advantage of the house, except one man, who reached his horse, cut the halter, sprang into the saddle, turned his horse down the lane, leaning close to the horn of the saddle, put spurs and made his escape. In the meantime the wounded man attempted to make his escape by taking advantage of the house and retreating. Capt. Alsup, when he saw the rebels were retreating, ordered a charge. The wounded man was again wounded, and fell to the ground, helpless. All the other rebels reached the woods, and made their escape.

Farris, the man who owned the house where the rebels were stopping, received a serious wound in the breast. They left sixteen horses with their rigs, saddle-riders filled with new clothing, in our possession. Gen. Burbrage retreated from the state, and the author reported to his command at Rolla.

Rescuing Union Families.

In the fall of 1862 some of the Union men whose families were still residing in Ozark and Howell counties went to the Federal post and were promised arms and ammunition in order to return and try to get their families out, as it had become almost impossible for their families to get through alone, on account of being robbed. About fifty of them procured arms and started for Howell county, from the outpost of the Federal authorities. They marched at night and lay by in the day, and on reaching the western part of Howell county, informed their families to get ready to move, still keeping themselves in hiding. About twenty families prepared for moving, and had assembled on the bayou, near where Friend's old mill was located. Just about the time they were ready to start, a bunch of rebels came up and opened fire on them. They returned the fire and held the rebels at a distance while they moved all their wagons up close together, and started in the direction of Ozark county. One of the men who had come to assist in the escort became excited upon the first fire from the rebels and ran, never stopping until he reached the Federal lines. The remainder of the men bravely repelled the rebels, while their families kept their teams steadily moving. On reaching the big North Fork of White River, and while the families in their wagons were in mid-stream, the rebels reached the bluff and opened fire on them. The Union men vigorously returned the fire. They all reached the opposite side of the river without one of their number being killed; some of the women and children had received slight wounds, but nothing serious. The rebels still continued to fire upon them until they reached the northern part of Ozark county, when further pursuit was abandoned, and about twenty families were enabled to reach the Federal lines. In a short time the Union men attempted to again reach their homes, for the purpose of helping destitute families to get out. They traveled only at night, keeping themselves concealed in day time. In this way they reached Fulton county, Arkansas, when the rebels found out that some of the Union men were in the country. The rebel forces at once became so strong that the Federals had to retreat without getting any of their families, passing back through the western part of Howell county, over into Ozark, and went into camp on the head of Lick Creek. Shortly after they got into camp the rebels slipped up on them and opened fire, mortally wounding a man named Fox and slightly wounding several others. They had to scatter at once to avoid being captured, and when they reached the Federal lines they were almost worn out. At this time all of the Federal posts had numbers of refugee families stationed near them, entirely destitute of food and raiment, and relying entirely for their preservation upon the small amount of help they received from the government.

General Price's Raid.

Upon my return from Batesville, Arkansas, in the spring of 1864, I commenced recruiting for the 16th Missouri Cavalry volunteers, the most of the regiment being composed of men who had been in the state service. The required number to form the regiment was soon procured, and the regiment was organized, electing for their Colonel, John Mahan. The author was elected Captain of Co. K. The regiment was at once placed in active service, being quartered at Springfield, Missouri, up to the time of Gen. Price's raid. Then the regiment was divided, one half of it being in pursuit of Price. The other half, which was known as the second battalion, was placed under my command and held at Springfield, it being expected that Gen. Price would change his line of march and attack the city. As soon as the fact was ascertained that Price was marching north and west of Springfield, orders were made to send every available man that could be spared from the post. Among the troops sent out was the author's battalion. We were ordered on a forced march in the direction of Utony, for the purpose of cutting off Price's retreat. We reached Utony about 10 o'clock at night, where they had a strong Federal garrison. Two thousand rebels of Price's command had just marched across the road before we reached the garrison, and gone into camp in sight of the town. Strong pickets were thrown out on each side. About daylight the Federal forces broke camp and moved on the rebel camp, soon coming in sight of the rebel forces, and fire was opened on both sides. The rebels commenced retreating, the Federals pursuing, and continuous firing and fighting was kept up until we came near the Arkansas line. A number of rebel prisoners were taken, besides some of their commissary wagons falling into the possession of the Federals. The Federal commander then ordered a retreat back to Springfield. Price's forces had torn up all the railroads as they passed over them, cutting off all supplies, and the soldiers and prisoners had been placed on quarter rations. The prisoners, numbering about three hundred and fifty, were ordered to be taken to Rolla, Missouri. After the first day's march from Springfield they met a Federal train carrying commissaries to Springfield and other western points. The men being then on quarter rations, the Colonel took possession of some of the commissaries and issued them to the soldiers and prisoners, for which he was afterward arrested and court-martialed. On reaching Lebanon, Missouri, I saw the quarter-master haul in about five or six loads of shucked corn, which was distributed to the soldiers and prisoners. I well remember that while they were distributing the corn to the prisoners, a general rush, which appeared to be almost uncontrollable, was made around the wagon. The corn was thrown out on the ground among them, they picked it up in their arms, and at once retired to their camp fires, so that they might parch and eat it. After leaving Lebanon, the prisoners were all placed in charge of the author. He remembers one rebel prisoner who had on a fine dress coat, with a bullet hole right in the center of the back, and the soldiers had to be watched closely to prevent them from shooting him, as they believed it to be a coat that had been taken from the body of some Union man, after he had been shot.

On reaching Rolla, the author turned over all the prisoners to the commander of the post, and they were sent directly to Rock Island, there to be held as prisoners until such time as they might be exchanged. I again returned to Springfield and reported to my regiment. A short time thereafter, the loyal men of the counties of Howell, Dent, Texas, Phelps, Ozark and Douglas, in Missouri, and of Fulton, Izard and Independence counties, in Arkansas, with a number of the officers and soldiers, including the commander at Rolla, petitioned Gen. Schofield, who was then in command of the western district, to have the author detached from his regiment, then at Springfield, and sent south of Rolla to some convenient place, and given command of a post, as it was almost impossible to send commissaries through from Rolla to Springfield, on what was known as the wire road, on account of the roving bands of rebels, who had complete control of the country, a short distance from the military post.

Capt. Monks Establishes a Post at Licking.

Gen. Schofield at once made an order that Capt. Monks be detached from his regiment and report at Rolla, with his company, for further orders. Gen. Sanborn, then in command at Springfield, informed the author of his final destination; that on reaching Rolla, he would be ordered by Gen. Schofield to Licking, Missouri, to establish a post.

It soon leaked out, and the rebels swore openly that if he established a post at Licking or at any other southern point, they would soon drive the post into the ground and annihilate him and his men. I went to Gen. Sanborn and requested that he send a telegram to Gen. Schofield, and ask him to countermand that part of the order that required Capt. Monks to report at Rolla for further orders, and order him to move directly from Springfield to Licking. The General hesitated for some time, as to whether it would be good policy, owing to the large numbers of rebels in the country through which I had to pass. He didn't believe that I would reach Licking with the one company, but he finally decided that if I was willing to risk it, he would ask Gen. Schofield to change his order. On Gen. Schofield's receiving the telegram, he made an order that I be detached from my regiment, be furnished two company wagons, be well supplied with arms, and proceed directly to Licking. On reaching Licking I was to report by courier to headquarters for further orders; and in obedience to said order, two company wagons, with tents, commissaries, arms and ammunition were at once furnished, and I set out for Licking, Texas county; passed Hartville, the county seat of Wright county, and struck the waters of Big Piney. There was considerable snow on the ground at the time. I took the rebels by complete surprise. While they were expecting me from Rolla to Licking, I struck them from the direction they least expected. On reaching Piney, I encountered a rebel force of about sixty men. We had a fight, two or three rebels were killed, and the rest retreated south. From that time until we reached Licking, we had more or less fighting every day. We would strike trails of rebels in the snow, where there appeared to be over one hundred men, but they were so sure that it was a large scout from Springfield that they did not take time to ascertain, but retreated south at once. On reaching Licking, I sent a dispatch to Gen. Schofield, telling of my arrival, and immediately received orders to establish a post and erect a stockade fort, and to issue such orders as I believed would rid the country of those irregular bands of rebels and bushwhackers and protect all in their person and property, especially loyal men. I immediately selected a frame building for my headquarters, with an office near by for the man acting as provost marshal; issued my order requiring all persons who claimed protection from the Federal authorities to come in and take the oath, and bring with them axes, shovels, picks and spades, with their teams, for the purpose of erecting a stockade fort. And further setting out in said order, requiring all persons who knew of any irregular bands of rebels or bushwhackers roaming or passing through the country, to report them at once; and if they failed to report them, they would be taken as bushwhackers and treated as such. In a short time I had erected a complete stockade fort with port-holes, and room enough inside to place all the cavalry horses in case of an attack by the rebels. I had these orders printed and sent out all over the country. In a short time, a man who had been known to be a rebel, but had stayed at home unmolested, but who had been giving aid and comfort to the rebels, came into the office and said: "Captain, I want to see you in your private room." On entering the room he said: "I have read that order of yours. You don't intend to enforce it, do you, Captain?" I said to him that I did or I wouldn't have made it; that the rebels and I could not both stay in that country. He said to me, "Captain, of all the post commanders we have had here, there never was one of them issued such an order as that. You know if I were to report those rebel bands they would kill me." I replied, "Very well; you have read my order, and I have said to you and all others that if you fail to report them I will kill you; and you say if you do report them, they will kill you; now, if you are more afraid of them than you are of me, you will have to risk the consequences; for, by the eternal God! if you fail to report them, I have said to you that I would treat you as a bushwhacker, and you well know how I treat them." He dropped his head for a few minutes, then raised it and said: "Well, it is might hard, Captain." I replied that there were a great many hard things now; asked him where all of his Union neighbors were. He said that they had been forced to leave their homes and were around the Federal posts for the reason that they claimed to be Union men. I told him that "a lot of you rebels have lain here in the country and made more money than you ever made before in your lives, and at the same time you have been giving aid, comfort and encouragement to all of these irregular bands—giving them all the information that they wanted, so that they might know just when to make their raids, and now I propose to break it up and stop it, unless they are able to rout me and drive me away. The government proposes to protect all of you who will come in and take the oath and comply with every requirement set out in the order. All I ask of you men is to give me information of these irregular rebel bands and their whereabouts, and you can again return home and your information will be kept a secret; but this much you are required to do." In a short time a large number of them had come in and enrolled their names, took the oath and went to work on the fort like heroes.

Occasionally one would come in and say "Captain, I want to procure a pass for me and my family through the Federal lines; I want to leave." I would ask him: "What's the matter now? You have stayed here all through the war, up to the present time, and now I have come among you, and offered to protect every one of you who will take the oath and comply with orders." He would reply with a long sigh, "Yes, Captain but that order you have made." I would ask him "what order." "You require all citizens, especially we people who have been rebels, and stayed at home, to report all of the roving bands of rebels and bushwhackers; if we don't do it, you will treat us like bushwhackers; if we were to report them, they would kill us." I said, "Now, you must choose between the two powers; and if you are more afraid of the rebels than you are of me, you will have to risk your chances. You say if you report them, they will kill you. Now, by the Eternal, I am determined to enforce everything that I have set out in that order. This day you must settle in your own mind whom you will obey." As soon as the first roving bands of rebels and guerrillas reached the country for the purpose of raiding the wire road between Rolla and Springfield, the night never was too dark but that this same class of men would come in and report them. I would at once make a detail, send these men right out with them. As soon as they would get near to the rebels, they would dismiss these men and let them go home.

The rebels, for several years, had been sending out a large scout from North Arkansas and the border counties of Missouri and when they would reach Texas and Pulaski counties they would divide into small squads and travel the by-ways and ridges; on reaching the wire road they would then concentrate and lay in wait until the wagon trains and non-combatants who were merchants, were moving through from Rolla to Springfield under the protection of an escort; and all at once they would make a charge upon them from their hiding places, rout the escort, capture the train and all others that might be in company with it, cut the mules loose from the wagon, take all the goods that was not cumberson, especially coffee, sugar, salt and dry goods, place them on the backs of the mules, travel a short distance, divide up again into small parties, take by-ways and mountains, travel fifteen or twenty miles, go into camp; on reaching the counties of Oregon and Shannon, Fulton and Lawrence, of Arkansas, they would concentrate their forces, go into camp, eat, drink, and be merry. As soon as their supplies would run short, they would make another scout of a similar nature. The commanders of the post, as soon as they would attack the trains, would order out a scout to pursue them. They would strike their trail and follow them a short distance to where they would separate and take to the mountains. They would abandon the pursuit, return and swear that the country wasn't worth protecting. In that way they completely outgeneraled the Federal forces and held complete possession of the country almost in sight of the post.

On one occasion, when the weather was very cold and bleak, I knew of their capturing some of the Federal soldiers within one mile of the fort, kept them until the coldest part of the night, just before day, stripped them naked, turned them loose, and they were compelled to travel a mile before they could reach a fire, and they were almost frostbitten. Every Union man was driven away from his home and moved his family to different posts.

The author had declared that he and the rebels could not both remain in the country together; that he would either rout them or they would have to rout him, and for that reason every man that remained in the country would have to aid him in the work. So, in every instance, when he would send a force in pursuit of those raiding bands, he would order the scout to follow them, and when they divided to still continue pursuit of the most visible trail, and when they came in sight to not take time to count noses, but charge them and pursue them until they were completely annihilated. They would go into camp and move at their leisure, but not so when my scouts got in pursuit of them. In a number of instances they would overtake them from twenty to twenty-five miles from the wire road, in camp, having a jolly good time, and the first intimation they would have would be the boys in blue charging in amongst them, shooting right and left, and they would scatter in all directions.

It was but a short time until they remarked to some of the rebel sympathizers that they had never seen such a change in the movements of the Federal scouts; that they used to consider themselves safe from a Federal scout as soon as they left the main road and divided into small squads; but now they were in as much danger in the most secluded spot in the mountains as they were in the traveled roads; therefore, their commanders would have to change their tactics in regard to the scouts, and abandon that part of the country, as almost every scout that they had made to the wire road had proved disastrous since "Old Monks" had been placed in command of the post. In a short time, the Union men, who had been driven from the country, began to return and go onto their farms, and about five months after I had been placed in command of the post, the civil authorities came and held circuit court, Judge Waddle, of Springfield, then being circuit judge.

Skirmishes with the Rebels.

Some time in the summer, Col. Freeman, who was commanding the rebels in northeastern Arkansas, whose headquarters were near the Spring River mill, made a raid and threatened to capture Federal forces that were then at the Licking post. I soon gained information of his intention, made every preparation to repel the attack, also informed the commander at Rolla of the intended raid. Col. Freeman, accompanied by other rebel commanders, concentrated all of the available rebel force then at his command, raided the country, came within about five miles of the post, learned that reinforcements had been sent to the post, countermarched and retreated to his headquarters near the head of Spring river.

A regiment of Federal troops, known as the Fifteenth Veterans, was sent as a reinforcement, with a part of the Fifth Missouri State Militia that was then stationed at Salem, with orders to remain at the post. I received orders to organize all of the available troops and pursue the rebel forces, and, if possible, reach the Spring River mill, in Fulton county, Arkansas, and destroy the mill, which Freeman was using at that time for grinding meal. The Federal force composing the scout, aggregating about three hundred and fifty men, moved from the post at Licking. The author divided his forces, ordering one wing of them to move through Spring Valley, in Texas county; the other wing to move directly in the direction of Thomasville, with orders to form a junction about seven miles from Thomasville, where there was a rebel force stationed. On reaching the Wallace farm, in Oregon county, we came onto a force of rebels, commanded by James Jamison, who had met for the purpose of receiving ammunition which had been smuggled through from Ironton. After an engagement, the rebels fled, leaving one man dead; James Jamison received a flesh wound in the thigh. The Federal force which had been ordered through Spring Valley had had an engagement near the head of the valley, which had delayed them. The plans of the author had been frustrated by coming in contact with the rebels sooner than he expected. As they had retreated in the direction of Thomasville, where the main force was said to be stationed, I continued my march, and in about one mile came onto a rebel camp, where the rebels had cabins erected for quarters; here another spirited engagement took place, the rebels retreating in the direction of Thomasville, the Federal forces still pursuing.

Just above Thomasville the command encountered a strong picket force, fired upon the command, intending to halt it, but being satisfied that there was a trap laid I ordered a charge. The picket force retreated to the left, up a steep hill, and at once the whole rebel force opened fire from the side of the mountain; the bullets flew just above our heads like hail, one ball passing through my hat. We still continued the charge and on reaching the top of the hill, routed the whole rebel force and they again retreated. The author marched into Thomasville, selected his camping ground inside of Captain Olds' barn lot, giving us the advantage of the barn, in case we were attacked by a superior rebel force. I at once dispatched a forage train with strong escort to gather in all the forage possible, as it was very scarce in the country. After we had been in camp about an hour I inquired of Captain Olds if he knew of any corn. He said he did not. In about a half hour my attention was called by one of the captains pointing to a large smokehouse, and on looking, saw the soldiers taking down any amount of first-class corn. I informed the captain that Captain Olds had claimed that he had no corn; to take the quartermaster and let him place a guard over the corn, to see that it was not wasted, and that it was properly apportioned. In a short time the author saw Captain Olds coming. He went to one of the other captains and inquired who the commander was. He was informed that it was Capt. Monks. He came to the author laughing and remarked: "You found my corn, did you? I told you that I had none; I had to secrete it in that building to keep it so that the rebels could not find it." I just remarked to Captain Olds: "You needn't try to hide anything from these lopeared Dutch, for I don't care where you put it they will find it." The men who discovered the corn were all Germans and belonged to a German company. He asked us to feed just as sparingly as possible and leave him a part of the corn, which we did. He then attempted to warn the author of his danger and asked him if he intended to camp there for the night; said that Colonel Freeman had over one thousand men which he could concentrate within five or six hours and that he would cut the author's command all to pieces. The author replied to the captain that that was his business, that Freeman had come up on the scout and claimed that he was wanting to fight; the author prepared for him and expected to accommodate him but he changed his notion and retreated, devastating the country as he went, and now the author was hunting him and his forces and wanted to fight. If he came up that night and attacked the author's command that it would save any more trouble hunting him.

Just about that time the author saw the other part of the command approaching and called the attention of Captain Olds and asked him if he thought that was a part of Freeman's command. After looking a few minutes he said to the author: "They are Federal troops." I asked him if he thought we would be able to remain there until morning? He said that he thought we would and invited me to come into his house and eat supper. While at supper asked if we intended to march any further south. The author informed him that if his information was correct in regard to Freeman's forces we were about as far away from home as we ought to get and that we had better move back in the direction of the post. The author ordered the command to be ready to march by early daylight, next morning broke camp and moved in the direction of Spring river. On reaching the head of Warm fork of Spring river, we encountered another rebel force; had a short engagement, and they again retreated. On reaching the head of Spring river about the middle of the afternoon, we again met a rebel force; after considerable firing they retreated.

The author moved up near the mill and went into camp. The mill was grinding corn with quite a lot of corn on hand, but the miller left and retreated with the rebels. The author soon placed a substitute in his place and the boys had a fine time baking corn cakes.

After supper, some of the men had just retired to rest, when the rebels again made a fierce attack; after fighting for twenty or twenty-five minutes they retreated a short distance and went into camp, the river dividing the two forces. During the night the two pickets would dare each other to cross the river. During the night there came a heavy rain and made the Warm fork of Spring river swimming; there was no way to cross except on the mill dam.

The next morning about daylight the author ordered them to take the millstones and break them up and destroy the machinery so it would be impossible to grind; dismounted about one hundred men, placed them in hiding and marched away a short distance, thinking the rebels would cross over and we would surprise and capture them. But on seeing the Federals break camp and marching up on the west side of the river, they broke camp and marched up on the east side of the river. The author then mounted his men and marched up the Warm fork to where he effected a crossing, marched about ten miles, went into camp for the purpose of getting breakfast. Just after breakfast, the author noticed the advance of a rebel force march out on another road; as soon as they discovered that the Federals were in camp, they fell back and the author at once mounted his men. On the other road, as there was a considerable hill that hid them from sight, he formed his men in two lines in a V; detailed a strong advance force, ordered them to move onto the rebels and charge them, and in case they found that they were too strong, to retreat back between the lines for the purpose of drawing the rebel forces in between the lines. After a fierce conflict, lasting but a few minutes, the rebels again retreated, leaving a rebel Major dead upon the ground. We then marched into Thomasville and had another running fight with the rebels, went into camp and the next morning marched back in the direction of the post at Licking, reaching the post about 10 o'clock that night. The author again took command at the post and the Fifteenth Veterans returned to Rolla.

Ridding the Country of Bushwhackers.

It soon became very rare to hear of a rebel scout north of the mountain. Both rebel and Union men who claimed protection by the Federal authorities began to repair and improve their farms again. During the time that the author was in command of the post, which continued up to the time that peace was made, his command had routed and completely driven from the country all irregular and roving bands of rebels and bushwhackers and had had numbers of small engagements in which there had been from eight to ninety of the most desperate class of men that ever lived, killed, which was shown in the adjutant general's report. After they had been driven out of the county, they located in the counties of Oregon, Shannon and Dent, and at once commenced pillaging and robbing all classes of citizens, irrespective of their political adherence. Col. Freeman sent a courier through the lines with a dispatch, stating the condition of affairs, and asking that an armistice be entered into between Col. Freeman's scouts and the scouts which might be sent out from the post, with an understanding that they were going to aid each other in routing and driving out these irregular bands.

While engaged in that work they were not to fire on each other, but to co-operate. The author was to enter into the agreement if it could be effected. Col. Freeman sent Capt. Cook into Oregon and Shannon counties to locate those roving guerilla bands, and in some way, unknown to either Col. Freeman or myself, they gained the information, and while Capt. Cook was in Oregon county locating them, they waylaid him and killed him. Col. Freeman, realizing the fact that they had come into possession of the whole scheme, came to the conclusion that we had better abandon the agreement. He organized scouts and captured and shot some of the most desperate characters that were leaders, while the author kept a vigilant watch to keep them from crossing over into Texas or adjoining counties. At the time peace was made, it was admitted by the law-abiding people, irrespective of party, that the command of Col. Monks had completely rid the country of all irregular bands of rebels and had made it safe, in a short time after had taken command of the post, for forage trains and all other classes of citizens to pass on the wire road from Rolla to Springfield unmolested, and that very often they passed through without an escort.

Battle of Mammoth Spring.

Col. Wood, commanding the Sixth Missouri cavalry, left Rolla on the 7th day of March, 1862, with about two hundred and fifty men, for the purpose of making a scout south into the counties of Oregon and Howell and Fulton county, Arkansas, to ascertain the strength of the rebel forces in that portion of the country; reached Licking and went into camp. The next morning he broke camp and marched to Jack's fork, in Shannon county, and on the morning of the 9th marched to Thomasville; on the 10th he marched to Mammoth Spring, Arkansas. On reaching Mammoth Spring they learned that there was a rebel force in camp on the south fork of Spring river, just below Salem, and on the morning of the 11th they broke camp and marched upon the rebels. On reaching the rebel encampment they found they had cut timber and blockaded the road, so that it was impossible to reach the forces, except on foot. In coming within a few hundred yards of the rebels, lying concealed behind the timbers, they opened fire on the advance of the Federal forces. The Federal forces had two small pieces of artillery that they unlimbered and brought into use. The rebels having no artillery, were soon dislodged from the first line of works, and they stubbornly fell back about one quarter of a mile, and went in behind the second fortifications that had been hurriedly erected. After fighting for an hour and a half or two hours the Federal force being greatly outnumbered, and the rebels having themselves so obstructed, Col. Woods saw that it was useless to further continue the fight and retreated. On the next night he reached Howell Valley just below West Plains and went into camp and on the morning of the 13th they broke camp and marched in the direction of Houston, Missouri, reaching Houston sometime after night. The Federal loss in the battle referred to was seven killed and wounded. The Confederate loss was said to be twenty-five or thirty killed and wounded. Colonels Coleman and Woodside were commanding the Confederates.

Col. Woods being in command of the post of Houston, learning that there was considerable of a rebel force, standing at West Plains, Missouri, under the command of Coleman and others, organized a scout and on the 24th day of February, 1862, broke camp and marched in the direction of West Plains, for the purpose of attacking the rebel forces stationed at that place, taking two small mounted howitzers strapped on mules, made a forced march, and in the early part of the day on the 25th reached West Plains. West Plains had a frame court house in the center of the square where the present court house is located. The road at that time led due north where Washington avenue is located until it struck the hill; also there was a road which led east where East Main street is now located and on passing what was known as the Thomas Howell farm, turned directly north in the direction of Gunters Valley. The rebels had a strong picket thrown out on both roads; a part of the rebel command was quartered in the court house. Woods being advised of the condition of the rebels and where they were all quartered, supposing that they would take advantage of the court house when the attack was made, selected a high position where the road first struck the hill, planted his artillery, divided his forces and made a flank movement, ordered them to strike the lower road and advance on the pickets and as soon as they were fired upon, to charge them, while he would remain with the other part of the force in readiness to dislodge them with his artillery in case they used the court house as a fortification. On the advance coming in sight of the rebel pickets, they fired and retreated with the Federal forces pursuing. The rebel forces at once rallied their forces and took possession of the court house. As soon as Col. Woods saw them file into the house he leveled his cannon and fired a shell which struck the house near its center and passed clear through; that was the first artillery that the rebel command ever had heard. They filed out of the house faster than they went into it; then Col. Woods moved with his forces directly upon the forces near the court house when a general engagement ensued. The rebels retreated west on the road near where West Main street is now located and a running fight continued for about one mile, when Woods abandoned the pursuit, marched back into West Plains, and again returned to Houston. The losses on both sides were light, several, however, being killed or wounded.

"Uncle Tommy" and His Crutches.

I will relate an incident which occurred during the fight. Old "Uncle Tommy" Howell as he was familiarly known, resided just below the town spring a short distance from the road; he had a sister living with him who was an old maid, and was known as "Aunt Polly." Howell being one among the early settlers of Howell Valley, had taken an active part in organizing Howell county, which took its name from him and he had been once representative of the county. The author heard him relate the circumstance in a speech delivered in West Plains after the war was over. He said when the fight came up that he was sitting on his front porch: all at once he heard firing commence, and heard horses feet and saw the rebel pickets coming on full gallop horseback, with the Federals close onto them with pistols in hand firing on them; he had been afflicted with rheumatism for years and one of his legs was drawn crooked and he hadn't attempted to walk without a crutch for several years; when he saw the men coming and the others shooting at them, he supposed that every shot was killing a man; he said they came right by his door and he never became excited while they were passing; as soon as they got near the court house they then made a stand, where it appeared to him that there were thousands of shots being exchanged every minute. They had all passed his house and he was sitting there unmolested, when his sister, who was known as "Aunt Polly" ran out on the porch and cried out at the top of her voice "Lord a massy, Uncle Tommy, run for your life; you have been a public man and they will kill you, sure." He said it so excited him that he sprang to his feet. All below his house the valley was covered with hazel brush and snow was lying on the ground. He first looked toward where the firing was going on and said "My God! they certainly have got them very near all killed in this time" for he was under the impression that every shot killed a man. He started southwest from his house, ran about a quarter of a mile, jumped over behind a log; he had hardly gotten still when he imagined he heard the horses feet of the Federals in pursuit of him; he raised up and looked, could not see any person, so ran about another quarter, jumped over behind another log and as soon as he got still, the first thought came into his mind that they were still in pursuit, for he could hear the horses' feet, but on reflecting a moment he found that it was his heart beating; he said he could still hear the firing and he thought they intended to kill them all before they quit. He had a son-in-law by the name of Hardin Brown living on the Warm fork of Spring river, about twenty miles distant, and he started on foot and never stopped traveling until he reached his house. On reaching the house, his daughter asked him how, in the name of God, he ever got there without his crutches. He said that was the first time that he had thought of his crutches. He began to notice his legs and the crooked leg was just as straight as the well leg. He said that it completely cured him of his rheumatism and he had the use of that leg just the same as he ever did the other leg, and never used a crutch afterwards. After the war he removed to Oregon county and was elected to the legislature, and died a member of the legislature.

Disposing of Union Men.

In the spring of 1862 there was a man by the name of Mawhinney, living about six miles below West Plains, in Howell valley, a Union man, but who had taken no part either way, except to express an opinion. About fifteen men belonging to a rebel scout went to his house, called for their dinners, some of them had him shoe their horses, and after they had their horses shod and got their dinner, they told him that they wanted him to go with them. His wife said to them "It ain't possible that after you have been treated as kindly as you have been you are going to take Mr. Mawhinney prisoner; you men certainly will not hurt him." They made no reply, carried him about one half mile from his home, shot him off of his horse, took the horse and went on, leaving the body on the side of the road. His wife with what other help she could get brought him in and had him buried.

About two weeks afterwards, in the spring of 1862, there was a man by the name of Bacon who lived near West Plains, who has some relatives living in this county at the present time. He was a Union man but had taken no part either way, except to express himself openly in favor of the Union. There came a scout of about twenty men and arrested him, started west with him in the direction of South Fork, and on reaching the vicinity where Homeland is located, left the road a short distance, shot him off of his horse. Went on to a house about one mile distant, called for their dinner. The woman in preparing dinner fried some bacon; after they were seated at the table she passed the bacon to them; several of them remarked that they didn't want any, that they had had some bacon, but had just disposed of it a short time before they reached the house. After Bacon had laid where he fell dead for two or three days he was found and being considerably decomposed a hole was dug and the body placed into it and covered up, where his dust remains until the present day.

Union Supplies Captured by Rebels.

In the spring of 1862, the department commander re-established the military post at Springfield. All of the commissaries and forage had to be conveyed from Rolla to Springfield, as the terminus of the railroad was at Rolla, by wagon trains, a distance of one hundred and twenty miles. It required a large escort of soldiers to guard the trains to prevent the rebels from capturing them. All of the country south of the wire road was in possession of the rebels. There was scarcely a wagon train that passed on the road without being attacked by the rebels. They made their attacks generally on the front and rear of the trains, and before the wagon masters could corral the trains, they would capture some of the wagons, make the teamsters drive into the woods, cut the mules loose from the wagons, take sacks of coffee, salt, sugar and other commissaries, tie them on the backs of the mules, divide into small bunches and retreat into the hills. Very often the escort would have to send back to Rolla for reinforcements. The train would be tied up from twelve to fifteen hours before it could move on. It became a mystery to the Federal commanders how the Confederates could concentrate a force of men numbering from fifty to three hundred, and the first intimation the escort would have, they, the rebels, would come out of the brush at some secluded spot, yelling, whooping and shooting, and charge upon the wagon train. They would generally capture more or less of the loaded wagons with the above results, and it became a question with the military authorities at Rolla and Springfield how to capture or rout these bands, and as to how they managed to keep that number of men near to the wire road and yet the Federals were unable to discover their hiding places.

About the 15th day of August, the department commander ordered Capt. Murphy to take five hundred men and two pieces of artillery and move south from Rolla; to go as far south as he thought it would be safe, without placing his men so far inside of the Confederate lines that they might be captured; and, if possible, to learn the rebel movements and location of their troops. Capt. Murphy broke camp at Rolla and moved south about fifteen miles, was fired on by the rebels from the brush, marched about twenty-five miles, went into camp; on the next morning resumed the march, hadn't marched more than five miles until they were fired on from the brush; they were fired on four or five times that day, and went into camp near Thomasville. The next day he threw out skirmish lines on each side of his command, and resumed the march down the Warm fork of Spring river. There was more or less skirmishing all day. He camped on the Warm fork and the next morning marched over to the Myatt, where we had quite a skirmish. The rebels again retreated in the direction of the Spring River mill, where they were said to have a thousand men.

Here the command countermarched back to Rolla, having captured fifty or sixty prisoners; the Federals had a few men wounded.

In the spring of 1862, the Federal troops advanced on Springfield from Rolla. The rebels retreated west and the Federals again established a military post at Springfield. The rebels continued to retreat west until they reached Prairie Grove, where they concentrated their forces and the memorable battle of that name was fought, the Federal troops being victorious. The Confederates retreated from the state.

The military post at Springfield being over one hundred miles west of Rolla, the terminus of the South Pacific railroad, three-fourths of the distance being in possession of the rebels, all the forage and commissaries had to be conveyed by wagon train. The main rebel forces having been driven from the state, and all of the country south of the wire road, with few exceptions, being in possession of the rebels, the Union men with their families having been driven from their homes. The leading Confederate officers met and held a council of war and decided to change their tactics. The first thing was to place two or three hundred well-armed Confederate soldiers south of and near the wire road leading from Rolla to Springfield, and so harass the wagon trains that the government wouldn't be able to get forage and commissaries through to Springfield, and thus force the Federals to abandon the post. In furtherance of this move, they ordered their soldiers to be taken near to the line of the road and divided into squads of from five to twenty-five men, conceal their arms and claim to be private citizens, live off the country and be so arranged that when a wagon train was about to leave Rolla, they could be called together on short notice; and when they wanted to make a more extensive raid, Confederate soldiers from as far south as the head of Spring river would march up and meet them and make a general raid.

The government had considerable trouble to learn the hiding places of these men, but they finally got officers who were acquainted with the country and men who were bona fide citizens, and knew who were citizens and who were not, and broke up their hiding places and drove them further south. It was learned that a part of this Confederate force was composed of men who claimed to be citizens when they were not making their raids.

Bravery of Captain Alsup.

In the summer of 1863, the Federal authorities established a military post at Clark's mill, in Douglas county, Missouri, on Bryant's fork of White river, erected a post and stationed some Illinois troops under the command of a Colonel, with Capt. Alsup's company, which was composed entirely of Douglas county citizens, in all about two hundred and fifty or three hundred men. Gen. Joe Shelby, a Confederate, with about five hundred troops, made a forced march from Arkansas and during the night time surrounded the fort, and the next morning had his artillery in readiness to open fire. He ordered a complete surrender of the garrison. The captain of the fort asked for a few minutes to consider the matter; at the expiration of the time, the Colonel in command agreed to surrender, stack up the guns and side arms in the fort, march his men outside and make an unconditional surrender. When the commander of the fort ordered his men and officers to stack their arms and march out, Capt. Lock Alsup and his company refused, and being cavalry, ordered his men to arm themselves and be ready to move whenever ordered. While the commander of the fort was having the remainder of the garrison stack their arms, Capt. Alsup and his company made a bold dash for liberty, came out of the fort shooting right and left, took the rebels by surprise, broke the rebel line, went through, being mounted on good horses, retreated up Bryant's fork with the rebels in pursuit. While going through an old field that had grown up to burrs about as high as a man's head, Fritz Krause, father of the assistant postmaster at

West Plains, was thrown from his horse, rolled under the burrs, the rebels passed by and never saw him. He laid in the burrs until dark, then made his escape and rejoined his company at Springfield. The rebels pursued them for about two miles, then returned to their command. Gen. Shelby paroled the prisoners, and such things as he could not carry with him he destroyed, the fort being burned. He resumed his march in the direction of Springfield and was reinforced by about five hundred troops. During this time, Capt. Alsup and his men had reached Springfield and, strange to say, hadn't lost a man; had a few slightly wounded. Gen. Brown, who was in command of the post at Springfield, was said to be a brother-in-law of Gen. Shelby, and on Shelby's arrival at Springfield he demanded the surrender of the garrison. The Federal troops held a consultation and concluded to fight. After a brief engagement, Gen. Shelby drew his troops off and moved north; there were several killed and wounded on both sides. Gen. Brown's arm was broken by a piece from a shell. Gen. Shelby continued his raid towards the Missouri river, had several small engagements and then retreated from the state. Capt. Alsup and his brave men should be held in memory by all comrades, especially by the loyal people of Douglas and Ozark counties, for their heroic action in charging through the rebel lines and making their escape after the post commander had attempted to deliver them into the hands of the rebels.

The fort at Clark's mill was never rebuilt. Capt. Alsup and the loyal men of Douglas and Ozark counties and part of Wright county built a temporary fort near the center of Douglas county, and old and young organized themselves into companies and armed themselves. With the help of Capt. Alsup's company, they appointed a few of their men as scouts, while the others worked in their fields. The scouts were out night and day along the state line and if a rebel scout attempted to raid the counties, notice was given all along the line and the men were all up in arms and ready to meet the raiders. It reminds one of reading the history of the early settlements along the Indian border. The settlers would build forts and put out sentinels; if the Indians were seen advancing, word was given and the families would hurry to the fort and the men arm themselves to drive the invaders back. So this organization, with some assistance from the post at Springfield, held Douglas and a part of

Ozark and Wright counties during the remainder of the Civil War, and after the war was over, Douglas county gained the title of "Old Loyal Douglas County." These old soldiers and comrades are fast falling and very soon there will be none left to tell of the heroisms and sacrifices they made for the country they loved. Will these comrades and their sons and daughters be so ungrateful that they will let their heroism and sacrifices die with them and be forgotten, never to be written in history? The answer will be no, a thousand times no. The history of their heroism and sacrifices shall be written and go down to their children and their children's children, and may "Old Glory" ever wave over the country that they love so well and for which they made so many sacrifices.

Bushwhacking in Howell County.

The writer wants to say that there was not a Union man nor a single Union family left at home, from Batesville, Ark. to Rolla, Mo., a distance of two-hundred miles. The writer especially wants to speak for Howell County, Mo. The rebels took quite a number of Union men from their homes and shot them, some of them being old men. I will name a few of them that were shot: Morton R. Langston, the father of T. J. and S. J. Langston, while he was hauling wood; Jeff Langston, one of the firm of Langston Bros. was riding on the wood at the time his father was shot. I asked a leading rebel after the war, why they shot Langston. His reply was: "He talked too much." Shot Mawhinney, Bacon and a number of others. Now I want to say right here, notwithstanding the treatment the Union men received from the rebels, not a single Confederate was ever taken from his home and shot or otherwise injured during the whole Civil War and no truthful Confederate will say to the contrary. There never was but one Confederate hurt after being taken prisoner in Howell County and he wasn't a citizen of Howell County; was said to be a north Missouri bushwhacker, charged with being one of the parties that shot old Mr. Langston, Mahinney and Bacon. A Federal scout in the year 1864 captured him below West Plains and the next morning they hung him to a smoke-house rafter. Notwithstanding a few of the friends of the bushwhackers will tell to strangers that the writer shot a man in this county, by the name of Hawkins, in the lap of his family, which is a positive lie; the facts are these: Hawkins was one of the worst bushwhackers and murderers that ever lived in Howell County and was commanding a company of bushwhackers at the time he was shot. A short time before he was shot he had captured one of his cousins, by the name of Washington Hawkins, a Federal soldier, and taken from him a fine mare with his saddle and rig complete.

In the spring of 1864, a battalion of the 11th Missouri Cavalry, commanded by Col. Woods, had been ordered to report to Col. Livingston at Batesville, Ark. The writer had been ordered to report at Rolla, Mo., with his command. Col. Woods had camped near West Plains the previous night, the next morning resumed his march towards Batesville; after he had passed West Plains a few miles, Hawkins and his bushwhackers fired on them from the brush and they continued to fire on them every few miles for sixteen miles. Our force met the force of Col. Woods at the state line where Col. Woods informed me how they had been firing upon his men all morning. He had taken a man prisoner by the name of William Krause, whom he turned over to me. Both forces resumed the march, he in the direction of Batesville, Ark., and I in the direction of Rolla, Mo. The prisoner told the writer that he knew the parties who had been firing on Col. Woods' command; that they had a camp by a pond in a secluded place, and were commanded by Hawkins and Yates; that it was about four miles almost west. I told Krause if he would place me on trail he could then go home. He did so and I then released him. Krause said there were about fifty rebels in the command.

We trailed them about two miles and came in sight of a house that belonged to old Mr. Newberry, a Union man. He and his family had been run off from home. I saw a horse hitched to the side of the door, and supposed there were more inside of the house; there was a skirt of timber that enabled us to get within about sixty yards of the house. I ordered my men, when we reached a given point, to charge upon the house, dismount and reach the wall of the house and demand the surrender of all persons that might be within. We were about fifteen feet from the door when Hawkins came out and attempted to mount his horse. The author demanded his surrender, but he drew his pistol to fire, the author having his pistol already in hand and presented, fired on him; the author was sitting in his saddle when he fired on him.

The men examined the house and found he was the only man in it. The horse he was riding was the one he had taken from his cousin, Washington Hawkins, a short time previous, with a government rig complete. Washington Hawkins resided at Bakersfield, Mo., and got his horse and rig again. We took the trail again, but dark came on us and we lost it. These are the facts surrounding the whole case, the killing of Hawkins, one of the worst bandits and guerillas that ever roamed through South Missouri and led the worst band of men in the state. I had previously taken him prisoner and he took the oath of allegiance, went right back and joined his command and, if possible, he was worse than before. I must say that there are few men in Howell county that claim to be Confederates, who tell strangers that Monks shot Hawkins down in the lap of his family and that he, Hawkins, was a good man. The writer wants to say that no truthful Confederate will tell any such thing; they will tell you that Hawkins was a bad man. Ask such Confederates as Capt. Howard, Mark Cooper, Judge Dryer, John Ledsinger, Harvey Kelow, Daniel Galloway, P. N. Gulley and a number of others, if Hawkins was a good man.

The writer wants to say that he don't believe all the Confederates were in favor of killing and driving out the families of Union men, but the most bitter element got in power and being backed by the order of Gen. McBride, to force all the Union men to join the Confederate service, or hang them, those Confederates who were opposed to such treatment were afraid to open their mouths for fear they would receive the same treatment. You don't hear these same men, that talked about Monks shooting Hawkins, say a word about Hawkins and his bushwhackers shooting Union men all over Howell county. There never were but two houses burned in Howell county by the Union men during the Civil war, and houses owned by these men had been previously burned by the Confederates. The town of West Plains was burned by the Confederates to keep the Federals from holding a post at West Plains.

The writer wants to say that on his return after the war, in the spring of 1866, he met rebels, both those that had been officers and soldiers, and never spoke a harsh word to them, asked them if they thought both parties could now live together; their answer was, that they thought they could. All that they asked was that they be protected. The writer assured them that both Federal and Confederates would be protected by the civil laws and all they would be asked to do would be to aid in a strict enforcement of civil laws, which they readily promised to do. The Union men who had returned to their homes and the late Confederates joined together and went to building and repairing old church houses and school-houses and soon were found worshiping together in the same church and sending their children to the same school-houses and the old ties that had existed before the war were being re-united. The country appeared to be prosperous and the old war spirit appeared to be fast dying out among the people.

I suppose the writer holds more commissions than any other man in the state, both military and civil and there never was a charge preferred against the writer of any failure to discharge his duties by the government or state. While in the military service thousands of dollars passed through the hands of the writer for forage and commissaries and ordinance stores and clothing, every dollar was accounted for and all contraband property was turned over to the government. I never converted, to my own private use, five cents of any man's property or money, before or after the war, in the war, nor since the war.

The writer is now residing within about twenty-five miles of where his father located in the year 1844 and there are several persons yet living that have been intimately acquainted with the writer since his boyhood up to the present time, namely James Kellet, Sr., Marion Kellet, present county treasury of Howell county, Washington Hawkins of Bakersfield, Mo., and quite a number of others that have been acquainted with the writer from forty to fifty years. The writer wants to say right here that he is not ashamed of anything he did before the war, in the war, nor since the war, and on his return home to Howell county on meeting the late rebels, he never spoke a harsh word to one of them, but received them kindly and said to them that the civil laws should be strictly enforced against all alike, Confederate and Federal.

In the year 1861, sometime in the month of September, after the Federals retreated from Springfield, Mo. and the Confederates had taken possession of Springfield, there was one Capt. Brixey who was captain of a company of home guards residing in the edge of Webster County, Mo.; soon after the Confederates took possession of the post, they ordered a captain belonging to a Texas regiment to detail one company and proceed to the residence of Capt. Brixey and arrest him. Capt. Brixey having no notice of the approach of the scouts, he and one of his men were sitting in the house; the first they knew they had a line within thirty yards of his door, hailed them and presented their guns and demanded their surrender. Capt. Brixey said, "The ———— you say." Both parties fired on each other about the same time, the man with Brixey fell dead, Brixey shot and killed the Confederate captain and wounded one or two other Confederates; he retreated through his house and into his orchard and made his escape; one of his arms was broken by the shot from the rebels from which he entirely recovered and lived many years afterwards, and has a son residing in this county at the present time.

Colonel Freeman's Second Raid.

Sometime in the Spring of 1862 Col. Freeman, not being satisfied with his first raid on the Federal troops at Salem, planned the second raid to attack the troops then stationed at Salem, Missouri; he organized his scout and compelled one Robert Bolin, who now resides in Howell County, to pilot him through the lines, as he, Bolin, had lived near Salem before the war. On reaching Salem, Col. Freeman halted his troops and planned his attack.

The Federal troops had no knowledge of the approach of any rebel forces; they were in squads around Salem. Freeman divided his forces and gave them a countersign and selected a spot near a deep ditch in the road and instructed them, if they were defeated and got scattered to concentrate at that ditch which was beyond the Federal lines a distance of some miles; on reaching the ditch they were to remain until they all were collected. After the first ones reached the place, it being dark, if they saw others approaching they would halt them and demand the countersign, and if they couldn't give it they were to fire on them without any further delay, knowing they were enemies. On reaching the public square they encountered a bunch of the Federal troops in a building; fired on them, wounded a few, a man by the name of Jacob Shoffler now residing in Howell County was in the house at the time, and they cut his clothes in about twenty different places with bullets and never drew blood; Maj. Santee was commanding, with one other officer. After they had rallied, all being in disorder, Maj. Santee ordered a charge on the rebels. Armed with an old pistol he met Col. Freeman of the Confederate side. Freeman had just shot out; Maj. Santee ordered his surrender. Col. Freeman started to run, Maj. Santee in close pursuit, snapped his old pistol, which failed to fire. He then threw the pistol at Col. Freeman, struck him somewhere between the shoulders, drew his sabre, and still continued the pursuit. There was a creek near by and a stone fence had been built along the side of it; the creek had been frozen over and a skiff of snow on it at the time. Just as Freeman reached the stone fence Maj. Santee made a thrust at him with his sabre, inflicting a slight wound; about that time, for the purpose of escaping, Col. Freeman sprang over the stone fence and lit into the creek. Maj. Santee, being on horseback, could not pursue any further. The rebels by this time were scattered in all directions, started to retreat. It being very dark, the first ones fifty or sixty in number reached the ditch, halted to wait for the remainder of them to collect. In a short time about thirty or forty more of them appeared in sight, retreating with considerable speed; they were halted, the countersign demanded. They had become so excited in the fight they had forgotten the countersign and failed to give it. So those who arrived first opened fire and wounded several of them, scattering them to the woods. They failed to concentrate until they had retreated south about 30 miles where they learned the mistake they had made and that they had fired upon their own men. Maj. Santee being of the opinion that he had seriously wounded Freeman with his sabre, concluded to investigate. On reaching the stone fence where he made his leap they looked over into the creek on the ice and (Col. Freeman being a large man) it looked like a large ox had been thrown over from the hole that he made in the ice. They saw that he had crossed the creek and reached the other side and saw no signs of blood. In the engagement there were about five or six wounded and killed.

In the summer of 1863 there was a Federal scout organized at Springfield, commanded by Col. Holland. It was ordered to move by way of Douglas county, get reinforcements then stationed at the fort, and from there march through the county of Ozark. They entered the county of Fulton, Ark., where they had several small engagements. After considerable fighting and capturing a number of prisoners, they returned to Springfield; loss, killed and wounded, very small.

In the fall of 1863, Col. Tracy, with a force of rebels, made a raid from Fulton county, marched up through Ozark county, and on reaching the Union settlement in Douglas county, he shot and killed nearly every man he captured, robbed houses, took everything in the house and out of doors, and burned the houses as he went. After raiding and pillaging a number of houses, he came to a house where a Union man by the name of Mahan and one by the name of McCarty were working in the blacksmith shop, with their arms near them. They were members of the home guard. The rebels demanded the surrender of the two men, and as it was generally believed that if a man surrendered to those irregular forces that it was sure death, they refused to surrender. When the forces of Col. Tracy commenced firing through the cracks of the shop, the men returned the fire. Mahan killed one rebel, and they wounded two or three others. The rebels shot McCarty down, shooting him eight or ten times after he fell, knocked the door down and rushed upon Mahan, disarmed him, took him prisoner and then continued their retreat. After reaching Fulton county, near the bayou, they took Mahan into the woods, stripped him naked and shot him, leaving his body lying on the ground unburied. Strange to say, in regard to McCarty, after he had been shot eight or ten times and left for dead, he recovered from the wounds and became hearty and stout.

Some time in the early part of the spring of 1864, a man by the name of Mahan deserted from the 11th Missouri cavalry, stationed at Batesville, and on reaching Howell county, about two miles from where Valley Star school house is now located, a bunch of bushwhackers commanded by B. F. Hawkins and Thomas Yates captured him, took him into the woods a short distance, stripped him naked and shot him, leaving his body lying on the ground, unburied. After he had lain there nearly a week, a man now residing in Howell county took a hoe and shovel and raked up some rocks and pitched them upon the decomposed body and threw a few shovels of dirt on him. As it was but a short distance from the road, the stench from the decomposing body was offensive to persons who traveled by.

Col. Monks Enforces the Civil Law.

In the month of July, 1865, the author was ordered to declare the civil law in force in the counties of Texas, Dent, Shannon, Oregon, Howell, Ozark and Douglas and report to his regiment again at Springfield for the purpose of being discharged. The long-looked-for and final result of the war had come with victory couched upon every man who had borne his flag to the breeze of his country, and to those who had lain themselves on the altar of their country and died that it might live.

There was general rejoicing among the loyal people, that there was not a foot of territory on American soil but where the stars and stripes once more floated unmolested, either by foreign or domestic enemies, and while the Confederates had fought manfully for what they conceived to be right, and had laid many of their sons on the altar and sacrificed them to a cause that they believed to be right, yet a large majority of them rejoiced when they learned that the cruel war was over. Although their cause was forever lost, yet the country that they had loved so well and the flag still floated and invited them back as erring sons.

The 16th regiment, with a large number of other regiments, was discharged at Springfield. Then a scene ensued that Americans had never witnessed before; the blue and the grey began to meet and greet each other as friends and seemed to forget that just a few months previous they had been meeting each other armed, for the purpose of slaying one another. A general amnesty proclamation had been granted by Gen. Grant to all the rebels who had surrendered. Their officers and commanders should discharge them and they should be allowed to retain their side arms for their own protection and return home for the purpose of again building up and establishing their homes; again meet their wives, their children, fathers and mothers, neighbors and friends, and once more be united in all the ties of love; to again reinstate churches, and instead of studying and practicing the art of war, they should beat their swords into pruning hooks and aid in establishing and building up society and good government.

But, lo! one of the most sad and heartrending scenes confronted many Confederates and Federals on returning to the places where they had once had happy homes and sweet families, they were not found. During the terrible war, many of the loved ones that they had left behind had been called from time to eternity. The home had disappeared and nothing was left but the soil; all of the improvements being entirely destroyed. But they, with the courage of heroes, gathered the fragments of their families, went to work improving and building houses, refencing their farms, reerecting church houses and school houses, and in a short time the men who had lately been enemies and borne arms against each other, were again neighbors and friends, associating together, sending their children to the same school, becoming members of the same church; all experienced the difference between a civil war and peace and fraternity. Many of them expressed themselves that they had read of civil wars, but never realized the effect of civil war until after they had passed through the present one; but they could not understand why they called it "civil" war, for if there was anything civil about the war they never experienced that part of it.

The author's family had been residing at Rolla during most of the time of the war. He commenced making preparations to return to his home in Howell county in the fall of 1865. He began to organize an immigration party of men who wanted to locate in Howell county and a number of men who had left their homes in that county. Just a short time before the parties were ready to leave Rolla for Howell county, he was met by several men who asked: "Why, Monks, ain't you afraid to go back to Howell county? You have fought the rebels so bitterly and contested every inch of ground during the whole war, and some of them hate you so badly, that I would be afraid that they would kill me." The author replied that he felt like Gen. Putnam, when the British attempted to bribe him and said that the colonies never could succeed in gaining their independence, and that he had better return and renew his allegience to the Crown. The General's reply was, "D——n a man that is not for his country." Now, my reply to you is, that I have forfeited almost all of my means and shattered the happiness of my family in contending and fighting for the preservation of the government; besides, myself and family have been exiled and banished from our home, and if the rebels had succeeded, all would have been gone. But now the government has been victorious in crushing the rebellion, liberty and protection have been once more guaranteed to every citizen, high or low, rich or poor, and, in the language of Gen. Putnam, I say, "D——n a man that is afraid to go back and enjoy the fruits of his victory."

Within a few days about twenty-five families left Rolla for West Plains, and on arriving at West Plains, went into camp. There was not a single building left in West Plains, as the Confederates had burned the whole town in time of the war, with the exception of one store building, which was burned by the Federal troops. The Confederates' object in burning the town was to prevent the Federals from establishing a post. The author procured some clapboards, built an addition to an old stable about two hundred yards south of where James' livery stable is now located.

Soon after we had reached West Plains and gone into camp, Capt. Howard, Capt. Nicks and a number of other rebels who were residing in the county, came in, met the author and said to him: "Captain, I am proud to meet you." The author replied, "I am proud to meet you. What do you think now in regard to the two parties living together?" They said that they were satisfied that both parties could live together, that all they wanted was protection. The author remarked that the rebels had been in control of the country for several years, but the loyal men were going to take charge of it and run it now, and as the loyal men had been contending for the enforcement of the law and claimed that every American citizen was entitled to the protection of the law, the author could promise them that, if they would fall into line and help enforce the law, they should receive equal protection with any other class of citizens; to which they replied that they were willing to do so, but there were roving bands of rebels and guerillas which had not been subject to the control of the Confederate authorities, and still refused to lay down their arms, and might yet cause some trouble.

The author was appointed sheriff of Howell county, W. Z. Buck circuit and county clerk and Peter Lemons, Judge Alsup and ——— were appointed county judges. There had been an old school house about a quarter of a mile east of West Plains that was still standing. They met at that school house, organized and set the civil government of the county in working order. Soon after, Governor Fletcher ordered an election and the author was elected to the state legislature, tendered his resignation as sheriff, which was accepted and W. D. Mustion was appointed to the vacancy. In a few weeks the author went to Jefferson City, tendered his credentials and was sworn in and became a member of the legislature.

Everything, so far as Howell county was concerned, appeared to move off quietly, while the counties of Oregon and Shannon, with a few of the border counties, were entirely controlled by irregular bands of late rebels, who openly declared that the civil law should not be enforced in those counties; that the Confederacy was whipped, but they were not and they intended to live off the government; they were armed to the teeth.

During the winter of 1865 and the year 1866, Howell county settled up faster than ever it had at any period before the war; the men who had homes in it and had been forced away on account of the war, mostly returned and commenced to improve their farms. Their houses, outhouse and improvements, generally, having been destroyed, the soil was the only thing left. The town also built up rapidly and in the year 1866 the inhabitants had increased to six or eight hundred.

In the fall of 1866 at the general election the author was re-elected to the legislature and Capt. Alley, who had been a Confederate all through the war, was elected to the legislature from Oregon county. The author again qualified and was present in the legislature during the whole time, when the great question was brought up before the legislature, as to what disposition the State would make of the first liens held by the state on the different railroads for aid that had been given to the rail-road corporations in the way of state bonds in 1850. In 1855 the state issued her bonds, delivered them to the companies and they went east and put them upon the market in New York and Boston to procure money to construct roads, and the bonds with all the accruing interest, were due the state.

Then for the first time the author learned that many of the men who had been selected to represent the people's interest in the State Legislature, failed to discharge the duties that their constituents had imposed upon them, betrayed their trust, and, through money, were entirely controlled in the interest of the railroad corporations. The author believing that it was one among the greatest duties that were imposed upon men of a representative government, to strictly contend and do all in his power to enact legislation in the interest of the people, therefore took a strong stand in favor of closing out all of the state liens against the different roads, held by the state. During the session of the winter of 1866 what was then known as the South Missouri Pacific, which terminated at Rolla, Missouri, was ordered to be closed out and the road declared forfeited. A resolution passed through both houses of the legislature ordering the Governor to seize it, and that said road be run by the state. In the meantime the Governor was to advertise and sell it. The Governor by authority of law advertised it and sold it for $550,000. Sometime in April the legislature adjourned, to meet in an adjourned session in December, 1867. The author returned home.

The immigration into the country rapidly increasing, prosperity appeared to be on every side; people had plenty of money, good crops, wheat was worth $1 to $1.50 per bushel, stock of all kinds brought first-class prices, peace so far as Howell county was concerned, prosperity and the bettering of the condition of society were moving hand in hand, and the author felt thankful that the war was over.

Outlaw Rule in Oregon and Shannon.

In the fall of 1867, the counties of Oregon and Shannon, were still controlled by those roving bands of outlaws who ruled the counties with an iron hand. A despotism, unequalled at any stage of the war, existed there. There was a public gathering in the fall of 1867 in Thomasville. Col. Jamison, one of the leaders of these outlawed bands rode into town at the head of about fifty men, well armed, shot two men's brains out, paraded the streets and swore that any man that attempted to enforce the civil law against them, would fare the same; rode out unmolested and there was not a single attempt made by the civil authorities to arrest one of them. In a few days Jamison with some of his men rode into town and a man by the name of Philip Arbogast, the father-in-law of Mr. Hill, one of the firm of Hill-Whitmire Mercantile Co., now doing business in West Plains, who had been a Confederate all through the war, remarked in the hearing of Jamison that the war was over, and he believed that the civil law ought to be enforced. Jamison at once dismounted, cocked his pistol, approached Arbogast and commenced punching him with the muzzle of it until he inflicted some wounds remarking to him that if he ever heard of him uttering a word again in favor of civil law being enforced that he would hunt him up and shoot his brains out.

Some time previous to that occurrence, two men who had been discharged from the Federal army and had once resided in Oregon county, came into the county to look at their old homes. Col. Jamison, with about forty men, arrested them, took them to the house of the sheriff, informed the sheriff that no "Feds" could ever reside in Oregon county, and no damn Black Republicans could ever cast a vote at any election that was held in the county; that they were going to make an example of the men, that others might take warning; that they were going to take them out far enough away that their stench would not annoy good Confederates. Accordingly, they started from the house, took them about one-half mile, stripped them naked, shot them to pieces, returned to the sheriff's house with the clothing, which was the uniform they had worn in the service, horse and mule and saddles which they had been riding; gave the mule to the sheriff, took the horse with them, published what they had done, and said that those men shouldn't be buried and that if any Confederate buried them, they would share the same fate.

Capt. Alley, who had been a Confederate all through the war, but was an honest man and wanted to see the law enforced, informed Governor Fletcher of the condition of the county. Governor Fletcher at once appointed him an enrolling officer, ordering him to enroll and organize the county into militia companies, to form a posse-comitatus to aid the sheriff in enforcing the law. As soon as he received his commission, he rode into the different townships, put up his notices requesting the people to meet him for the purpose of enrolling. Jamison, with about forty men, rode into the township where the first meeting was to be, posted another written notice on the same tree, the purport of which was that if Capt. Alley, the old, white-headed scoundrel, appeared on the day to carry out the orders of the Governor, he would meet him and shoot his old head off his shoulders. Alley, being satisfied that he would carry out his threat, went to the place before daylight and concealed himself nearby. About 10 o'clock on the day appointed, Jamison and about forty followers came charging in on their horses, revolvers in hand, cursing and declaring that they would like to see the old white-headed scoundrel put in an appearance so they could make an example of him; that they didn't intend to let any man enforce the law against them. As soon as they retired Alley returned home and wrote to the Governor again, stating the acts, conduct and threats that Jamison had openly made, and that troops would have to be sent into the counties to aid him and others in organizing, so the civil law could be enforced. He asked the Governor to appoint Capt. Monks to command the troops which he might send.

The author received a letter from the Governor informing him of the condition; also stated in the letter that while Howell county was peaceable and law abiding, that her citizens were not safe, by any means, while such a desperate band of outlaws were right at their very door, bidding defiance to the civil law, committing all manner of crimes from murder down and begging the author to consent to his being appointed Major of State troops; that he would make an order for the author to organize the men in the county of Howell and include Howell county in his order, declaring them to be under martial law especially when it had been requested by Capt. Alley, who had been a life-long Confederate. The author took the matter under advisement, and as Jamison, with his band of men, had threatened time and again to raid Howell county and kill the author with other Union men, he decided to give his consent to the Governor, wrote him while he reluctantly would consent to accept the appointment he had thought that he had discharged his duty in the late war and would not be required to take part in any further military operation.

Colonel Monks Commissioned by the Governor.

The governor at once appointed and commissioned the author Major of state troops and ordered him to at once proceed and organize a company of militia, and at the same time sent one hundred Springfield rifles and one hundred rounds of ammunition for each gun. And soon as it was organized, he was to proceed to Oregon county, for the purpose of aiding and supporting Captain Alley who had been appointed enrolling officer of Oregon county, to enroll and form companies for the purpose of aiding the sheriff in enforcing the civil law. He was to pursue, arrest and drive out those roving bands of murderers from the counties of Oregon, Shannon and Dent. The author at once organized a company in Howell county, composed of men who had been in the Confederate and Federal service. On Jamison and others in Oregon county learning that the author had been appointed Major and that he was organizing, and the state was arming the men with orders to enter the counties of Oregon, Shannon and Dent to drive out the murdering bands and aid Captain Alley in organizing a posse comitatus to aid the sheriff in enforcing the civil law, they publicly declared that "old Monks" might get into Oregon county but that he would never get out alive.

At that time there was a secret order in the counties of Oregon and Shannon known as the Sons of Liberty. The author was informed that on a certain night they would hold a meeting on Warm fork of Spring river. The author made a forced march and, on reaching the place where they had assembled, surrounded the house and took all the inmates prisoners, among them being the sheriff of the county and a few other prominent men. The next morning Capt. Alley met the author, put up his notices ordering every man to come in and enroll his name. The author remained over the next day near the place, got in possession of their papers, with a secret oath placed upon them, and the aims and objects, binding themselves together to prevent the enforcement of the civil law, and further binding themselves to capture or take property from any man who had been in the Federal army, and, when it became necessary to enforce it, to shoot men down. They claimed to have lawyers connected with it, so that if they should be arrested they were to make a pretense of a trial and allow no man to go onto the jury except those who belonged to the order.

Capt. Greer, who had been a Captain in the Confederate service all through the war, and afterwards was elected to he state legislature, remarked that, "I can soon tell whether those grips, obligations and oaths were in the organization known as the Sons of Liberty"; said that "Old Uncle Dickey" Boles, a short time previous, came to him and informed him that the Sons of Liberty were going to hold a meeting in a big sink on the mountain and they wanted him to come and join it; that he was looked upon as a business man and he didn't know anything about what was going on right at his door; that if he would come and join it, in a few years he would be a rich man. Capt. Greer said he replied to him, "Uncle Dickey, I have always been an honest man and have worked hard, and if a man can get rich in two or three years by joining that order, there must be something dishonest in it." Old Uncle Dickey replied: "You won't be in a bit of danger in joining it, for we are so organized that the civil law can't reach us." Capt. Greer said he had a son-in-law who was requested, at the same time he was, to attend the meeting, and that after the meeting he saw him and asked him what kind of an organization it was. He said his brother-in-law told him, "I dare not tell you; I took the bitterest oath that I have ever taken in my life not to reveal the workings of the order on penalty of death. But I will tell you enough; Captain, I know that you are an honest man and that that organization is a damn jay-hawking institution, and you want nothing to do with it." Captain Greer at once sent for his brother-in-law; he came, and the signs, grips and by-laws that were captured at the place of the meeting were submitted to him and he said he believed they were word for word the same, and contained the very same oath that they swore him to on the night that he went to their meeting.

The author was informed that Jamison was then lying in wait on the road that led from Warm Fork to Frederick Fork township, the next place where Alley had notified them to meet, waiting for the author to pass with his men so that he might fire on them from the brush. Then the hardest task confronted the author that he ever had had to meet, to study out a plan to prevent Jamison firing on his men from the bush as he marched by. He held four men as prisoners, whom he knew were Jamison's right-hand bowers; he had just been informed that Jamison had a spy then on the ground to learn the time the author would break camp and move in the direction of Fredericks Fork. He ordered a wagon brought up with three spring seats, took the four prisoners and set them in the two front seats, tied a small rope around their bodies and around each seat, with two guards in the back seat; then arrested Jamison's spy, informed him what his business was, which he admitted and said that Jamison was lying in wait to learn what time I would move out, and that he intended to fire on me as soon as I came within reach. I took him to the wagon and asked him if he was acquainted with the prisoners. He said that he was. "Well," said I, "I am going to release you and I want you to go and tell Jamison that, just as certain as he fires from the brush and kills one of my men, I will retaliate by killing these four men, whom I know are his right-hand bowers." The author also wrote a letter containing the same statement, and sent another man, who was a Confederate, with Jamison's spy, to see that the message was delivered.

On reaching Jamison, they delivered the message and informed him of what I had said, and told him that there was no possible chance for these men to escape, for there was a rope tied around each man's body and fastened to the spring seat, and they were also under a strong guard. The man who went to carry the dispatch said that after Jamison read it, he appeared to be in trouble and remarked: "Well, we will have to desist and not fire, for just as certain as we fire on him and kill some of his men, he is sure to kill our men." One of the prisoners, after he was placed in the wagon and heard the message sent to Jamison, remarked to the other prisoners: "We are dead men, for Jamison is sure to fire on them." We soon broke camp, and on reaching the place where Jamison had been waiting, saw the camp fire and where their horses had been tied and fed, but there was not a man to be seen, neither was there a gun fired.

On reaching Fredericks Fork township, Capt. Alley made a speech to the people and said, among other things, that the counties of Oregon and Shannon had been controlled by one of the most desperate class of men that ever live. That they had ridden through the country on horse-back, heavily armed, defying the enforcement of the civil law, intimidating the people, both Federal and Confederate alike, and committing all manner of crimes, robbing and murdering the people and boasting openly that the damn Confederacy was whipped, but that they were not and intended to live off the damn "Feds." Now the war is over and all good citizens, be they Federal or Confederate, should be in favor of the enforcement of the civil law. "I am ordered by the governor of the state to enroll all able-bodied men in the county to form a posse to aid the sheriff in enforcing the law in Oregon county; I am to organize companies to enforce the civil law. These bushwhackers and thieves have terrorized this county long enough. The governor has sent Capt. Monks, a man who is not afraid of bushwhackers and thieves, into this county to arrest these bushwhackers, thieves and murderers and bring them to justice. If the people of this county want the civil law enforced, they should aid Capt. Monks and his men to hunt these fellows down and either arrest them or drive them from the county. Our people have been present and saw these men commit all manner of crimes, from murder down to the smallest crime known to the criminal code. They have done this openly and the people were afraid to open their mouths or say a word against it, on penalty of death. I wrote the governor, stating the condition of affairs in this county, that neither person nor property were safe, and to send Capt. Monks to this county. And he has sent him and we have got the right man in the right place."

One of the prominent men of Oregon county went to Jefferson City to see the governor to procure the removal of the writer and have Col. A. J. Sea appointed in his place. He said to the governor that Capt. Monks was arresting some of the best men in Oregon county and had them prisoners. The governor showed him some of Capt. Alley's letters that he had written to the governor. The letters stated among other things that persons and property were at the mercy of these desperadoes and the county was being terrorized by James Jamison and his men; that they were robbing whom they pleased openly; that a day or two before he, Alley, wrote the

COL. AND MRS. MONKS AT CLOSE OF WAR.

letter, that Jamison shot a man's brains out in Thomasville, and dared any man to say he was in favor of the enforcement of the civil law, that he would serve him the same way. The governor asked him if those things were true, and he replied that they were; the governor said to him: "You are a leading man in that county and a citizen of Thomasville and never a word have you written to me that such terror and lawlessness existed in your county." He replied, "Governor, I was afraid to." The governor replied to him, "when I send a man down there that is not afraid to handle those men without gloves, then here you come with a howl. Now I expected when I sent Capt. Monks down there, if he did his duty, that there would be a howl raised; I am satisfied that he is doing his duty. I am responsible for his acts and you men want to get rid of him; go home and tell your people to organize companies under Captain Alley and aid Captain Monks and his men in arresting and driving those bushwhackers and bandits out of your county and whenever Captain Monks reports to me that the person and property of your citizens are secure and that the civil law is being enforced, he will be removed, and not before."

They then employed Colonel A. J. Sea as an attorney. Some time during the night, while we were encamped on Fredericks Fork, some of

COLLECTING BONES OF TWO FEDERAL SOLDIERS SHOT BY COL. JAMISON AND MEN IN OREGON COUNTY.

the soldiers took the sheriff out and put a rope around his neck to make him tell where the bones of two soldiers were, who were murdered by Jamison and his men. He admitted that he knew where the bones of the two Federal soldiers were; that after they shot them Jamison gave him the mule and saddle that one man was riding; that he was afraid not to take them and promised as soon as the command reached Thomasville to go and show the bones. On the next morning after our arrival at Thomasville I procured a big box and placed it in a wagon and brought the sheriff from the guard house and set him on a box under strong guard. About that time Colonel A. J. Sea came up and asked what we were going to do with that man. I told him, "That is my business; when you was in the military service did you inform the civilians of your object and aims? You are a civilian now and I will give you five minutes to get outside of the lines or you will go into the guard house." He took me at my word and left at once.

The sheriff piloted the scout to the bones of the men that had been murdered, and the sheriff, aided by the scout, picked up the bones and placed them in the box. On examination it was found that three bullets had passed through one of the skulls, and the other skull appeared to have been shot all to pieces. I brought the bones in and caused them to be buried in a cemetery, about one mile west of Thomasville.

Captain Alley had completed the organization of two companies, one commanded by Captain Lasley and the other by Captain Bledsaw. The companies were mostly composed of men who had been late Confederates, as there were very few Union men in the country. They immediately fell in with my soldiers and a vigorous search was at once made for Jamison and his men. Being aided by men who were thoroughly acquainted with the county and knew just where to look for Jamison and his cut-throats, they agreed to keep on Jamison's track and arrest him and his men if possible, in Oregon county. I moved my troops up into Shannon county to prevent Jamison and his men from crossing over into Shannon and scouted that county to keep them from hiding there. The Oregon county companies shot and killed some of them and arrested others. Jamison and the others left the county and never have returned to it since.

But they left some of their sympathizers in the county, and the only weapons left them were their tongues; having no conscience or principle, and instigated by the wicked one, they began lying and preferring all manner of charges against the writer and his men who went into the county and, by the aid of the law-abiding citizens, drove out and arrested one of the worst set of men that ever lived, the savage not excepted, and restored the civil law, so that every citizen was secure in person and property.

The writer informed the governor that a large majority of the citizens, both Confederate and Federal, had nobly responded to his call, had organized two companies of militia to aid the sheriff in the enforcement of the civil law; Jamison and his bushwhackers had either been arrested, killed or driven from the county, and the strong arm of the military law was not needed any longer.

On December 25, 1867, the writer was ordered by the governor to withdraw his forces from the counties that had been placed under martial law and declare the civil law to be in full force and effect. I accordingly returned to Howell county and disbanded my soldiers.

During my march and stay in the counties of Oregon and Shannon, it was admitted by all honorable Confederates that I had enforced a strict discipline over my men and protected all classes of citizens in person and property, had paid the people for all forage and commissaries that were required for the soldiers, and had driven out the worst set of bushwhackers, thieves and murderers that ever lived.

Reminiscences

In the spring of 1866 the loyal men had mostly returned to their homes; among them, Benjamin Alsup, who had been taken prisoner by the rebels in 1861 and confined in the penitentiary at Little Rock, Ark. He was released in 1865, when peace was made. There was but one house left in West Plains, an old school house about one-quarter of a mile east of the town spring, which was used for a court house. Judge Van Wormer, who resided at Rolla, was judge of the circuit court and Mr. Perry was circuit attorney. A short time after the return of Mr. Alsup, a public meeting of the loyal men was called, signed by several loyal men. At the date set the writer was present. The meeting was called to order and Mr. Alsup was elected chairman. He stated the object of the meeting, and among other things said: "The rebels have hung, murdered, imprisoned and driven all the Union men from their homes, and *by the living,* they didn't intend that a single rebel should live inside the limits of Howell county." He was in favor of giving them ten days' notice to leave the county, and if they were not gone by that time, to shoot them down wherever found. Someone introduced a resolution that the rebels be notified to leave with their families inside of ten days or they would force them to leave. The resolution was seconded, I got the floor and spoke as follows: "If that course is pursued, it will ruin the county; peace has been made and Gen. Grant has ordered the rebels to return home and become good citizens. Admitting that everything Mr. Alsup has said is true and we were to turn around and do the same that they did, we would be just as guilty as they were, and it would be a question of might and not right; and I want to say here now, if any man injures a late rebel, except in self-defense or in defense of his family or property, I will prosecute him to the bitter end of the law." Mr. Alsup called another man to the chair and replied to what I had said, saying: "*By the living,* I am surprised at Captain Monks, a man who has been treated by the rebels as he has, who now gets up here and says he will defend the rebels; *by the living*, I want Capt. Monks to understand right here, now, that if any loyal man kills a rebel and has to leave the country, and has no horse to ride, I will furnish him a good horse to ride off on; and *by the living*, let him prosecute me; he will have a sweet time of it." The next man that took the floor was a Mr. Hall, who resided about eight miles south of West Plains. He said: "I am just like Uncle Ben; if any loyal man kills a rebel and has to leave the country, I will furnish him a good horse to ride off on, and let Captain Monks prosecute me if he wants to; I don't think it would be healthy for him to prosecute me for killing a rebel or helping a man who did kill one." The resolution was put to a vote and lost by a good majority.

Later in the spring, there was a man by the name of Finley living seven or eight miles south of West Plains; the family was composed of husband and wife, both of them about sixty-five years of age, a daughter of twenty-two years and a son of about eleven. They had been rebels, but were very quiet and peaceable citizens; they were residing on government land, had good improvements and a good orchard. There was a man by the name of Frederick Baker who had homesteaded the land Mr. Finley was living on. Baker notified Finley to leave in ten days; if not out in that time, they would be killed. Mr. Finley wanted pay for his improvements before giving possession. At the expiration of ten days, very early in the morning Mrs. Finley went into the lot to milk the cows; Baker slipped up to the lot and with a Colt revolver shot the old lady dead. The daughter saw her mother fall, ran to her and he shot her; she fell by the side of her mother. The old man ran to the door, reached up to get his gun out of the rack, when Baker placed his pistol against his body and shot him dead. The pistol was so close to Finley when discharged that the powder set his clothes on fire. The boy was the only one of the family left; he ran to the nearest neighbor for help and when they got back to the house they found the old man and his wife dead and the daughter shot through the breast, maimed for life. The old man's clothes were still on fire when the neighbors arrived.

Hall made his words good for he furnished Baker with a first-class horse, saddle and bridle, to leave the country on and aided Baker in making his escape. As soon as the writer learned of the murder he caused an affidavit to be made and procured a warrant for the arrest of Baker and had it put into the hands of the sheriff and did all in his power to cause Baker's arrest, but by the aid given him by Hall and others he made his escape. The writer reported the murder to the Governor and the Governor offered a reward of three hundred dollars for Baker's body, dead or alive. Baker never was arrested.

The writer was appointed assistant prosecuting attorney by Mr. Perry, who was Circuit Attorney at the time. After I qualified I caused an affidavit to be made against Mr. Hall charging him with being an accessory to the murder before the fact and caused his arrest. I was at once notified that if I attempted to prosecute Hall I would meet the same fate as the Finley family. Hall was arrested, and the day set for his preliminary trial at the school-house east of town. On the day set for trial there were quite a number of persons present; the writer appeared, armed with a good pistol, laid it by his side during the progress of the trial; it was proven by the state that he, Hall, was guilty as charged. The justice held him over to wait the action of the grand jury and ordered him to enter into a recognizance of two thousand dollars for his appearance at the next term of the Howell county circuit court, which he readily filled and was released. Soon after his release he took the fever and died. Baker never was captured. It was one among the dirtiest murders that ever was committed in Howell county.

Gen. McBride, before the war, resided in Texas county, on a farm, and was circuit judge of the 18th judicial circuit, which included Howell county. He enlisted in the Confederate army and was placed in command of the Confederate troops at West Plains. The Union men well remember his famous order, given in the spring of 1861, that all Union men join the Confederate service, and if they didn't join the Confederate army he would hang them as high as Haman. After his term of service expired, he moved his family to near Batesville, Ark., where he resided up to near the close of the war. He had taken sick and died in the spring of 1866. Some of the friends of the widow in Texas county sent after her and her family to bring them back to her farm. Reaching West Plains on their return, they were out of money and provisions. They asked the people to help them and a donation was taken up for her in West Plains; I donated five dollars to help her back to her home in Texas county.

After the loyal men had returned to their homes and the civil law had been fully restored I brought suits by attachment against the following persons, to-wit: William Nicks, N. Barnett, for aiding the parties in arresting and taking me from my home and abusing me while a prisoner. I attached their real estate which was well improved and valuable; procured a judgement of $8,000.00 against said real estate, procured an execution and ordered the sale of said real estate. Before the time for the sale Barnett and William Nicks came to me and admitted that Barnett was 1st Lieutenant and Nicks 2nd Lieutenant of Capt. Forshee's Confederate company, while I was held prisoner by said company and that I was shamefully and cruelly treated while a prisoner, but they were sorry for what they had done and hoped I would forgive them. Nicks further said to me, that he had saved my life; that while I was a prisoner, he overheard some of the Confederate soldiers agree that on the next night while I was asleep they would slip up and shoot me in the head, and he got his blankets and came and slept with me. I knew that Nicks brought his blanket and slept with me one night, but did not know why he did it.

Nicks and Barnett further said, "Captain you have us completely at your mercy; we believe you are a good man and were friends before the war. You have a judgement against our homes and if you sell them you will turn us and our families out of doors and leave us destitute without any homes for our wives and children." I said, "I know it is hard, for my wife and children were driven from their homes because they were loyal to their government; but children shouldn't be held responsible for the acts of their parents and I will say to you now that I won't sell your homes, I will give them to your wives and children; we are commanded in the best book of all books to do good for evil; you men can each one pay me a small sum for expenses and I will satisfy judgement." Barnett paid me $150. Nicks made a deed to some tax lands and I entered satisfaction on the judgements. They both said to me that they ever would be grateful for what I had done for them.

The country begun to settle up and the people, irrespective of past associations, formed new ones, especially the sons and daughters of those who wore the blue and gray, and seemed to forget that they had ever been enemies. As time sped on these attachments ripened into love. I had but two daughters living. Nancy E. Monks, the oldest, married

V. P. Renfrow, the son of a Confederate; they have two children, a son, Charles, and a daughter, Mattie M., now grown. Mary M. Monks, who married H. D. Green, whose father, a Confederate colonel, died in the service. They have five children living and one dead, one girl and four boys. Their children are Mattie E., now Mattie E. Bugg; Will H. D., Frank, Russell and Dick. Adeline Turner, whom I had raised, married Jacob Shoffler, a Union soldier, and has ten children, four boys and six girls. Abraham Roach, a boy who had made his home with me since infancy, married Mattie Hunt, a daughter of Jesse Hunt, a Union soldier, has three children living, two girls and one boy, Maggie, Frank and Bernice. I don't believe that there is any person that loves their children better than I do, and I don't see any difference between my grandchildren and my own children; I love my sons-in-law as well as my own children; I love the girl and boy that I raised, and their families feel as near to me as my own. They are flesh of our flesh and bone of our bone, and our highest duty to God and them is to teach them patriotism and loyalty to their government and that their first duty is to God and their second duty to their country.

God forbid that we ever have any more civil war. War is the enemy of good society, degrades the morals of the people, causes rapine and murder, destroys thousands of lives, brings misery and trouble upon the whole people, creates a government debt that our children will not see paid, makes friends enemies. God forbid that any more sectional strife ever may grow up among the people; may there be no North, no South, no East, no West, but let it be a government of the whole people, for the people and by the people. May the time speedily come when the civilized nations of the earth will know war no more; when the civilized nations meet in an international congress, pass an international law that all differences between nations shall be settled by arbitration. May this nation in truth and in deed become a Christian nation and every man speak the truth to his neighbor and adopt the Golden Rule, "Do unto others as you would have them do unto you."

I take pleasure in giving the names of some of the loyal men who resided in Howell county in 1861, at the commencement of the Civil war, who stood for the Union in the dark hour when patriotism and loyalty to country were tested: John McDaniel, sr., John McDaniel, jr.,

FRANK GREEN AND CHARLES RENFROW.

Jonathan Youngblood, George Youngblood, David Nicholass, Thomas Wallace, Martin Keel, Thomas Nicholass, Newton Bond, William Hardcastle, Siras Newberry, William Newberry, David Henson, John Black, sr., Daniel Black, Peter Lanons, Thomas Brisco, Morton Langston, Stephen Woodward, Seth P. Woodward, Dr. D. D. Emmons, Alfred Mustion, W. D. Mustion, John Mustion, Wesley Cordell, Hugh Cordell, William Maroney, Henry Maroney, Collins Coffey, John Coffey, William Coffey, John Chapin, Silas Chapin, Benjamin Alsup, Andrew Smith, Andrew V. Tabor, Josiah Carrico, Josephus Carrico, John Dent, Esau Fox, Thomas O. Brown, Jacob Shoffler, Thomas Rice, sr., Thomas Rice, jr., John W. Rice, Nathaniel Briggs, Captain Lyle, ———— Rhodes, Jesse Hunt, Joseph Spears, James West, Jesse West, Dent West, Thomas Kelley.

I will give the names of a few of the men of Douglas county who remained loyal to their country in 1861: Joseph Wheat, John Wheat, Ervin King, John Coats, Locke Alsup, William Alsup, Thomas Alsup, Jack Alsup, Shelt Alsup, Aaron Collins, William Collins, Toodie Collins, Doc Huffman, Jariah Huffman, Madison Huffman, William Huffman.

I will give the names of a few of the men who resided in Ozark county, at the commencement of the war, who remained loyal to their country in the dark days when it tried men's souls to be loyal: James Kellet, sr., Marion Kellet, Washington Hawkins, Jesse James, William James, ———— Brown, R. R. Gilliland, Nace Turley, Washington Webster, Dick Webster, Macajar Foster, Jacob Foster, Henry Saunders, Stephen Saunders, Allan Saunders, Alexander Huffman, James Hall, Bennett James.

I would love to have space to tell of the patriotism, heroism and devotion to their country, besides their good citizenship, of the men of Howell, Douglas and Ozark counties, but suffice it to say that there never was the same number of men, at any time, who made more sacrifices for the preservation of their country than did these men in its darkest hour. These patriots are growing old and will soon be gone and their lips closed in death, and there will not be one left to tell of their sacrifices and the services they rendered to their country in its extreme need. History only will tell of the hardships, privations and service that they rendered to the government. Will there be no history left to tell of the heroism and devotion to their country in its darkest hour? The answer will come from ten thousand tongues that their history shall be written and go down to our children's children, that they may learn of the heroism, privation and sacrifice that was made by those brave men and women, that their country might live and not a star be dropped from its banner. While history is being written and monuments being erected to the Confederate soldiers for heroism, shall we be so ungrateful to the loyal men and women, after they are dead and gone, and not tell the rising generation of the heroism and sacrifice they have made, that their country might live? The answer will come from every loyal heart: No; a thousand times no; it shall be written and perpetuated for generations not yet born.

Has Known Col. Monks Thirty Years.

I have known William Monks for thirty years or more. I have been in court with him and a more kind and obliging man I never knew or had dealings with. He is very considerate in regard to the feelings of others, always willing to help those who need help. In later life he joined the church and preached; since he began the Christian life, I have never heard of any conduct that was not in conformity to his profession of Christianity. Had he had the school advantages that others have had, he would have been a power in the community where he lived.

The writer of this was born in Lancaster county, Pennsylvania, April first, 1824. His father immigrated west and landed in Pittsburg in 1837. Then the writer of this migrated southwest and finally landed in Tennessee. At Springfield he met Catherine Ebbett, or Abbott, as they now call it, and married her March 20, 1856. She was born in Reesville, Kentucky, and is still living, aged 76 years last January.

J. B. WINGER,
West Plains, Mo.

MR. AND MRS. J. B. WINGER.

Dr. Dixon's Long Acquaintance.

I will state that I came to Howell county in the year 1866 and settled on Hutton Valley near where the town of Willow Springs now is. The present townsite was then a small field without a fence and one small log cabin. I followed the practice of medicine up to the present date. I was 83 years old the 20th of August, 1906, and the picture I send you was taken when I was 81 years old. I was born in McMinn county, East Tennessee, and remained there until I was eleven years old when I left there and have gone through many changes and experiences since then. I served in the Mexican war. I married near Louisville, Ky., in 1849. My wife is still living and is nearly eighty-five years of age and in pretty fair health.

I will state that I have known Col. Wm. Monks and wife for over forty years and know them to be good and true people. I will further state that there were said to be but seventy-eight families in the entire county of Howell, and four families in the town of West Plains in May, 1866 and Col. Wm. Monks was one of the four. Now I believe there is a population in West Plains of over 4,000 and there is room for many more. This is an educational town, fine colleges and high schools besides quite a number of ward school houses, almost entirely built of brick. Schools last about nine months in the year.

Respectfully yours,
Dr. J. C. B. Dixon,
West Plains, Mo.

DR. J. C. B. DIXON.

Union Woman Leaves Arkansas for Missouri.

Mrs. Giddens, a widow, before the war resided in Conway county, Arkansas. She had two sons, Brad and John, who were about grown at the commencement of the war. This was a Union family and these two boys, with others, kept themselves hid until the Confederates issued a general order to hunt down all Union men and either force them to join the Confederate army or hang them. The boys at once saw that they would be arrested and forced into the Confederate service. They held a consultation with their mother and decided to try to reach Federal lines near Rolla.

Their mother took a couple of wagons with a large yoke of oxen to each wagon, and loaded them with her household goods, wearing apparel and provisions to last them through. In the spring of 1864 they started for Rolla. The boys traveled at night until they reached Missouri, and on reaching Taney county they met some Federal troops and made their way to

S. B. GIDDENS AND WIFE, MARY DEWETT, AND STILLEN STELMAN.

Rolla, where they enlisted and joined the 16th U.S. Cavalry Volunteers, and were attached to company K, commanded by Capt. Monks, and served until peace was made and they were honorably discharged at Springfield. Both of them are still living and are active ministers of the church of Christ.

Their mother aimed to reach Rolla by way of West Plains, and on reaching Howell county, near what is known as the Newt Bond farm, the bushwhackers stopped her wagons and robbed her, and ordered her to exchange her large cattle for smaller ones and her large wagon for a small, light wagon, so that the small cattle could pull it. Finally, after being stopped several times by the Confederate authorities, she reached Rolla and found that her sons had enlisted in the Federal army. She saw the stars and stripes unfurled and it appeared like a complete change of country. Here she located and remained until her sons were discharged from the United States service.

SAMUEL B. GIDDENS,
Summerville, Mo.

All Union families were forced to leave Texas county. The illustration contains the pictures of S. B. Giddens and wife, who were driven out; also Mrs. Mary Dewett, now over seventy years of age, who was forced to leave all she had and flee for her life; Mrs. Stillen Stellman, whose father went to Rolla and got the Federal soldiers to guard him while he removed his family.

Union Men Killed in Izard County, Ark.

Moody, Mo., September 26, 1906

Prior to and when the war of the rebellion broke out the writer of this article was a citizen of Izard county, Arkansas; the few loyal people that lived in North Arkansas, had a hope that war would be averted and when Ft. Sumpter was fired upon they realized the awful condition and consequences of war at their very doors; those who favored a dissolution of the states had given notice in no uncertain way. And when the news was flashed over the country that there had been a clash of arms, the persecution of the loyal people began in the South and Central states by those that favored secession. They organized themselves into companies and went from house to house notifying all those that seemed not to take sides either way, that the time had come when the sheep and goats had to be separated. The Union element was arrested and many were sent to the penitentiary at Little Rock, Arkansas, from the counties of Izard, Fulton and Independence. Those people were robbed and plundered as long as there was anything worth taking and some of them, after they had got all the Union people had, commenced arresting and hanging the Union men. They arrested a young man and placed a halter around his neck to hang him; he broke loose from them and was run one mile before he was caught; then he was taken to a stooping ash tree and hung. The writer was creditably informed that a man who was a prominent member of the Baptist church, scratched the dirt from under his toes in order that he might hang clear of the ground. I have seen the tree he was hanged on many times.

Another brutal murder was perpetrated upon the person of Rube Hudson, a Union man who had been run from home and returned home in the winter of 1865; from an exposure, he took sick with pneumonia, his wife had secreted him under the floor near the chimney and fire place; the news got out that he was at home, the rebels raided his house; every thing in the way of beds and what little they had left was turned upside down and they gave up the hunt and started away; a spell of coughing came on him, for he was very ill and he was heard coughing by them and they came back and tore up the floor and found him; they dragged him out and took him about one hundred yards from the house; there he was beaten and hung to make him tell of others who might have come with him; finally he was hung and shot to death, where the family could hear him pleading for his life; he made a special appeal to one of his near neighbors calling his name and asking him to intercede for him and save him. The only consolation he got was "you are a goner, Rube; you are a goner, Rube," he was left hanging for the family to cut down and bury. He met his death for no other cause than that of being a staunch Union man.

Another bloodcurdling murder was perpetrated upon the person of Minor White, for no other cause than that of being loyal to his country. He was honest and upright in his dealings with his fellow men, but he was arrested, taken to the county seat of Izard county, tried and was released. Before he started home a friend told him not to go the road for they would follow him and kill him, he said: "I have always been free to speak my sentiments; I have done nothing that I have to slip back home through the woods. I am going to take the public highway, if I am killed." He was overtaken about a mile out by the mob that took him there; he was shot and otherwise mutilated and left hanging to a tree.

I could mention many things that were done to the Union men and women in Northern Arkansas that make me shudder to think of, and if I were to undertake to relate all that came under my own observation, and many incidents that took place in the counties mentioned that were related to me by others who are entitled to credit for honor and truth. There was not a Union family left at home in the counties above referred to.

I am opposed to war on general principles: first, it never settles the issue; second, it is always a poor man's fight and a rich man's fuss; third, if the poor soldier is fortunate enough to get back alive, the debt is his to pay.

J. M. DIXON.

The Ku-Klux

The lawless bands that had been roving through the counties of Howell, Oregon, Shannon and Dent had been captured, killed or driven out of these counties by the officers of the law, aided by the militia forces of the state. All classes of persons and men of every political faith were secure in their person and property. The civil law was enforced to the letter and the people generally looked to the bright future of Missouri.

In the fall of 1868, in the month of September during a political campaign that was being made in Howell county, while a political speaking was going on at Black's store in Benton township in the southwest part of the county, a courier came with a dispatch stating that Captain Simpson Mason, registering officer of Fulton county, Arkansas, had been shot and killed from ambush, near the state line adjoining Howell county, by men who styled themselves Ku-klux, and had ordered all Union men, and especially the officers of the law, to keep inside of their doors and to tender their resignations as such officers or they would fare the same as Mason had. It was stated that the law-abiding citizens were without arms and that the Ku-klux were raiding the whole country; the whole country was being terrorized by said men and in God's name asked us to come and bring men and arms to aid the civil officers to enforce the law. The writer advised the people to be cool; that if there was an organization in the state of Arkansas to overturn the state government and the loyal people of said state were helpless, since the rebels at the commencement of the Civil war had had no regard for state lines I thought that we would have the same right to go down and help our loyal brethren to enforce the civil law.

A committee of twelve men was selected to say what action we would take; among the committee were Benjamin Alsup, Rev. Adam Wright, Rev. John Collins, David Nicholass. Old men were placed on the committee. The committee retired to deliberate upon the matter, and in a short time returned and made the following report: "That we,

ADMINISTERING KUKLUX OATH.

the loyal people of Howell county, go at once with all available men and arms." The writer had in his possession at that time one hundred Springfield rifles, with one thousand rounds of cartridges for each gun. During the night and the next day about seventy-five men were organized into a temporary company and were placed under the command of Uncle Benjamin Alsup. On the night following we made a forced march, reaching the Widow Pickrum's farm, situated on Bennet's river, in Fulton county, Arkansas, the next morning. We found Captain Richardson, with one company of state guards, fortified in a barn. On our arrival we offered our services to Captain Richardson, which were readily accepted. They were looking for an attack to be made by the Ku-klux at any moment, as Colonel Tracy was said to be at Jackson Port with three hundred and fifty well armed Ku-klux.

While waiting for further orders from Governor Clayton a vigorous search was commenced for the murderers of Captain Mason. We soon learned that on the day previous to the murder of Mason he was registering the voters on the Big North Fork, at what was known as the

Calhoun mill, and on the next day he was to meet the people at the Harbor Precinct for registration. And on the previous night the Kuklux, according to a general move that was to be made throughout the state, met at Colonel Tracy's, at the Widow Pickrum farm. Among them were Colonel Tracy, Dow Bryant, U. R. Bush, and about forty others; they selected about twenty men to do the shooting and divided them into three bunches and erected three blinds, as they did not know which road Captain Mason might travel. They placed about seven well armed men in each blind, who had been sworn by the Kuklux and after they had been placed in their blinds one of the men who did the shooting said, "Let him come; I am sure to get him for I can hit an old gobbler's neck that distance." The blind was erected where the road made a short curve with very thick brush on the left side of the road. When Captain Mason and posse approached within about thirty yards of the blind they fired a volley, five of the shots taking effect in Mason's body. Captain Mason fell from his horse and expired in a few moments. The assassins fled through a thick bottom growth. Bryant, Bush, and two or three others were arrested, charged with being a part of the men who did the shooting. They were arrested by the state guards, as the civil officers were afraid to issue a single warrant on account of the threats of the Kuklux. On an investigation it was proven that Tracy, Bryant, Bush and about forty others were present the night before Mason's murder. And that Bush was the man who remarked after he had gone into the blind, "Let him come. I can get him. I can hit an old gobbler's neck that far."

In the meantime, the governor had gotten a dispatch through to Capt. Richardson that the Kuklux in large numbers were organizing and threatening to attack the state officers; that he and the state officers were barricaded in the state house and that he was organizing the state guards as fast as possible. Capt. Richardson was ordered to recruit every available man and protect the civil officers as far as possible; that he had made arrangements to send arms and ammunition up White river on a boat. I suggested to Benjamin Alsup and others who had come down from Missouri that the only way we could make our acts legal would be to join the state guards and be mustered into the state service, to which proposition my old friend Alsup objected and remarked: "That's the way with Monks; he is afraid he will hurt some rebel, contrary to law. Now, by the living, I came down here to hang some of these rebels and murderers to the first limb we come to, and if we have to join the state guards and wait on the civil and military law to punish them, they never will be punished. I am going back to Missouri." About two-thirds of the men who came down enlisted in the state service; Alsup and others returned to Missouri.

As soon as Governor Clayton learned that the writer had come into the state with men and arms, he sent another dispatch stating that he and all the law-abiding people of the state would ever be grateful to him for furnishing men and arms at a time when they were entirely helpless and at the mercy of a secret and bloodthirsty enemy, bent on overthrowing the state government; that if I would remain in the state with my men and arms he would make me lieutenant-colonel of the seventh regiment of state guards.

We were watching the movements of the Kuklux, and in about eight or ten days after the murder of Capt. Mason, late one evening, the deputy sheriff of the county came to headquarters and informed Capt. Richardson that there were three hundred and fifty Kuklux, well armed, in camp at Salem, the county seat of Fulton county, and intended to attack Capt. Richardson before day, the next morning; they had ordered him, the deputy sheriff, under penalty of death, to bring Bush and turn him over to them. A brief consultation was held by the officers, and being satisfied that they were not able to meet the force of Kuklux then marching upon them, it was agreed that the writer should take the men from Missouri and recruit men for the service and get all the arms and ammunition that were left at home and return with all possible speed. In the meantime, they would retreat to some secluded place and watch the movements of the Kuklux. They turned Bush over to the deputy sheriff and he started in the direction of Salem, and Capt. Richardson broke camp and retreated. The deputy sheriff had not traveled more than two miles when a posse of armed men met and demanded Bush, and he, supposing that they were a part of the Kuklux command, turned him over. They took him about two hundred yards and shot him to death. The next morning, before daylight, Col. Tracy charged upon the late camp of Capt. Richardson, but found it had been vacated.

The Kuklux began a regular, organized system of raiding the Union men's houses, especially the officers of the civil law, posting written notices, ordering their resignations at once, and if they attempted the arrest of any Kuklux, death would be the penalty. They posted a picture of a coffin with the notice, at the same time ordering all influential Union men to leave the state at once, under the penalty of death. In about two weeks the governor ordered a part of the seventh regiment of state guards to Fulton county, to be stationed on Bennett's river, and to complete the organization of the regiment with all possible speed; Col. Dail was placed in command.

After my return home, I organized three companies, commanded by Capt. F. M. Monks, Capt. Nicolas and Capt. Rice. About three days after the regiment reached Fulton county, the writer rejoined his regiment with three companies, one hundred Springfield rifles and one thousand rounds of cartridges for each gun, and soon completed the organization of the regiment; he was commissioned lieutenant-colonel of the regiment.

The governor had sent arms and ammunition up White river, but the Kuklux captured and sunk the boat with all the arms and ammunition. The governor said that my arrival saved the north part of the state from the control of the Kuklux, as he would not have been able to procure arms for months. The regiment began an active campaign at once, by which they came into possession of the intentions, aims, secrets and oaths of the order; found that the order extended up into Missouri, along the state line. It was a complete military organization. The intention was to overturn the state government by intimidating the civil officers of the state, and with this purpose in view they procured a human skull and two thigh bones, and while the member was looking on these bones the following oath was administered by the grand cyclops:

"We (or I, as the case might be) do solemnly swear before Almighty God and these witnesses, and looking upon these human bones, that I will obey and carry into effect every order made by any cyclops or assistant cyclops, and if I fail to strictly conform and execute every order made as above required of me, unless I am prevented from some cause which shall be no fault of mine, or if I shall give any information to any person or persons except members of this order, that the doom of all traitors shall be meted out to me, and that my bones may become as naked and dry as the bones I am looking upon. And I take this oath voluntarily, without any mental reservation or evasion whatever, for the causes set out in said order, so help me God."

After the oath had been taken the persons taking said oath were ready for duty. The intentions and aims of this organization were to intimidate the civil officers and, if necessary to the accomplishment of their aims, to kill and murder all officers of the state by assassination or drive them from the state. All civil officers of the state were at once notified to tender their resignations and to cease to discharge their official duties as peace officers, and if they failed to comply with said order, death would be the penalty. The governor and all the state officers received the same order; all Union men that were influential in the state were ordered to keep themselves in doors or be driven from the state, or be murdered by assassination. The following words, with pictures of coffins, were attached to said notices:

"If you fail to comply with this notice, this coffin will be your final resting place."

The Kuklux organization, having but one object and aim, to turn the state government over to the control of the late rebels or Democratic party of the state, was a complete secret military organization with the most desperate means to-wit: Murder, by assassination whenever ordered by a cyclops or assistant cyclops.

A grand cyclops took the place of a colonel. An assistant cyclops lieutenant-colonel. An order from one of these officers to shoot any man was final, from which there was no appeal; and men were selected to execute said order by the most desperate oath known to man or history. This kind of warfare, being inaugurated throughout the whole state, with a thorough understanding that their organization would revolt against the civil authorities of the state government, and had the day set throughout the whole state.

On the same day that Captain Simpson Mason was assassinated in Fulton county, Kuklux attempted to assassinate Governor Clayton in Little Rock. They were seen in considerable numbers near the state capitol, after night, all wearing masks. They notified the governor, that they intended to capture and take possession of the state capitol by a force, if he did not resign his office as governor; the danger became so great that he barricaded the state house, as he had but few state troops. The whole state was invaded by the Kuklux at the same time and they commenced raiding the state in bands of from twenty-five to two hundred and fifty men; all wore masks and large rubber pouches concealed by a cover. They visited the Union men and colored men's houses and raided the whole country generally, proclaiming that they were dead rebels who had been shot on the different battlefields during the civil war and that they had come back to rid the state of black republicans and carpet-baggers.

They would claim that they were very thirsty, that they never had a drink of water since they had been killed at the battles of Gettysburg, Corinth, Vicksburg, and other big battles. They would call on the colored people to bring them a bucketful and one of their number would pour the whole bucketful into his pouch and called for more water, making the colored people believe that they drank the water; then they would give the colored people orders not to be caught off their plantations, and if so caught, the penalty of death would be inflicted; many of the influential colored people were shot down. The author saw a number of fresh graves of the colored people that had been shot by the Kuklux; saw holes in windows in houses in towns and villages that had been shot through after night, while men were reading, who had been notified to resign their offices or stop using their influence in favor of the enforcement of the civil law.

The author remembers passing some colored people on the side of the road; one old colored woman cried out at the top of her voice "Lawd, massa, massa are you men hunting dem dar Kuklux? Wi, da told us dat bullets wouldn't kill them. I fought we could fight live men but when it come to fightin' dead men, don't know what to tink about it. Wi dey come to our house, rode up to de fence called for water; said they hadn't any water since the battle of Shiloh. Wi, one man drank a bucketful, and den call for mo. I thought to my soul that they would never get enuf water." The author replied, "Auntie, when these rebels are killed, they never get back here; the bad man keeps them to build fires for him. These Kuklux are the men that ran away from the battle of Shiloh and have just crawled out of their dens. That's why they are masked." The old woman said, "Dat what I thought bout it." While the Kuklux were raiding the country they visited an old darkie's house and gave him three day's notice to leave the country; and if he failed to leave they would visit him again and death would be his penalty. In about three or four days, twenty-five or thirty Kuklux rode up to his cabin in the night and called for him; he was armed with an old U.S. musket; he fired into the crowd and killed one of the band and then ran and made his escape.

Part of the regiment received orders to report to General Uphan, who was stationed at Cottonplant, on White river, leaving Captain Richardson in charge of the forces in Fulton county and Captain Toney in charge of the troops in Izard and Sharp counties. The regiment broke camp and marched by way of Jacksonport and on their arrival went into camp on the Wadel farm, two miles below Jacksonport. The Kuklux had declared that we should not march through Jacksonport. A brother-in-law of Mr. Wadel from North Missouri invited the writer to supper; the writer believing that a trap had been fixed to decoy him outside of the lines took one lieutenant and a posse of men and went to his house; on our arrival, we found a bountiful supper; had every thing that a hungry man could wish; had eggnog served in silver cups with silver spoons. The residence was about forty-two by twenty feet; two large rooms with a ten-foot hall between, with kitchen on west side, fine portico, with about ten or twelve negro cabins, about sixty to one hundred feet from the dwelling-house. Just before supper I noticed eight or ten men come in on foot dressed in gray clothing. I at once ordered my men to be ready at any moment and to not let them get the drop on them. Just about the time that most of my men were through eating supper, I noticed that some of the men that came in to the supper table had arms on their persons and noticed that the negroes were excited. I stepped out at a back door and just as I entered the hall door I saw the landlord approaching the room where my men were seated at the table with a navy pistol cocked in his right hand, holding it behind his back. Just as he attempted to open the door where my men were seated at the supper table, I sprang forward and grabbed his pistol and wrenched it out of his hand, and said to him, "Don't you dare to attempt to shoot one of my men." He turned around facing me and said, "I went all through the Civil war and you are the first men that ever disarmed me." In a moment my men had pistols in hand ready for action, and I noticed some of the men that came dressed in gray had pistols in their pockets. I remarked to them:

"I came here on an invitation; I am here as a guest. I wish to treat all persons as gentlemen, especially the landlord and his family; but this hostile move made upon the part of the landlord and the presence of these armed men shows me that there is something wrong. I ordered my men to fall in line and return to the camp. His wife appeared to be a perfect lady and her husband appeared to be under the influence of whiskey. He agreed that if I would release him, he would go into his room and stay there until my men had all returned to the camp. After he had gone into his room, I gave his revolver to his wife on her promising not to give it to him until the next morning.

I learned from Mr. Wadel's brother-in-law that he came from northern Missouri at the commencement of the war and at about the close of the war he married his sister; that he was a cyclops and came to Fulton county in the Kuklux raid, and that the men who came that evening were all Kuklux, that if I had gone alone to his supper, I would have been killed.

The next morning we broke camp and resumed our march. On the regiment arriving at Cottonplant, Col. Dail reported to Gen. Upham and we were ordered into camp. As soon as the citizens of the city learned of my arrival, they requested Gen. Upham that I be invited to deliver a speech in the city hall; that they had heard and read of Col. Monks and they wanted him to deliver an address to the people at early candle-light on the present condition of the state. There were about seven or eight hundred men stationed at the post. After supper, the adjutant sent an order by an orderly to detail fifty men for a patrol guard; that the soldiers had broken into the warehouse and were taking out whiskey and other articles. I ordered the detail to be made and report at headquarters for further orders. Our headquarters were not more than forty yards from the warehouse. I spoke in an audible voice, "Now, we claim that our mission as soldiers is to protect persons and property. I want you to see that your guns and pistols are well loaded, and go direct to the warehouse first and arrest all soldiers that you find in or about the warehouse and take them to the guard-house and there keep them safe until further orders, and patrol the city closely. Order all soldiers and officers who have not passes to be inside of their quarters in thirty minutes, and if you find any soldiers on the street after thirty minutes, arrest them and take them to the guard-house; if they resist you, shoot them; and if you have to shoot, shoot to kill." About that time some man near the warehouse called out: "Who in hell are you? This whiskey is Kuklux whiskey, and we will take what we please." I replied, "If we cannot enforce discipline over the soldiers, we will go back home and send others; you will find out who I am if you wait until the patrol gets there."

I ordered the officer to sound the reveille. Inside of thirty minutes every soldier was inside of his quarters. The citizens said that such a thing had not occurred since the post had been established. Capt. Sharp was reckless when drinking; he had mutinied and the men that were disposed to be wild had terrorized the people of the city. Gen. Upham had failed to enforce discipline over Capt. Sharp and his company. Capt. Sharp had ridden up and down the streets before the regiment had arrived and proclaimed, "when Colonel Monks arrives we will clean all the Kuklux up." The citizens were considerably frightened on my arrival in August, but after they saw how completely I enforced discipline everything became quiet, they appeared to be perfectly secure in person and property.

On the next night, at early candle-light, the large hall was filled. After being introduced by Gen. Upham, I spoke in part as follows:

"Gentlemen and fellow citizens of Arkansas: I am from your sister state, Missouri, and I am very sorry to find you people in the state of war. War is not very pleasant; it has its effects upon society; demoralizes the morals of the people, besides the great sacrifice of life and property. Besides this, it ailenates those who should be brethren and makes them bitter enemies. Your people may ask the question, what right have you Missourians to come down into our state? My first answer will be, Captain Simpson Mason was but recently assassinated in Fulton county, near the state line, while in the discharge of his official duty. At the commencement of the civil war he was a citizen of Fulton county, Arkansas, and I was a citizen of Howell county, Missouri. Both of us were unconditional Union men. Both of us were driven from our homes and posses of men from your state, regardless of the state lines, scouted our county, murdering and driving out Union men, women and children and hung and shot down loyal men. Captain Mason and I met in the early part of the war of the rebellion and soon became fast friends. Served together during the war. When peace was made we determined to go back home. Men would meet us and say, 'If you men go back among the old rebels who hate you so badly they will kill you.' Our reply would be, 'Damn a man that is afraid to go back and enjoy the fruits of his victory.' We met and pledged our sacred honor to each other that if, after our return to our old homes, either one of us was killed by the late rebels, the other would do all in his power to bring the guilty parties to justice. A better and truer man never lived than Captain Simpson Mason. Each of us came back with the olive leaf in his mouth. Now I don't say that all rebels are Kuklux, but I will say all Kuklux have been late rebels and have organized a secret organization, the objects and aims of which are to overturn the civil government of your state by murder and intimidations, through the most vile and desperate means known to man, the savage not excepted. Besides your organization extends into the border counties of Missouri and as the rebels thought right to cross the state line during the Civil war, we think it right to cross it now to help our loyal brethren, and these are the causes that brought us to your state. We don't want booty. We want to see the civil law enforced, and we ask your cooperation, and promise you that all law-abiding citizens, be they Union or rebel, shall be protected in person and property during our stay in your state and we intend to enforce the strictest discipline among our troops. I hope by the cooperation of the people of your state this unholy war will soon cease." At the conclusion of the speech they gave three cheers for Missouri troops.

On the third day after our arrival at Cottonplant, Captain J. B. Nicholas' and Captain Sharp's companies were ordered to be detached from the regiment and placed under the command of the author and ordered to march at once and report at Marion, the county seat of Crittenden county for further orders. On our arrival at Marion we were ordered to proceed directly to Osceola, the county seat of Mississippi county, Arkansas and to erect a military post and issue an order ordering all the persons that were armed to come in and take the oath. On our arrival at that place to report the same to the Governor of the state. I issued the following general order:

"To the people of the state of Arkansas, especially the citizens of Mississippi county; greeting; whereas a part of the people, disregarding

MAKING A PLEDGE—COL. WM. MONKS AND CAPT. SIMPSON MASON.

their duties as good law-abiding citizens, have by and through a secret organization known as Kuklux revolted against the civil government of the state of Arkansas and are now armed and attempting by murder and intimidations to overthrow the civil government of the state, now therefore, by the authority in me vested and as commander of said post, do order all persons who may be in armed hostility to the present government and those who may be by act or deed aiding or encouraging those who are in arms against the legal constituted laws of the state to return to their allegiance and aid in enforcing the civil law. And any person who may be found from and after this date armed or aiding or abetting those who are in arms against the civil law of the state will be promptly arrested and punished to the extent of the law.   WM. MONKS, commanding the post."

When I arrived there was not a single civil officer in this county. They had either resigned or had kept themselves indoors. I at once commenced a vigorous campaign and soon learned that there were two men charged with being cyclops; one of them resided about thirty miles down the river on an island; he was charged with killing eight or ten colored people. I made a detail of about fifty men and placed them in charge of Captain Sharp and ordered him to go down and arrest both and bring them up to headquarters. The second day after the scouts started they returned by steamboat with both men, as well as several other prisoners. After the boat arrived Captain Sharp came to headquarters and suggested the release of one of the men as he didn't think he was guilty. I ordered the prisoners brought to headquarters at once. There was a man by the name of Edington who resided in Osceola, one of the wealthiest men in the county; he was well acquainted with one of the men, as he had been sheriff of the county in which he resided and a colonel in the Confederate army. He asked me to parole him to the limits of the city and he would go on his bond for one thousand dollars until said charges could be investigated. In a few days after he was paroled Mr. Edington came into the office and informed me that after his arrest and while on the boat coming up the river Capt. Sharp came to him in the presence of the captain of the steamboat and remarked, "Well colonel, you have got a hard man holt of you now; if you will pay me one hundred and fifty dollars I can use my influence with Col. Monks and have you released." The colonel said to Captain Sharp that he didn't have the money with him. The captain of the steamboat said to the colonel, "I have the money, I will loan it to you." The colonel paid Captain Sharp one hundred and fifty dollars. Captain Sharp agreed to have him released and let him go back on the boat. Mr. Edington said he had watched all my proceedings since I took command of the post and had become satisfied that my highest aim was to protect every person in his person and property.

I ordered the orderly to arrest the colonel and bring him to headquarters. I told him that I had been informed that after his arrest and while in custody of Captain Sharp on the steamboat he paid Captain Sharp one hundred and fifty dollars and Captain Sharp was to release him and let him return home on the boat. He admitted that he paid the money and made a full statement of all the facts that caused him to pay the money. I notified Captain Sharp to appear at headquarters at once. Informed him of what I had just learned, that while he had the colonel prisoner, coming up on the steamboat, that he, the prisoner, paid him one hundred and fifty dollars to procure his release. Captain Sharp admitted that it was true; I asked the captain if he had the money. He said he had. I asked the colonel if he had a friend that he could pay the money to; that I could not pay the money to him, that he might bribe another one of my officers. He said that I could pay the money to Mr. Edington. Captain Sharp paid the money to Mr. Edington by the order of the colonel. I ordered the colonel to the guardhouse for bribing my officers. I ordered Captain Sharp to report at headquarters the next day at ten o'clock. The Captain promptly appeared at the hour set. We went into the back room of my office alone. The captain and myself took seats. I said to the captain, "I am very sorry that this thing occurred; that you have allowed one of your prisoners to bribe you and you have betrayed that confidence imposed in you by the state. It become my painful duty to place you under arrest and of all crimes known to the criminal calender the worst is that one of treason. We claim that we are hunting violaters of the law and if we become violaters of the law then it will devolve on the state to place a new set of men in the service so that all violaters of the law can be arrested and brought to justice. Now I have been informed that while you composed a part of the command stationed at Cottonplant under General Upham you was arrested for disorderly conduct and you caused your company to mutinize. Now I want to say to you that I am going to put you under arrest and disarm you and I will parole you to the limits of the city and your first lieutenant will be placed in command of the company and if you cause your men to mutinize I will arrest the whole company and send them to Little Rock."

I ordered the whole company to appear at headquarters and informed them of what I had done. I then sent the orderly and brought out the colonel and paroled him to the limits of the city under one thousand dollar bond. I never had a more obedient set of soldiers in all my service than Captain Sharp's company and they were as true and as brave men as ever lived. Captain Sharp said he was sorry for what he had done and I had done my duty and in about one week I returned his arms and placed him in command of his company. And during the remainder of service Captain Sharp discharged every duty with honor to himself and his state. While I was in command of the post I made a vigorous campaign. Arrested or drove out all the armed Kuklux and had the civil law fully put in force and the ministers of the gospel reorganized their churches and business of all kinds was resumed. Intimidations of the people, of the civil officers, and of the county by the Kuklux was a thing of the past. I received orders from the adjutant general at Little Rock to declare the civil law enforced in Mississippi county and to report with my command to the commander of the post at Marion, Crittendon county, Arkansas, for further orders. My command was conveyed by steamboat to Hopefield and from Hopefield we marched to Marion.

And in obedience to said orders I issued the following order: "To all whom it may concern, especially to the citizens of Mississippi county, Arkansas, I send greeting. It affords me great pleasure to say to the people of Mississippi county that the Kuklux organization is completely broken up and there is no armed opposition to the enforcement of the civil law. Therefore, by the power in me vested I declare the civil law from this date in full force and effect in said county. And I invite all good citizens to aid in the enforcement of the civil law.

WM. MONKS, Commander of the post.

And when the people of the city learned that my command had

been ordered to leave the city they at once presented the writer with a new suit of clothes. And on the arrival of the boat and while we were loading our camp equipage, arms and ammunition, about three of four hundred persons composed of men, women, and children assembled on the bank of the river to bid us goodbye. And as the boat moved out they waved their handkerchiefs and hats and gave three cheers for the soldier boys and their commanders.

On our arrival at Marion we turned over our guns, ammunition and camp equipage and were ordered by the adjutant general to proceed to Jacksonport for further orders and on our arrival at Jacksonport the writer was ordered to leave his command at Jacksonport and to report in person to the governor at Little Rock. On my arrival at Little Rock I was informed by the adjutant general that the governor was dangerously sick and confined to his room. The legislature of the state being in session I was invited by both houses to deliver an address to the legislature. Both bodies met in the lower house. The writer was introduced by the speaker. Spoke as follows:

"Mr. President of the General Assembly of the State of Arkansas, it affords me great pleasure to have the honor of addressing this august body of men assembled in this hall. Men who have been elected by the people of the whole state. Men who have the interest of the people at heart. Men who have the confidence of the people. Men who are intelligent and know what kind of laws the people need. Men who are determined to do your whole duty; men who have the courage, patriotism and love of country at heart, who have stood by your post while one of the most secret organizations, known as Kuklux, bound by one of the most desperate oaths to overturn your state government by intimidation and murder of all the civil officers of the state and to kill and murder the loyal citizens of your state. The intention of said organization was to overturn the legally constituted laws of the state, but through the untiring effort of your governor and his subordinate officers and the loyal people of your state and the valor and patriotism of your soldiers, this organization has been completely routed and broken up and the civil law is again declared to be enforced in your state. Now may your wisdom as legislators guide you and your successors in all duties that you may be called upon to perform in the legislative capacity. And may you always have the interest of the whole people at heart. And may all the laws that may be enacted by this legislature or your successors be in the interest of the whole people. And may patriotism and the love of both state and nation grow in the hearts of your people and may they become so united that nothing can sever that cord of love for their state and nation. May God's blessing guide and direct every one of your public acts, and go with you to your homes and families and now that your state is once more at peace and the civil law is being enforced, and your people are secure both in person and property, I therefore will return to Missouri to the bosom of my family. I bid you all good bye."

The whole house rose to its feet and gave three cheers and pressed forward to give the writer a good, parting handshake.

The governor continued to grow worse. The doctors would not admit any person to his sick room. The adjutant general informed me that the governor wanted to see me in person. That I had come to the rescue of the people with men and arms, when the loyal people were completely overpowered and saved the northern part of the state from the control of the Kuklux. He said the governor was well pleased with my services while in the State; that even the rebels spoke in the highest terms in regard to the discipline that I enforced over my men; that I had protected the person and property of both Union and rebel, and that I had given general satisfaction to all classes of persons that were favorable to the enforcement of the civil law and that it was the desire of the governor to promote me to a brigadier-general for the valuable services that I had rendered in the state, and place me in command of the northern district. I said, "You can tell the governor when he gets well that I was very sorry to find him sick, that it would have been a pleasure to me to have met him in person. And the offer that he has made to me to promote me to brigadier-general for the meritorious services that I have rendered to the state places me under many obligations to his honor for the high esteem and confidence he imposes in me, as touching my military service, and as a private citizen while in this state. And while I thank him for his offer to promote me to the rank of brigadier-general and place me in command of the northern district of Arkansas, I must decline the offer and return to Missouri for I love the people of my state, I love my home and my desire is to become a private citizen. The only thing that impelled me to come into your state was to aid the state in enforcing the civil law and protect your people from assassination and murder and to do all in my power to aid in bringing violaters of law to justice. This being accomplished and civil law again being enforced in every part of the state, my services as a soldier and an officer not being needed any longer I will ask you again to give my respects to the governor and will ever hold his memory sacred, and may God's blessing rest upon the people of your state and your chief executive. So I will bid you good-bye."

I returned to Jacksonport and rejoined my command and marched directly to West Plains. There my men bid each other goodbye and returned to their homes, hoping that this thing of war would be over forever.

On my arrival home I found, to my great surprise, a new political organization, composed of men who styled themselves Liberal Republicans, and democrats and rebels; and through some of the most vicious and unprincipled rebels, they charged me with being a thief and a murderer. My friends came to me and requested that I at once institute suits of slander against them, for they knew that it was false from the beginning to end. During the intervening time they had called an indignation meeting and publicly denounced me as a thief and murderer. I instituted a civil suit for slander against all persons who took part in said indignation meeting. I also instituted suit against one other man on the same charge. The county of Howell at that time, especially the judicial circuit, was presided over by a judge, who was an extreme democrat. The defence made application to the judge for a change of venue from this judicial circuit; he ordered the change sent to Laclede county, to the city of Lebanon, before Judge Fian. The defence then set about taking depositions. I was notified to meet them in Sharp county at Evening Shade for the purpose of taking depositions. When we met at Evening Shade they commenced hunting around for witnesses to prove their charges, but failed to find a single one. But every person they interviewed touching the charges declared that they were false and that Colonel Monks enforced discipline over his men while he was in their state and protected every one in person and property and that all classes of persons regarded him as being perfectly honest and a good military officer; they failed to procure a single witness at that place. I next was notified to meet them in Oregon county, at the court house, for the purpose of taking depositions. I accordingly armed myself with two good navy revolvers and went to Alton, the county seat of Oregon county; the circuit court being in session at that time, on my arrival I put up at a boarding house conducted by Alfred Harris, who still resides in that county. Circuit court being in session I went into the court room and remained until recess. Just after recess the judge came and told me that he had been informed that a mob then had the court-house surrounded and was going to mob me whenever I entered the square, and to remain in the court room for a few minutes and he would try and have the mob removed; in eight or ten minutes the deputy sheriff returned and informed me that the mob had been removed, and that I could go down and go to my hotel. As I passed down I saw about fifty or sixty men in front of the saloons, swearing at the top of their voices, "He fought us during the civil war and he shall not be allowed to come into this county and live." After reaching the hotel, Mr. Harris with several other friends urged me not to meet the parties, who were going to take depositions in one of the rooms in the court house, for they believed the mob would kill me. I laughed and told them that I reckoned not and that I thought the war was over and that they couldn't play that game on me, to notify me to meet them to take the depositions and then prepare a mob to prevent me from appearing, so that they would be able to manufacture evidence in the case. And I would either be present at one o'clock, the time I was notified to meet them, or I would die in the attempt. So I appeared promptly at one o'clock, the time set, but not one of the opposite party, either attorney or client put in an appearance. I remained there until four o'clock and still no appearance had been entered by the defendants or their attorneys, and I again returned to my hotel, after circuit court had adjourned for the day.

While we were seated at the table eating supper, a man rapped at the hotel door and called to Mr. Harris, the landlord, that he wanted to see him privately for a few moments. Mr. Harris soon returned and remarked to the writer that he had been ordered to deliver a message; that he had just been informed that a mob of about one hundred men then had the hotel surrounded and they would give me ten minutes to get out of town or I would be shot to death. I replied to Mr. Harris, "In the first place, I am too old to run; and in the second place, if these bushwhackers have not shed enough innocent blood, they will have the best opportunity now that they will ever get; tell them that I don't intend to leave or run." Mr. Harris said that he would deliver the message to the bearer.

There were two Confederates seated at the table, eating. They said, "What does this mean? We thought the war was over." They got up and left the table. After the writer finished his supper, he retired to the sitting room, which adjoined Mr. Harris' library. Mr. Harris immediately came in and offered to barricade the doors and windows. I objected. He then remarked that the mob would shoot in through the windows, that he would blind the windows. I consented to his putting blinds on the windows, but that the doors shouldn't be interfered with. There was but one door entering the sitting room except the door that came through the library. I took my seat on a bench where I could reach the knob of the door with my left hand and hold my revolver in my right hand. Mr. Harris proposed to blow out the lights, to which I objected. I told him that if the mob came I wanted the light so that I could see how to shoot. He then took his seat and entered into conversation. In a few moments some person took hold of the knob of the door. I rose to my feet with my revolver cocked, in my right hand and let the door open just so that one man could enter at a time. Mr. Maxey, of Howell county, an attorney-at-law, had come in to get a book out of the library, not knowing that there was any trouble up. As he came inside of the room I had my pistol cocked and presented on his left breast. When I recognized Mr. Maxey I lowered my pistol and remarked to him, "Your face has saved your life." Mr. Maxey became very much excited, walked across the floor once or twice, and inquired what was up. I informed him of the notice of the mob and the time that I had been given to leave the hotel and that the time had then expired, and that when I heard him take hold of the door, I supposed the mob was coming. Mr. Maxey remarked that "This thing will never do, I'm going to see if it can't be stopped." I requested him to say to every person that might be disposed to come into the house to make themselves known outside of the door before entering the house.

LOYAL WOMEN OF HOWELL COUNTY.

In a short time the circuit judge and deputy sheriff, with two or three others, came to the door and made themselves known and came in. The circuit judge said: "Colonel, I have been informed that you have been notified by the mob to leave the town in ten minutes or you would be shot to death, and I have come to see if you wanted a guard." I replied that I didn't. "If these God damn bushwhackers haven't shed enough innocent blood and are still bloodthirsty, they will never have a better opportunity; so just let them come." The judge and sheriff and those who came with them left the room. I remained in the room until the usual bedtime. I heard them cursing outside and declare that they would take me out before daylight. I thought of my horse that was in the stable, a few yards away. I remarked to Mr. Harris that I was going to the stable to look at my horse. He begged me not to go out, that I would be shot down. I said to him that it was a game that two or more could work at.

On reaching the stable, I heard the men quarreling on the public square. A man by the name of Jones, who had been a Confederate and then was prosecuting attorney of the county, and another citizen, who appeared to be leading the mob, were having an altercation. Jones remarked to the other man that he had never met Col. Monks until to-day and that he appeared to be a perfect gentleman, that the war was over, and that he had the same right to come here and transact business as any other man; to which the other declared, with an oath, that a man who had fought them through the war shouldn't come there, and they intended to take him out and shoot him before daylight; and further charged that Jones was not a good Confederate. Jones then gave him the lie. The two appeared to be about to come together, but others interfered to keep them separated. I returned to the hotel and said to Mr. Harris that the seat of war had moved up onto the square.

Mr. Maxey informed me that just outside of the door of the hotel he met the mob, and they declared that they intended to take Monks out and shoot him before daylight. He replied to them that they might do it, but they had better take their stretchers along, for some other persons would have to bring some of them out; that he had just been in the house and in a moment he was confronted by Col. Monks with a revolver presented at his left breast and the very devil was in his eye, and if they entered the room he would shoot as long as he could move a finger.

When bedtime came, I was placed in an upper room and locked the door, expecting that if they located my room they would shoot through the windows. I could still hear them cursing and threatening to take me out until late in the night. The next morning everything was quiet. I went to the stable and took my horse down to the spring to water; a number of men were standing at the side of the street, and one said: "Where do you suppose the captain and his men are?" I remarked to them that they were just like a pack of wolves; they were in the brush this morning, waiting for night to again renew their howling. There was one, Capt. Wagoner, who resided in town, who remarked to me the next morning that he never was as proud of anything in his life; that if they could have scared me and I had attempted to leave town in the night, they intended to murder me.

After circuit court convened, I went into court, and at noon of that day the court adjourned. And I, with a number of others, went to Thomasville, put up at the hotel, had my horse fed and took supper.

While on the road, the man that led the mob passed me on his way to Thomasville, where he resided. The defendants and their attorneys failed to produce a single witness to testify in the case. I returned home to West Plains.

I was notified to meet them at other places in the country, to take depositions in said cause. The political feeling was strong then between the parties, and they sent the suits to a county over a hundred miles distant from where the suits were instituted; this county, at that time, was completely controlled by the democratic party.

When the suits came up to be tried, over half of the jury had been late rebels, yet they failed to introduce a single witness to support their charges, and I recovered a verdict in each case. Judge Fian, who tried the case, said that he was never so surprised in his life; that he opened up the floodgates and let them bring in all their evidence from the beginning of the war up to the time of the trial. Judge Fian had been a colonel on the Federal side in the Civil war.

On the account of the failure to get any proof the juries were compelled to give a verdict in both cases for Col. Monks, although it was against the will and feeling of them. It cost the defendants between five and seven hundred dollars. After the trials, all parties returned to Howell county. The defendants, after they had procured a change of venue to Laclede county, boasted openly before trials, that they were going to beat both cases, that they had got them into a democratic county. The defendants being beaten at all points, returned, but not being satisfied, and being backed by the late bushwhackers and Kuklux (the most desperate set of men that ever lived,) at the next term of the Howell county circuit court they procured the appointment of a special prosecuting attorney, who had been a late rebel and selected a jury of men composed of liberal Republicans and so-called democrats, with the express purpose of indicting the writer for killing one of the most desperate bushwhackers and rebel desperadoes that ever was in South Missouri. The men who composed the jury knew well that he was killed in an open hand to hand fight during the Civil war. The writer soon found out that they were trying to get a bill of indictment against the writer, so the writer watched the proceedings of the grand jury. On Saturday the grand jury came into court and turned in their indictments and reported to the court that they had no more business. The court discharged them.

At the same moment the writer asked the court if there was any bill of indictment preferred against him. He ran over the indictments and informed the writer that there was an indictment against him, for murder in the first degree. The Judge said that he was sorry that I had called it out for he wanted to go home until Monday. I told him, "Just adjourn your court and go home. The sheriff is here." I remarked to the jury that they needn't have put the county to any cost hunting witnesses; if they had come to me, I could have told them that I killed him and the only thing that I was sorry for, was that I hadn't killed a lot more of the bushwhackers. I would love to ask this jury if they have indicted any of the bushwhackers and rebels who have hung and murdered Union men all over Howell county, irrespective of age; the most of those men were killed at their homes or taken from their homes and afterwards killed. A part of the men who did these things are still living in Howell county and that jury knows it.

The sheriff and the judge stepped out of the court house and in a few minutes returned, and the judge remarked, "I will turn you over to the sheriff." He then ordered the sheriff to adjourn the court until the next Monday. The sheriff remarked to the writer, "You can go where you please and report to the court at ten o'clock next Monday." The writer remarked, in the presence of the judge and sheriff, "I did not know that a man indicted for murder in the first degree could be paroled." The sheriff adjourned the court and he and the judge left the court house together. When I met a number of my friends (as there was a political meeting going on that day) and informed them that I had been indicted and paroled until next Monday, I couldn't make some of them believe it.

I appeared at ten o'clock the next Monday morning and before the court was convened, Edward Seay, and attorney-at-law, one among the ablest lawyers at the bar, a strong rebel sympathizer, came to the writer and said, "It is a shame that you have been indicted. It has been done for political purpose and I want your consent to file a motion to quash the indictment." I remarked to him that I would rather be tried before a jury of my country so that I could show the intention and aims of those who caused said indictments to be procured. He still plead with me to let him file a motion to quash it, that it would not cost me one cent. I at last told him to use his own pleasure in regard to it, so he filed a motion to quash it, and submitted the motion to the court without any argument, and the court sustained the motion and quashed the indictment. So ended that charge of murder against the writer. They saw they were beaten again and their schemes were again exposed to the whole people and they fell back sullen and become desperate.

In a short time the writer was informed that they were threatening to assassinate him and to be continually on the watch. I put men on their trails. Several attempts were made to decoy the writer into their nets, but they failed. They then employed one Dr. Beldon, who made an attempt to shoot the author in his own dooryard, but the writer saw him in time to prevent his shooting, and he left the county at once. Shortly after, the author was again warned to be on the watch, that they were still making threats.

There was a man by the name of W. H. McCowen, who had been a Confederate colonel, living in West Plains. He was known to be a very dangerous man when drinking and was an uncompromising rebel. The writer then resided in the house south of the town spring, known as the West Plains House, and the street ran within a few feet of the gate, which opened into a hall between the house and kitchen. There was a saloon about forty yards west of the house, on the same street, run by a man by the name of Jackson, another uncompromising rebel. This saloon appeared to be headquarters for these would-be assassins. I had just brought my horse from the stable and tied him by the gate, with the intention of going to my farm. Mrs. Lasater, who still resides in West Plains, had just come over to my house and was there at the time of the shooting. Mrs. McCowen, the wife of Col. McCowen, came to my house that morning, came in the back way, and appeared to be very much excited, and informed me that certain men were going to assassinate me that morning; that to her knowledge they had been plotting for three days. They had been using every inducement, making her husband drunk and trying to work him into it. She had shut him up and locked the doors to keep them away from her husband, but they would raise the windows and come in. She had done all she could to keep her husband out of it, and she thought it was her duty to come and let me

CAPT. WILL H. D. GREEN, GRANDSON.   LIEUT. MARK SPRINGER, CO. K.

know that they had agreed to shoot me that morning. I thanked her for the information and said to her that I would ever be grateful to her. I further said to her that I did not want to hurt the colonel or any other person, but they must not come to my house on that kind of business if they didn't want to get hurt. In a few moments she returned home, going around the back way.

I at once sent to S. P. Woodworth, a merchant who resided in West Plains and a strong Union man, for his double-barreled shotgun. I had two good navy pistols. He sent me his gun and said it was well loaded with buckshot and was sure to fire. I advised the women, if they came, to keep cool and go into the back room so they would be out of danger. I raised the two front windows of the sitting-room about two or three inches, so I could shoot under them, keeping close watch on the saloon. In about thirty minutes after Mrs. McCowen left, I saw two of the men leave the saloon and come in the direction of my house. They came to the gate, opened it and stepped onto the porch. My wife went to the door and begged them to leave. One of the men said that the wanted to see the colonel. He was armed with two first-class pistols, one of the pistols belonging to Col. McCowen. I cocked both barrels of my shotgun and stepped out on the porch with my gun presented and ordered him to turn around and leave my premises in one minute. Just at that moment my youngest daughter, now the wife of Mr. Green, sprang forward and caught my gun. I said to her: "For God's sake keep away from me." But she stood by my side. During this time he had passed outside of the gate and had gotten behind a tree; had his pistol cocked and presented at me and in a moment I had him covered with my shotgun. He would attempt to get sight of me and would dodge his head back behind the tree. Not knowing where the other man was, I watched his head and when he attempted to take sight I fired at his head; at the crack of the gun he fell. Then six or seven men commenced jumping out at the door of the saloon. The first thing I thought of was, "They will pretend to arrest me and give the mob a chance to shoot me after I am disarmed." I sprang on my horse and rode east and in a few moments five or six men came to my door and asked my wife who shot first. She ordered them to leave the house. They soon found that one of the would-be assassins was shot. On an examination it was found that one of the shot had struck him in the right side of the forehead, the right side of the brim of his hat was torn into fragments and the tree had caught a part of the load. The tree is still standing in the yard. Immediately afterward I sent them word that they had again opened the ball and I was ready to fight it out. I never saw men begin to plead for peace as hard in my life. The sheriff and others would come to me and say: "Colonel, why didn't you shoot some of those fellows long ago? That is just what they needed." I asked them why they hadn't arrested some of the assassins long ago.

When the Union men learned that an attempt had been made by these would-be assassins to assassinate me about two hundred and fifty of them headed by such men as J. F. Reiley, Esau Fox, Andrew V. Tabor, David B. Nicholass, John B. Nicholass, Josiah Carico, Chas. Long, J. Youngblood, and Geo. Youngblood rode into town well armed and publicly notified these assassins and those who were aiding and abetting them, that if another attempt was made to assassinate Colonel Monks, or if they did assassinate him it would take ten of their leaders to pay the debt and they knew just who they were. On an investigation, it was proven that on the night before they attempted the assassination about ten or twelve of these would-be assassins met together in the town of West Plains, and one of their leaders set out among other causes why Colonel Monks would have to be killed; that they had tried to scare him away from the country but found they couldn't scare him and the only way to keep the republican party from going into power again in this county was to kill Colonel Monks. Some of the men that were present were hired to do the shooting next morning and paid the money. They drank a health to each other on the death of Colonel Monks next morning. The man who advised and instructed them and paid them a part of the money is still living in Howell county. This failure in their attempt to assassinate me and the action taken by the loyal men appeared to put a quietus on their idea of assassination; if they ever made any further effort the writer never learned about it. They had been defeated in every attempt made either to slander or murder me.

I want to say here that I shall ever hold sacred the memory of Mrs. McCowen, for I owe to her the preservation of my life, and may God's blessing ever follow her and rest upon her.

The bushwhackers and Ku-klux element were not yet satisfied and had but one way to vent their spleen against me. That was to get right down to hard lying. Having failed to prove a single one of their charges against me in the courts they were bent on injuring me and damaging my character. With no regard for the truth they would go around secretly and tell strangers who knew nothing about me that I was a murderer and a thief. The better element among those who had been Confederates declared openly that these statements were false from beginning to end. Many of them have said that I was an honest man, and that if any one wished to employ an honest lawyer Monks was the man to go to, for no one could buy him.

Sometimes I would be informed that a late Confederate would say: "I believe Col. Monks was a good man and an honest one. But I dislike him because he fought us so hard during the war." I would reply: "Tell him that I couldn't please them in any way at the commencement of the war; I didn't want to take up arms. I was an unconditional Union man, and they, the rebels, came to my home and arrested me, took me into their command and swore that I should fight; that they would make me fight and attempted to force me into the Confederate lines, and when I found that nothing else would do them but to fight, and I went to fighting, then they turn about and curse me for fighting."

Again I would be informed that some of those persons, who had no regard for the truth, would secretly charge me with being a murderer. In reply I would inform them that every part of the country where I had performed military service was now in the control of the Democratic party and there was no limitation to the crime of murder.

Henry Dixon Green.

Henry Dixon Green was born in Henderson county, Ky., in the year 1851. His father, H. D. Green, was a colonel in the Confederate army, and died while in the service. In 1876, the younger Green left his native state, taking Horace Greeley's advice, and went west to grow up with the country. He located at West Plains, Mo., and soon began reading law in the office of Hon. A. H. Livingston. He was admitted to the bar, and formed a co-partnership with Mr. Livingston in the practice of law, which continued for several years. Afterwards he formed a partnership with Judge B. F. Olden. This firm was for years the local legal representative for the Kansas City, Fort Scott and Memphis Railroad Company, now part of the Frisco System. Mr. Green acted as claim agent for this railroad, and afterwards had charge of the claim department of the Missouri Pacific Railroad Company for the territory of Kansas, Nebraska, Colorado and Indian Territory, but resigned to resume the general practice of law at West Plains, Mo. He served as Probate Judge of Howell county.

Mr. Green was married in 1878 at West Plains to Miss Mary M. Monks, daughter of Col. Wm. Monks. Mrs. Green is a strong republican while Mr. Green is a strong supporter of the principles of the democratic party; but their home life is perfectly peaceful and happy. Five children have brightened this home, a daughter, now Mrs. Arch Bugg, and four sons, Will H. D., Frank, Russell and Dixon. The children all take their politics from their mother. The oldest son, Will, has been admitted to the Howell county bar and is now practicing law with his father. He is also Captain of Company K, the local military company of West Plains. The second and third sons are also members of the company. Frank works and studies at present in his father's law office, and the other boys are in school.

RUSSELL GREEN AND DIXON GREEN.

Index

Militia, xxvii
Smith, 15–16
Smith, A. J., xxxiii
Smith, Andrew, 95, 147
Smith, Andy, 95
Sons of Liberty, 134–35
Spears, Ed, xxxix
Spears, Joseph, 64–65, 147
Springer, Mark, 182
Springfield, Mo., 60–61, 101, 102, 116, 117, 119, 127
Spring River, Ark., 109–10
Stellman, Stillen, 153, 154
Stevens, John W., 87
Stinnett, 20
Stratton, 19
Sylamore Creek, Ark., 84

Taber, Andrew V., 27, 184
Texas County, Mo., 154
Thomasville, Mo., xxiv, xxxii, 27, 28, 108, 117, 137, 139, 178–79
Thompson, Steve, 45
Toney, Capt., 164
Tracey, N. H., xxxix, xl
Tracy, Joseph H., xxxix, xl, 126, 158, 159, 160
Treverbaugh, Joseph, 46, 47
Turley, Nace, 147
Turnbo, Silas C., xvi
Turner, Adeline, 145
Tutt-Everett war, xvii, 18–19
Tutt, Hamp, 19

Unionists, xx, 39–42, 57–60, 62–70, 115–16, 119–20, 126, 145, 147, 153–56
Upham, Daniel P., xliii–xliv, xlvi, 164, 165, 166
Utony. *See* Newtonia, Mo.

Van Wormer, Aaron, 141

Waddle, Judge, 107

Wadel, 164, 165
Wadle, John S., xxxi
Wagoner, Capt., 178
Walker, Andrew J. "Hell Roaring," lii
Wallace, Thomas, 147
Ware, Jehoida J., li, 86
Weatherford, Col., 85
Weaver, Garrett, 43
Webster County, Mo., 123–24
Webster, Dick, 147
Webster, Washington, 147
West Plains, Mo., xiv, xvi, xxi, xxiii, xxx, xlvi–xlvii, 24, 27, 28, 33–35, 36–37, 71–75, 77–80, 89, 91–93, 112–14, 115, 121, 129, 141–42, 151, 157–58, 181, 183–84, 186
West, Dent, 147
West, George, xxv
West, James, 147
West, Jesse, 147
West, Nathan, xlv
Wheat, John, 147
Wheat, Joseph, 147
whiskey, xvii, 12
White, Minor, 156
wildlife, 6–8
Willow Springs, Mo., 151
Winger, J. B., 149–50
Wolf, John Quincy, xvi
women, 8, 52, 62–63, 66–70, 81–82, 83, 177
Wood, Samuel N., 112–13
Woods, Col., 87, 89, 121
Woodside, Col., 112
Woodward, Seth P., 147
Woodward, Stephen, 147
Woodworth, S. P., 183
Wright, Adam S., 1, 157

Yates, Thomas, 88, 121, 126
Youngblood, George, 147, 184
Youngblood, Jonathan, 147, 184